TURN YOUR HOBBY INTO A BUSINESS — THE RIGHT WAY
Tax and Legal Tips to Avoid IRS Problems

TURN YOUR HOBBY INTO A BUSINESS — THE RIGHT WAY
Tax and Legal Tips to Avoid IRS Problems

John Alan Cohan, Attorney at Law

Self-Counsel Press Inc.
(a subsidiary of)
International Self-Counsel Press Ltd.
USA　　Canada

Library of Congress Control Number: 2008930915

Self-Counsel Press is committed to preserving ancient forests and natural resources. We elected to print this title on 30% postconsumer recycled paper, processed chlorine-free. As a result, for this printing, we have saved:

12 Trees (40' tall and 6-8" diameter)
4,400 Gallons of Wastewater
8 million BTUs of Total Energy
565 Pounds of Solid Waste
1,060 Pounds of Greenhouse Gases

Self-Counsel Press made this paper choice because our printer, Thomson-Shore, Inc., is a member of Green Press Initiative, a nonprofit program dedicated to supporting authors, publishers, and suppliers in their efforts to reduce their use of fiber obtained from endangered forests.

For more information, visit www.greenpressinitiative.org

Environmental impact estimates were made using the Environmental Defense Paper Calculator. For more information visit: www.edf.org/papercalculator

Self-Counsel Press Inc.
(a subsidiary of)
International Self-Counsel Press Ltd.

1704 N. State Street	1481 Charlotte Road
Bellingham, WA 98225	North Vancouver, BC V7J 1H1
USA	Canada

CONTENTS

INTRODUCTION   xv

PART I: THE BASICS OF TURNING YOUR HOBBY INTO A BUSINESS   1

1   THE HOBBY LOSS RULE   3

    1.   Your Honest Intention   5

    2.   Importance of Documentary Evidence   5

    3.   The Start-up Phase   6

    4.   Safe Harbor Rule   6

    5.   Establishing a Shift from Hobby to Business   7

    6.   Chapter Summary   7

2   A BUSINESSLIKE APPROACH PRIOR TO STARTING YOUR BUSINESS   9

    1.   Investigating the Market   9

       1.1   Consulting with experts   11

       1.2   Are you an expert?   11

    2.   Permits, Licenses, and Zoning Requirements   12

    3.   Business Plan   12

    4.   Choose a Name for Your Business   13

    5.   Should You Incorporate Your Venture?   13

6.	Business Checking Account	14
7.	Business Phone Line and Phone Listing	14
8.	Budget, Income Projections, and Other Financial Records	15
9.	Chapter Summary	15

3 CREATING A BUSINESS PLAN 16

1.	Why Should You Create a Business Plan?	16
2.	What Is a Business Plan?	17
	2.1 Highlights of a business plan	17
3.	Prepare Your Business Plan Now	18
4.	Suggested Format of a Business Plan	19
	4.1 Summary of plan	19
	4.2 Mission statement (optional)	19
	4.3 Marketing plan	19
	4.4 Operational plan	20
	4.5 Financial projections	20
	4.6 Long-range plan	21
5.	Chapter Summary	21

4 OPERATING YOUR BUSINESS 22

1.	Day-to-Day Business Records	23
2.	Importance of Accuracy of Business Records	23
3.	Making Changes in Methods of Operation	24
4.	Improving Your Skills and Expertise	25
5.	Appraisals of Assets Used in the Activity	26
6.	Written Contracts	26
7.	Keeping a Time Log	27
8.	Travel, Automobile, and Entertainment Expenses	30
	8.1 Travel expenses	30
	8.2 Automobile expenses	30
	8.3 Entertainment expenses	30
9.	Chapter Summary	31

5 ADVERTISING AND PROMOTION

	33
1. Advertising	33
1.1 Word of mouth	33
1.2 Website	34
1.3 Public speaking, organizations, and trade shows	34
1.4 Contact the customer directly	34
1.5 Sponsorship of an activity	35
1.6 Creative advertising	37
1.7 Socializing as a means of advertising	38
2. Document Your Marketing Efforts	39
3. Chapter Summary	40

6 HOME OFFICE DEDUCTIONS

	41
1. Regular and Exclusive Business Use	42
2. Principal Place of Business	42
2.1 If you do most of your business at home	42
2.2 If you do only administrative work at home	43
3. Meeting Clients or Customers at Home	43
4. Using a Separate Structure for Business	43
5. Storing Inventory or Sample Products at Home	44
6. Chapter Summary	44

7 HOW TO HANDLE AN IRS AUDIT

	45
1. Election to Postpone an Audit	46
2. Preparing for an Audit	46
3. Initial Interview	47
4. Substantiation	49
5. Questions Presented by the Auditor	50
6. Best Evidence	51
7. Formal Appraisals of Property	52
8. If You Are Assessed a Deficiency	52
9. Penalties	53
10. Offers in Compromise Policy of the IRS	53
11. Chapter Summary	53

PART II: CREATIVE BUSINESSES   55

8   ACTORS, FILMMAKERS, AND MUSICIANS   57
1. Actors   57
2. Filmmakers   60
3. Musicians   63
     3.1 Sponsorship and Management Agreements with Children   65
4. Chapter Summary   66

9   ARTISTS AND PHOTOGRAPHERS   68
1. Artists   68
2. Photography   74
3. Chapter Summary   78

10   WRITERS   80
1. Conduct Your Writing Venture in a Businesslike Manner   80
2. Research Projects by Educators and Scientists   89
     2.1 Special rules for educators   89
     2.2 Scientific research   89
3. Chapter Summary   90

PART III: AGRICULTURAL AND ANIMAL BUSINESSES   93

11   TREE FARMING AND GREENHOUSES   95
1. Tree Farming   95
2. Greenhouses   101
3. Chapter Summary   104

12   AGRICULTURAL FARMING   105
1. Family Farms   105
2. Chapter Summary   111

13   DOG BREEDING   112
1. Successful Dog-Breeding Cases   113
2. Unsuccessful Dog-Breeding Cases   116
3. Pet Stores   118
4. Chapter Summary   119

14 COMMERCIAL FISHING   120

1. Unsuccessful Commercial Fishing Case   120

2. Successful Commercial Fishing Case   121

3. Chapter Summary   122

PART IV: AUTOMOBILE, AIRCRAFT, AND BOAT BUSINESSES   123

15 CLASSIC CAR RESTORATION   125

1. Restoration   126

    1.1 Depreciation of restoration costs   128

    1.2 Restoration of vintage cars for rental   128

    1.3 Restoration for vintage car races   130

2. Chapter Summary   131

16 AUTOMOBILE RACING   132

1. Ways to Make Money as a Race Car Driver   132

2. Racing for Profit   133

    2.1 Motorcycle racing   133

    2.2 Car racing   135

3. Racing Sponsorship for Advertising   136

4. Chapter Summary   139

PART V: SPORTS AND GAMBLING BUSINESSES   141

17 SPORTS   143

1. Fishing Tournaments   143

2. Boat Racing   145

    2.1 Sponsorship of boat racing   146

3. Golf   148

4. Volleyball   149

5. Sponsorship Advertising for Sports   150

6. Chapter Summary   152

18 GAMBLING   153

1. Professional Gamblers   153

2. Proving Gambling Losses   154

3. High Rollers: Comps   155

4. Chapter Summary   156

PART VI: OTHER BUSINESSES

157

19 COLLECTIBLES
159

1. Deductions for Costs Associated with the Management or Conservation
of Your Investment Collection 160

2. Art and Antiques 160

    2.1 Antique shops 164

3. Rocks and Crystals 166

4. Stamps and Coins 166

5. Model Railroads 169

6. Chapter Summary 170

20 TREASURE HUNTING
172

1. Shipwrecks 172

2. Gold Prospecting 174

3. Chapter Summary 175

21 VACATION RENTALS AND TRAVEL CONSULTING
176

1. Bed-and-Breakfasts 176

2. Resorts 177

3. Travel Consulting 181

4. Chapter Summary 182

NOTICE TO READERS

ACKNOWLEDGMENTS

I would like to acknowledge my dear mother, Ilona, who has always been supportive of my writing endeavors.

I also wish to acknowledge the enthusiastic encouragement of the many faithful readers of my legal column that appears in magazines throughout the country.

And, I extend my thanks and appreciation to Tanya Howe, who provided insight and spiritedness into her excellent editing of this book.

INTRODUCTION

About one million new businesses are started each year in the United States. Many of these new endeavors are undertaken by people who have converted their hobbies into business ventures.

If you are reading this book, it shows that you are passionate about your hobby and may be considering taking the next step and making your hobby into a business. You are a candidate for converting your hobby into a business if the following applies to you:

- You really enjoy your hobby.

- You spend a lot of time working on your hobby.

- Other people seem to be making money doing the same or a similar hobby.

- You understand that there are tax benefits associated with operating as a business.

This book will provide you with important knowledge about turning your hobby into a business. If you are sincere in your intention and follow the advice given in this book, you will be eligible to take tax deductions on your expenses, and thereby offset your gross income from other sources. Of course, if you eventually make a profit — and most everyone would prefer a profit to a loss — your new endeavor will not be a tax shelter, but a cash cow.

Operating a former hobby as a business is easier than you think, and the rewards from a tax standpoint are the same as with any other business — you are entitled to deduct your expenses against other income.

A tax deduction (also called a tax write-off) is the amount you are entitled to subtract from your gross income (all the money you make), thereby reducing your taxable income. The government has decided that entrepreneurs don't have to pay tax on income they spend for business purposes. The more deductions you have, the lower your taxable income will be and the less tax you will have to pay.

So, if you turn your hobby into a business, you can take advantage of tax deductions that otherwise would not be available. This means you can deduct the expenses from the income earned in your day job.

1. The Difference between a Hobby and a Business

What is a business and how is it different from a hobby? For tax purposes, a business is any activity in which you regularly engage *primarily* to earn a profit. You don't have to show a profit every year to qualify as a business. As long as your *primary intention* is to make money, you can qualify as a business, even if you incur losses.

You do not want the IRS to think that your activity is a hobby, because as a hobbyist you cannot take the tax deductions that a business is entitled to. Instead, you will only be able to deduct your hobby-related expenses from the income the hobby generates. On the one hand, if you don't have income from the hobby, you will not receive deductions. On the other hand, if you make the hobby a business, any losses associated with the activity are tax deductible against your other sources of income.

Many successful ventures started out as hobbies. Martha Stewart realized a pipe dream by converting her passion for home entertainment into an enormous company. Ely Callaway used his passion for golf to develop golf clubs with hickory-wrapped steel shafts and formed the Callaway Gold Company, which has earned billions of dollars in revenue!

Scuba divers have turned their passion into lucrative treasure-hunting ventures.

John Grisham dreamed of becoming a writer. He squeezed in time to write a manuscript in the morning and at night, around his day job. Eventually he became one of the most commercially successful authors in modern times.

The vast majority of people who convert their hobbies into businesses are ordinary people who simply want to do it the right way and avoid problems with the IRS.

You might be approaching retirement age and be thinking about how to keep active in a way that could also supplement your retirement income. You might want to move into a new career, such as acting or writing, while retaining your day job. Or, you may be fresh out of college and want to venture into a field such as art, music, or photography, which means that you will have to start at the bottom and, while you earnestly work your way up, take a day job.

For more than two decades I have advised countless individuals on how to convert a hobby interest into a business and this book is a treasure-trove of my secrets. Part I discusses the basics of turning your hobby into a business, while Parts II through VI examine real-life case studies culled from the US Tax Court. By reading the case studies, you will learn from the successes and mistakes of others. This book will allay fears and clear up misconceptions, and will give you the courage to make the move from hobby to business.

The CD that comes with this book includes a resource section to help you further your research about turning your hobby into a business. The CD also includes bonus case studies.

2. Converting Your Hobby into a Business

Not every hobbyist should convert their activity into a business; not because it is too intimidating to do so, but because they may not want to operate in a businesslike manner. Many people are bored with financial details, which is understandable! I have encountered wealthy individuals who do not care about the financial details of their hobby activities and they can afford to subsidize the costs over an extended period of time. Individuals who have a cavalier attitude about their activities are better off simply keeping the activities as hobbies.

Transitioning from hobby to business requires an adjustment in the way you pursue your activity. You will have to take greater care in record keeping and other elements, which will be discussed in this book. The key word is *documentation*. I remember a professor in law school who told the class how miraculous documents are in the eyes of the law. A witness can testify with self-serving facts about something, and that has a certain degree of credibility depending on the demeanor and sincerity of the witness. However, if the testimony is backed up by documents, the court has a clear and objective account of the facts. You don't need to rely on the witness because you have something far more precious to go by. This issue will be explored in some detail throughout the book.

The main distinction between a hobby and a business is that the owner hopes to make a profit in a business, but not in a hobby. So, the main difference between a hobbyist and a businessperson is that there is a different focus concerning the economics of the activity. In a business, you have to consider whether or not the activity will be profitable, and therefore must take an interest in the finances of the endeavor.

If you take stock of the advice laid out in this book, you will have a good chance of making a profit in your former hobby and you will be able to deduct the costs of the venture against other sources of income.

PART I
THE BASICS OF TURNING YOUR HOBBY INTO A BUSINESS

1
THE HOBBY LOSS RULE

One of the most powerful weapons of the IRS is the hobby loss rule. The hobby loss rule is a way for the IRS to deny tax deductions to those who claim to be operating a business, but who are in fact carrying on a hobby.

The hobby loss rule ascertains your motive for conducting an activity that has the trappings of recreation or pleasure. One US Tax Court case described the rationale behind the hobby loss rule this way:

"Where the activity is not the taxpayer's principal means of livelihood and is of a sporting or recreational nature, then indeed, if he incurs losses in it, the question of motive becomes acute. The taxpayer is required to demonstrate that the appearance of a pleasure-seeking motive is misleading and that instead the motive for the activity was profit making. The difficulty inherent in so elusive a test as motive has resulted in the search for objective guideposts." [*Imbesi v. Commissioner,* 361 F.2d 640, 645 (3rd Cir. 1966).]

Under the hobby loss rule, only taxpayers who operate a bona fide business can take business deductions. To the IRS, a business is a venture operated to make money and is run in a professional, businesslike manner. In contrast, a venture that consistently loses money, has elements of personal pleasure or recreation, and is operated in a haphazard manner could be classified as a hobby. In that case you will not be allowed to deduct your expenses against other sources of income.

The hobby loss rule provides guideposts to see if your activity *reflects a profit motive* even if there are losses. The profit motive must be the *primary* motive.

The IRS uses the hobby loss rule mainly to analyze activities that bear features of recreation or pleasure for which the taxpayer takes write-offs. The IRS does not use the hobby loss rule for clear-cut business ventures, even if there are significant losses. For example, many Fortune 500 companies incur periods of significant losses. The airline industry is a prime example. This makes stockholders unhappy, but the IRS doesn't attack the fact that they are engaged in a business, not a hobby.

In converting your hobby into a business, it is important to establish that you *intend* to derive a profit from the operation of the activity. The IRS looks at all the facts and circumstances in evaluating whether the activity is one for profit despite the fact that losses occur. Since tax deductions are a matter of legislative grace, the taxpayer bears the burden of establishing the requisite profit objective.

The three most important factors of the hobby loss rule are as follows:

1. **How you carry on the business.** The principal element that distinguishes a hobby from a business is the manner in which you carry on the activity. Among other things, this means maintaining good books and records, and conducting the activity like any other business.

   The IRS tends to regard the "shoebox method" of record keeping as an implication that you are not taking your business seriously: People will throw receipts and other records into a shoebox and extract them to prepare their tax returns. They don't use these items for financial planning or to help gauge how their business is faring.

   If you are reasonably vigilant in maintaining good books and records of your activity, you will satisfy this component of the hobby loss rule. Also, keeping businesslike records helps you to analyze the strengths and weaknesses of your activity, to recognize what might be changed to improve the chances of making a profit, and to track the costs of the venture. The trick is to use your records for *quality control* purposes.

2. **Your expertise or that of your advisers.** You may already be an expert in your field. If you are not an expert, the IRS contemplates whether or not you have consulted experts to determine the feasibility of making money in your type of venture. This issue will emerge in various case studies throughout the book.

3. **The time and effort you put into the activity.** The IRS believes that if you assiduously apply yourself in an enterprise rather than dabble like a dilettante, you are engaged in a business. This factor is discussed quite often in case studies that will be explored in this book.

These are the three main factors of the hobby loss rule, and these and other factors of the rule will become more and more apparent as you progress through this book. The bottom line is that if these factors are not adequately met, the IRS will take the view that you are engaged in the activity primarily for the recreation or pleasure it affords, and that it is a hobby, not a business.

No single factor is controlling. Rather, the facts and circumstances of your situation are taken as a whole. If you are weak in one factor, it can be overcome if you are strong in another factor.

Many people are careless and ignore the hobby loss rule, and they only have themselves to blame if the IRS denies their tax benefits. Others, including you (since you are reading this book) are more inclined to take stock of the hobby loss rule, so that your former hobby activity can be treated as a business.

The whole purpose of this book is to support you in treating your activity as a business and fully deducting your losses, even if you don't earn profits for many years in a row. You want to be able to convince the IRS that earning a profit — and not having fun or accumulating tax deductions — is the primary motive for doing what you do. At the same time, nothing says that you cannot also take pleasure in your venture. A business is not a hobby merely because the owner finds it pleasurable. A famous tax case said, "Suffering has never been made a prerequisite to deductibility." [*Thomas W. Jackson v. Commissioner,* 59 T.C. 312 (1972).]

1. Your Honest Intention

Under the hobby loss rule, if you have an honest intention of making a profit from your venture despite the odds against it, you may take tax deductions just like any other business. The philosophy of the IRS is that people are entitled to pursue their dreams in whichever field of endeavor they choose, however speculative the activity might be.

In order to conduct your former hobby as a business and take write-offs, you should be prepared to show that you are engaged in the activity with the primary, predominant, or principal purpose and intent of realizing an economic profit independent of tax savings. The test is whether you engage in the activity with the honest objective of making a profit, *not* whether there is a reasonable expectation of making a profit. The hobby loss rule requires that you sincerely and in good faith hope and expect to make a profit, despite high odds against this coming true.

Put another way, you may conceive of and embark on an enterprise of your choosing no matter how impractical, idiosyncratic, or questionable of success it may seem to others. There is such a thing as a sincere and honest speculative business in the business world.

A prime example is investing in wildcat oil wells. Under tax regulations, an investor in a wildcat oil well who incurs very substantial expenditures can be in the venture for profit even though the expectation of a profit might be considered unreasonable. The chances of making a profit on an individual well might be remote, but

the entrepreneur still has an honest goal of making money. So too, an artist, actor, writer, or musician might have only a slight chance of yielding a big chunk of income, yet in these fields one has to start at the bottom and exert one's best efforts in moving towards success.

In converting a hobby into a business it is most everyone's ultimate objective to make a profit, but many people who turn their hobbies into businesses might rarely, if ever, make a profit from the venture.

As you will see, with some activities profits are elusive and difficult to attain — such as dog breeding or car racing. Still, if you observe the criteria of the hobby loss rule, you will be entitled to deduct these losses against your "day job."

2. Importance of Documentary Evidence

What matters, if you are audited, is proving your *intention* to be engaged in a business. Now, just what is intention? Intention pertains to the inner workings of your mind — what you personally believe is the truth. To ascertain intention is a pervasive problem of the law. Judge Learned Hand remarked, "Nothing is more frequent in human relations than the effort to learn what goes on in others' minds." [*United Business Corp. of America v. Commissioner,* 62 F.2d 754, 756 (2nd Cir. 1933).]

The IRS gives greater weight to objective evidence than to an individual's statements regarding his or her intention to be engaged in a business. *Objective evidence* consists of documents, logs, copies of email messages, correspondence, contracts, and other business records. *Subjective evidence* consists of self-serving statements made by the taxpayer as to intention; these statements are also important, but are accorded less weight than objective evidence.

The IRS is aware that the taxpayer may tend to give self-serving or evasive answers to certain questions, and that it is not uncommon for individuals to exaggerate facts, or even lie. So, it is important to maintain documents in the course of conducting your venture. These records can be important in helping you withstand IRS scrutiny if you are audited.

How much evidence is good enough? Actually, it is quality rather than quantity that matters. The amount of documentation you will need to support your businesslike approach will vary under the circumstances. For instance, the amount of business records in a stamp or coin collecting activity will be small in comparison to that needed to support your intention regarding a horse farming venture.

If your business records are in shambles, or altogether missing, it will be hard to convince the IRS that your former hobby activity is a business. The IRS won't simply take your word for it. Objective evidence is what usually helps people withstand IRS scrutiny in hobby loss cases, as you will see later on in this book.

3. The Start-up Phase

The process of converting a hobby into a business often entails a period of years in which there is no actual profit, but significant losses. It is usually expected in the business world that you will lose money in the start-up phase, and you are entitled to utilize these losses as write-offs.

Numerous US Tax Court cases have talked about a start-up phase for various types of ventures. For example, it can take ten years before a citrus grove is productive enough to be profitable and it can take from five to ten years before a horse-breeding venture might be profitable — or longer, depending on many variables.

In the hobby loss area, the IRS sometimes audits people who are clearly in the start-up phase — perhaps even in their first or second year of the activity. Why this is so is not entirely clear. Sometimes it is easy for the IRS to zap people in the start-up phase because of the well-known fact that many taxpayers do not realize the importance of carrying on the activity in a businesslike manner.

Regardless of which stage you are in with the activity, and even if you are in the start-up phase, it needs to be operated in a businesslike manner if you claim the activity is a business rather than a hobby.

4. Safe Harbor Rule

The safe harbor rule means that if you have three profit years in a five-year period, (or two profit years in a seven-year period for activities that consist of breeding, showing, training, or racing horses — see Chapter 15) the IRS will assume that you are engaged in a business and not a hobby. Any profit, no matter how small, qualifies as a profit year.

A profit means that your gross income from the activity is more than your tax deductions. Some people engage in careful *profit-year planning* to help the venture show a profit for the year. That might entail minimizing costs during that year so as to enhance profitability. People sometimes do this, quite properly, by deferring payment of expenses until the next year, or prepaying some expenses in the preceding year. Any time you operate more efficiently, or cut down on costs, you improve your chances of making a profit. It should be noted that the IRS frowns on *creative accounting* methods that might make it appear, improperly, that you have realized a profit year.

5. Establishing a Shift from Hobby to Business

In turning your hobby into a business, it is important to be able to show how you decided that you could make money in what was formerly a hobby. One of the favorite questions the IRS asks in a hobby loss audit is, "What research did you conduct into the economics of the activity prior to the commencement of the activity?"

Again, documentary evidence is what you need to establish this. It is helpful to document *how* you came to this decision. For example, you consulted with individuals who were making money in the field, you analyzed trade and marketing materials, or you consulted industry experts about the feasibility of making money in this area. You would be wise to maintain a file on your marketing research, copies of correspondence or consultations with advisers, copies of articles you researched, and any other materials that prove you did your due diligence.

What you must avoid is the implication that you entered the venture blindly, or that you decided overnight that you were no longer conducting a hobby but instead a business. You want to show that you conducted market research about the venture. When you start any type of business you are expected to conduct an investigation to ascertain its profit-making potential and to uncover any possible obstacles to its producing a profit. This is not to say that you are held to the standards of an investigator for a new Disney World location, but if you make no inquiry, or inquire only in a desultory manner, the IRS will discount your later claim of a profit-seeking motive.

If you have little or no prior experience in the field, it is particularly important to show that you have gone to some lengths to study the field prior to entering it. As one US Tax Court case stated, "Preparation for an activity by extensive study of its accepted business, economic and scientific practices, and consultation with those who are expert therein, may indicate that the taxpayer entered into the activity for profit." [*Seebold v. Commissioner,* T.C. Memo 1988-183.]

If you have no prior experience in the activity, and receive no expert advice, this will weigh heavily against the assertion that you are engaged in a business rather than a hobby.

6. Chapter Summary

Everyone is entitled to make a living in any way that is lawful. People are entitled to make a living in highly speculative ventures. In a democratic country, everyone benefits from other peoples' risk-taking. People prize entrepreneurial spirit and the freedom of individuals to take risks, even if they might end up with poor results. One reason the economy does so well is that people take gambles, and sometimes these gambles pay off in spectacular ways.

The hobby loss rule seeks to ferret out people who are carrying on a personal activity (a hobby) and claiming it is a business. The qualities that make one person pass IRS muster and the next person fail are fairly straightforward. Understanding the hobby loss rule is a way to know what the IRS expects of people who are carrying on a business activity in a field that people often take to be a hobby.

To convert a hobby into a business you must have the primary, predominant, or principal purpose and intention of realizing an economic profit independent of tax write-offs. Your main motivation must be to make a profit rather than to engage in a personal pursuit. The test is your honest intention, not whether it is reasonable to expect to make money from the venture. Reasonableness is not the test, but rather *actual* and *bona fide* intention, however unreasonable the venture.

Your honest intention of making a profit is something that is demonstrated in several broad areas:

- The manner in which you carry on the activity.

- Your expertise or that of your advisers.

- The amount of time and effort you spend on the activity.

Thus, business records are key to complying with the hobby loss rule. A business, under the hobby loss rule, should be operated much like any other sort of business. The next chapter will explore the types of business records that are important for people who decide to convert their hobbies into businesses, or for anyone who decides to launch a new venture in an area that traditionally might be thought of as a hobby.

2

A BUSINESSLIKE APPROACH PRIOR TO STARTING YOUR BUSINESS

When you are ready to convert your hobby into a business, or to start your new venture, it is important to proceed in a businesslike manner. This chapter will highlight the major areas of concern for new businesses that the IRS and the US Tax Court have singled out in hobby loss cases.

1. Investigating the Market

As mentioned in the last chapter, the IRS may ask in a hobby loss audit: "What research did you conduct into the economics of the activity prior to the commencement of the activity?"

You should be able to prove that you gave consideration to the business aspects of the venture before plunging into it. If you don't conduct some sort of preparation or research of the business aspects of the field before embarking on your venture, the IRS will argue that you proceeded in an unbusinesslike manner.

If you have prior hobby experience with the activity, you may know a lot about how people can make money in the activity. If you have little or no prior experience in the area, it is particularly important to show that you have gone to some lengths to study the field prior to entering it, or else it will look as if you are engaged in a hobby.

There is no particular formality when conducting market research. You should undertake a basic investigation of the factors that would affect making a profit. Your research should provide you with knowledge such as —

- what the ultimate costs might be,

- the amount of revenue you could expect,

- what risks are involved, and

- how you might achieve some degree of cost efficiency.

In conducting market investigation, it is important to consult with industry experts about making money in the field, and to analyze trade and marketing materials. What you must avoid is the implication that you entered the venture blindly. Rather, you want to show that you conducted market research in advance. When you start a business you are expected to conduct an investigation in a businesslike way to learn of its profit potential, and to uncover any possible obstacles to producing a profit.

There are numerous things you can easily do to investigate the economics of your chosen field. You can —

- read and study industry journals about the economics of the activity,

- surf the Internet,

- attend trade meetings,

- find a mentor, and

- consult industry experts.

It is important to document your research. You should gather your findings and keep them in a file to help show what sort of market research you conducted. You would be wise to maintain documentary evidence of your research including —

- copies of correspondence,

- emails and notes from consultations with advisers,

- copies of articles you researched,

- evidence of attendance at industry seminars (e.g., registration receipts, copies of programs, notes you took, and names of contacts you met),

- evidence of trade shows you attended (e.g., registration receipts, hotel receipts, and brochures collected at the events), and

- any other materials that prove you did your due diligence in researching the activity.

If you are ever audited, this evidence of research you conducted can make or break your case. The IRS will be impressed if you have a file that shows how you conducted market research before you started the venture.

If you can find financial forecast information (e.g., an article in the *Wall Street Journal* that says

that stamp collecting has a great future), include it. If you have information that suggests new developments that significantly impact the dynamics of your activity, include that information. For instance, if there is new technology that will enhance the desirability of your product or services, keep information about it in your file. Or, if there is technology coming available that will cut down the costs of your operation, put information about it into the file.

For example, if you want to convert your interest in photography into a business, you should research *how* to profit in this field — what sort of photography activities could be profitable (e.g., travel photography, tinting old photos), what your marketing strategy might be, whether you might be able to sell pictures on the Internet, whether there are art galleries that might consider showing your work, or whether you could publish a book of photographs and market it.

Even if you have significant prior experience in photography, it is important to undertake research as to the economics of running the activity as a business. You might know a lot about the techniques of photography, but making money in the field is a separate matter — and that is where you should focus your research.

The amount of market research you need to do will depend on how much you already know. Some people are experts in their field and are quite familiar with the economics involved, so they will not need to conduct much market research. Others are attracted to a particular field but have little prior experience in it and want to start something fresh. In this situation it is particularly important to gather a good deal of information about how to make money in the activity.

It is important when doing research to focus on the economics of the venture, rather than only the technical or logistical aspects of the activity.

For instance, if you are going to start a boat charter venture, look into how others make money doing that rather than how to improve your boating navigation skills, although the latter is important as well when maintaining an ongoing venture.

You should keep your research files indefinitely. If you are audited, even many years down the line, the IRS may ask how you decided to enter your field, and you will want to show that you were diligent in the way you approached it.

1.1 Consulting with experts

Part of the evidence of a businesslike manner of operating a venture is your expertise or that of your advisers. Both before and after launching a venture it is important, particularly if you are not an expert in the subject, to consult others who are experienced in the field and to follow the advice received.

The IRS will want to know how you figured you could make money in the venture. It will be important to show that you obtained advice from experts, particularly on the business aspects of the field, before starting the venture. If you have no prior experience in the activity and you obtain no expert advice, this suggests you are engaged in a hobby, not a business.

Usually it is necessary to pay a consultation fee for advice obtained. Sometimes it is possible to obtain expert advice from government sources, for example, Agriculture Department officials for those involved in farming.

Avoid "expert" advice from friends or relatives. If the only advice you obtain is free advice given by friends and relatives, the IRS will say that this is evidence you are conducting a hobby, not a business.

If you get good advice about how to move your venture closer towards making a profit, you should follow the advice. If you don't follow the advice, the IRS will want to know why. In one case, a dog breeder was advised by his attorney to obtain a zoning variance in operating a kennel out of his home. He didn't follow the advice and later lost his US Tax Court case. [*Thomas C. Burger v. Commissioner,* T.C. Memo 1985-523.]

1.2 Are you an expert?

Expert in the context of the hobby loss rule is a loosely formulated term. It does not mean the same thing as someone qualified to testify in court as an expert witness — but is a less rigid formulation.

People frequently become experts in their own right over a period of years of participation, experience, and study in their chosen field. You may acquire considerable knowledge in many facets of the business by hands-on experience, studying of trade magazines and books, attending industry events and seminars, and taking courses relevant to making money in your field. A stamp collector, for instance, may become quite knowledgeable about industry trends, the pricing of stamps, what the market will bear, where deals can be made, and what sort of advertising venue is worthwhile.

If you become an expert you will have a thorough knowledge of your field, so you are entitled to make business decisions in your field of endeavor on your own, without the need to consult outside experts.

Evidence of your personal expertise, particularly in the business aspects of the field, helps prove that your principal intention is to engage in a business, not a hobby.

If you have little or no prior experience in the field, it is particularly important, in addition to obtaining expert advice, to learn as much as you can about the business end of things in your field.

2. Permits, Licenses, and Zoning Requirements

Prior to starting your venture it is important to investigate what legal requirements exist for engaging in the particular activity. If you do not have proper licenses and permits, or if you are violating the zoning ordinance, the IRS will argue that you are not operating in a businesslike manner, and that your activity is a hobby, not a business.

Licenses and permits for various enterprises are handled by the state, city, and county governments. You have to check with your particular city, state, and county for what permits, licenses, and zoning variances are necessary to engage in your venture. For instance, if you are planning on breeding dogs, you may need to get a kennel license even if you operate out of your home, and you must check to see if your location is zoned for this type of activity.

Sometimes getting a permit, say, for a dog kennel, is a relatively simple procedure in the city or county in which you live. However, sometimes it may be necessary to spend considerable time and effort to comply with certain legal requirements.

There may be times when you do not get a straightforward answer from authorities on the question of licenses or permits, which can be daunting. You might get different answers from different authorities as to whether a permit or license is required for your particular activity. You should do your best to find out what is or isn't required. It is useful to check the state attorney general's office, the city clerk's office, trade associations, and with others who are conducting the same type of business in your area.

Certain activities such as building or operating a resort, bed and breakfast, or recreational facility require numerous permits and licenses, and sometimes even a zoning variation. Sometimes the situation is too burdensome and time consuming to make it worth one's while.

If you are selling anything, it is usually important to get a sales tax permit from the state in which you operate.

Almost all businesses are required to obtain a city business permit or license. This is imposed by most cities as a way of raising revenue. Even individuals who operate out of their homes are technically required to file for these business licenses. The city issues an annual certificate indicating that the person is authorized to conduct business in the jurisdiction. In many jurisdictions the resources for enforcement are limited and people who operate businesses in their homes are not hassled by the city if they fail to obtain business licenses.

However, if you don't have a city business license, the IRS may find this to be unbusinesslike and it could harm your case. The annual fee for a city business license varies, depending on your gross receipts. In many jurisdictions there is no fee if your gross receipts fall below a certain threshold.

3. Business Plan

Prior to starting the venture, and once you have gathered information about the economics of the activity (including any permits, licenses, and other legal requirements), you should implement a written business plan.

The next chapter discusses business plans in some detail to assist you in writing one of your own. For now, just note that the IRS *Audit Techniques Guide* requests that revenue agents ask taxpayers in hobby loss audits whether they have a business plan. If you don't have one, the IRS will argue that you are not operating in a businesslike manner. This could result in denial of your tax benefits, particularly if you have a history of losses.

Ideally, your business plan will be written before you start the venture, rather than partway through it.

4. Choose a Name for Your Business

Choosing a name for your venture is important for the practical reason that people will come to identify the name with your business or service. It is helpful if you can choose a name that stands out. The name of a business can be a significant attraction if skillfully selected.

If you can't think of something clever, it is always appropriate to simply use your own name, such as "Jones Dog Breeding" or "Timothy's Boat Charters."

You should file a Fictitious Business Name Statement (also known as a "doing business as" or DBA form) in the county in which you are doing business. This form is easy to file. The form and instructions are available from your county clerk's office. If the name is already being used by another business, you may have to select another name. Sometimes you can use a variation of the name that someone else has already registered if you are operating a different type of business. For instance, "Big Boy Landscaping" can be registered even though there is a "Big Boy Art Gallery."

5. Should You Incorporate Your Venture?

I am frequently asked whether it is advisable to operate a newly formed venture as a corporation or a limited liability company (LLC), and if so, whether to incorporate in Nevada or some other state that has corporate-friendly laws. The answer depends on the individual situation. Most

businesses operate as sole proprietorships because this is the easiest way in which to operate.

Some people prefer the corporate or LLC entity because it seems more businesslike. As a practical matter, operating as a corporation or LLC often makes a stronger impression on the public at large. Also, your personal liability is limited if you operate a venture as a corporation or LLC. For instance, if there is a judgment against the entity, the claimants usually cannot enforce the judgment against you personally, but only against the assets of the entity. However, in some situations you can be held personally liable even though you are operating under the auspices of a corporation or LLC, so it is not a cure-all.

Corporate procedures are flexible so that with a closely held corporation or LLC you can utilize losses from the venture to offset your principal source of income. It simply is reported in a different manner and your tax return will have more forms to complete.

Most people do not like operating as a corporation or LLC because of additional paperwork and the need to transfer ownership of assets into the entity. There is a filing fee to register a corporation or LLC with the Secretary of State in the state where you operate. Sometimes it is necessary to register in other states where you conduct business.

Operating as a corporation or LLC requires more attention to business records than operating sole proprietorships. You must maintain a Minute Book and other formalities associated with corporate law. One of the formalities includes conducting annual meetings of the Board of Directors (even if you are the sole shareholder-director), which must be recorded in the Minute Book. Many small businesses fail to properly maintain Minute Books and only update them when the IRS requests to see them.

Operating as a corporation or LLC can be, for many people, a kind of trap. It can be difficult to maintain the formalities expected of these entities. The IRS, in an audit, might find fault with how your books and records are kept for the corporate or LLC entity. For instance, the IRS will want to verify that your bank account is in the name of the entity, that you obtained a taxpayer ID number for the entity, and that you transferred assets into the entity. For many people, the formal requirements are too much trouble.

Keep in mind that throughout this book you will see many instances where people have won their tax cases as sole proprietors. The IRS looks to the overall businesslike manner in which you conduct your activity, and an overwhelming number of situations do not involve corporate or LLC entities.

Your decision to incorporate should be based on practical considerations for, as mentioned, your ability to withstand IRS scrutiny under the hobby loss rule, which really depends on the overall businesslike manner in which you operate.

Many resources are available if you are interested in learning more about incorporating your business. See *Limited Liability Company*, published by Self-Counsel Press, for more information about LLCs.

6. Business Checking Account

A surprising number of US Tax Court cases have faulted taxpayers for not having separate checking accounts. The idea is that by having a separate bank account, you are differentiating between personal and business expenditures. If you use the same bank account for personal and business purposes, this means you are commingling funds, and to the IRS this is unbusinesslike.

Keep in mind that if you fail to have a separate checking account, this will not usually make

or break your case, as long as you are operating the activity, overall, in a businesslike manner. But if your overall manner of conducting the venture is haphazard and unbusinesslike, then commingling funds will be the nail in the coffin if you are audited by the IRS.

If you insist on having one bank account for both personal and business activities, then you should maintain a ledger that clearly differentiates checks that are for personal purposes and those that are for business purposes. The better approach is to have a separate checking account for the venture and not to use that account for personal expenses. You may need to transfer personal funds into the business account from time to time to help with cash flow, and that is entirely appropriate.

7. Business Phone Line and Phone Listing

In some hobby loss cases, the taxpayers have been ruled against because, among other things, they did not have a separate phone line for the venture. It is always important to have a separate phone number for your venture and to have it listed in the White Pages (and, if appropriate, in the Yellow Pages). A separate phone line is a lot more businesslike than using your personal phone number for the venture.

The practical importance of having a Yellow Pages listing under the appropriate category is that people can look up your business by category (e.g., Pet Stores, Antique Dealers). It seems like a minor point, but several US Tax Court cases have faulted taxpayers for failing to operate in a businesslike manner because, among other things, they weren't listed in the Yellow Pages.

Some people simply do not need to have a separate business line for their activities because they might have a low volume of incoming calls.

For instance, an author working on a manuscript might not need to have a separate phone line for the writing activity. It depends on the circumstances.

8. Budget, Income Projections, and Other Financial Records

The IRS will be impressed if you have a budget, income statement, balance sheet, income projection, or other financial data that helps you evaluate the overall performance of the activity.

As you will see in the next chapter, some type of budget or projection is necessary in order to have a complete business plan.

Most people who are audited under the hobby loss rule do not have much to show by way of a budget or cost projections. In order to withstand IRS scrutiny, it is important to present a budget, or something similar, as evidence that you know how much you need to spend, what your break-even point is, and what categories of expenses might be reduced in future years.

Even the simplest type of budget will be helpful to prove that you are mindful of the economics of the venture, and that you are operating a business, not a hobby.

To help you formulate a budget or other economic analysis, you might consult industry data relevant to your field, which can refine your projections. The budget should show how much money you anticipate spending on various categories of expenses. The budget should also project the amount of income you realistically expect to generate. You can highlight the break-even point. This will enable you to determine how and when you might reasonably expect to make a profit.

The budget should be as detailed as possible. Some people hire an accountant to make a formal budget, but this is not necessary. Most people can create a half-decent budget on their own.

If you are willing to take the time to do so, you might want to prepare a five-year economic analysis. This would show a budget, cost projections, a break-even point, and other economic data for a five-year period. The IRS will find this to be a very businesslike approach because you would have taken the trouble to project well into the future to help you seriously consider the costs involved and how much income you will need to make a profit.

9. Chapter Summary

Some of the elements discussed in this chapter may seem daunting. If you comply even partially with the businesslike elements discussed here, you should be in a position to convince the IRS that you are operating a business, not a hobby, even if you have a history of losses.

For instance, numerous taxpayers have won their cases even though they did not have a separate bank account for the activity. However, in those cases they had good overall records that indicated a businesslike concern for the venture, including ledgers, balance sheets, cost projections, or other documents to show their concern for the economics of the activity.

Remember that it is important to conduct a basic investigation of the industry and to document what you learned prior to your initial entry into the activity. Your records should show market research, other economic analysis you considered, and advice obtained from people you consulted in the industry.

It is also important to have business cards for your activity (showing your name, the business name, address, and phone number), as well as business stationery and envelopes.

The next chapter discusses the business plan, which is one of the most important aspects of making your venture businesslike.

3
CREATING A BUSINESS PLAN

In hobby loss audits, most people are caught off guard when asked by the IRS whether they have a business plan. People usually have general ideas in their minds as to how they are operating their activities and where they are headed. Some people will say they have the plan all in their heads, but then they are unable to articulate what the plan is. Other people will say their activities are very basic, that they know what they are doing, and that they don't need a business plan.

Many small businesses do not have a written business plan; for example, some beauty parlors, restaurants, or candy stores. The plan is in the heads of the owners. The IRS does not harass them about business plans if they are audited, because they are clearly in a business pursuit. However, if you are in a venture that has elements of a hobby, it becomes crucial to have a business plan in order to withstand IRS scrutiny.

Because so many people fail to have a written business plan, the IRS uses this as a wedge to argue that they really don't have a plan, and so

they are not conducting the venture in a business-like manner.

In addition to the plan, the question will arise in an audit as to whether you are actually operating according to the plan that you have formulated. A business plan is something that you *utilize* to improve the profitability of your activity. The plan, along with other records, should be used to analyze why losses recurred over a period of time, and whether any possibility of recouping the losses exists.

1. Why Should You Create a Business Plan?

A written business plan is important evidence that you are operating a business, not a hobby.

Most people who start small businesses such as beauty parlors or car washes do *not* have a formal business plan unless they are seeking venture capital funds, or wish to establish a commercial lending relationship with a bank. For them, a business plan is a tool to garner interest on the part of investors or lenders.

The US Tax Court has said that in hobby loss cases you should have some type of plan for your venture. In the IRS *Audit Techniques Guide* on hobby loss audits, revenue agents are advised:

"The taxpayer should have a formal written plan. The plan should demonstrate the taxpayer's financial and economic forecast for the activity. The plan should not be a 'fantasy Schedule F or C.' In other words, some taxpayers may wish to submit a business plan that is nothing more than a Schedule F or C, which unrealistically overstates the expenses for the activity. This is not an acceptable business plan."

Legally speaking, the IRS does not *require* that a business plan be in writing. The US Tax Court has said that a business plan need not be in writing and can be evidenced by the taxpayer's actions. However, in my opinion, it is crucial to put the plan in writing. If you have it "in your head," the IRS will decide that this is unbusinesslike and claim that you really don't know what your plan consists of.

Some people spend thousands of dollars to have professional business plans drafted. There are numerous resources, some good and others not, to assist you in drawing up a business plan. This chapter will enable you to draft a business plan on your own.

Writing a business plan forces you to think about how you need to go about making a profit. It forces you to look at the product or service you are offering, how you will price it, how you will handle your competition, and how you will target your customer base.

Keep in mind that a business plan is a document that the IRS views with respect, because most people do not have one. It is one of the best items of evidence to show your intention is to operate a business, not a hobby. It is evidence that you have considered the dynamics of your particular market before embarking on your business journey.

2. What Is a Business Plan?

A business plan sets forth the strategy for the success of your venture. It is a guide for carrying your idea forward into a successful business operation. It formally states the strategic direction of your venture. A business plan describes the nature of your products or services and how you intend to sell or market them. It outlines the overall market that you are targeting and how your products and/or services compare with competitors.

The IRS takes the view that a written business plan demonstrates your businesslike concern for the success of the venture. People engaged in a hobby do not have business plans. One of the most important things that distinguishes a business from a hobby is the existence of a written business plan.

The business plan narrates what your business is all about, what kinds of opportunites you see, and how you intend to make money. The length and breadth of the plan will depend on how much time you want to put into developing it.

The language of a business plan should be simple and non-technical. As mentioned, usually individual taxpayers write their own business plans.

2.1 Highlights of a business plan

If you are preparing your own business plan, the document should be in your own words, well-written in simple, non-technical style, and well-organized. It should be conversational in tone. Needless to say, the document should not contain spelling or grammatical errors.

The plan should state why you are qualified to undertake the venture, which means explaining your background and possible expertise, the advice obtained from others experienced in the field, the nature of your competition, and how you can distinguish yourself from your competition.

The business plan essentially puts your strategy into writing. If you have not developed a strategy or direction for your venture, then you should start by making an outline of how you believe you can make money in this field.

Much of the plan will consist of information you already have in your head from your experiences when you conducted the activity as a hobby. It is good to put anything relevant that you know from your personal experience into the business plan.

Preparing the plan helps you to focus on your ideas more clearly, which intensifies them. Forming a business plan helps you think through your strategies, balance passion with facts, and set a clear guideline as to what your objectives are. By going through the process, even if you are not a good writer, you will be forced to think through various potential situations and learn more about how your venture will go forward.

Many individuals find that writing the plan is easy because of their prior experience in their fields. Some people also find the experience to be fun and creative.

There are thousands of Internet sources for assistance in writing a business plan. If you choose to select one of these sources for assistance, proceed with caution. Some of my clients hire others to write their business plans, but they use well-recommended and reputable individuals, some of whom charge good-sized fees for their work. A professionally-prepared business plan by someone qualified in the field is usually more impressive than a plan you yourself would write. Still, the great majority of business plans that pass IRS muster are written by individual taxpayers.

Part of a business plan should consist of some sort of financial projection that shows how much you will have to spend to get going, what property you are going to bring into the venture (e.g., a stamp collection), how much it will take to run the venture, when a break-even point will be reached, and how much revenue you reasonably expect to generate.

3. Prepare Your Business Plan Now

Don't wait to get audited. It is too late to create a plan once you are audited. The IRS is aware of "canned" business plans that people try and pass off as thoughtful business plans. The IRS wants to see business records that are maintained in the ordinary course of your activity, not those that you might suddenly decide to prepare for an audit. As mentioned in the previous chapter, your business plan should be written before you start the venture.

If you are audited, it is too late to put together a written business plan unless you honestly date it and admit that you have prepared it in connection with your audit. That is better than nothing. You can explain that the plan has always been in your head, and you thought it would be best at this time to put it in writing so that your intentions could be made clear.

Of course, you should never backdate documents. It is dishonest and illegal. In one case, the US Tax Court found discrepancies in the dating of the taxpayer's business plan, and with that the taxpayer's credibility was presumably reduced to nothing. [*Hastings v. Commissioner*, T.C. Memo 2002-310.]

Remember, your business plan is evidence to be used in the event of an audit to show the businesslike manner of your venture. The IRS will always regard a written business plan as more credible than your verbal claims about the plan.

It is important to update the plan every year or two to indicate how well you are meeting your overall objectives, and to show that you are mindful of changed circumstances, setbacks, or other situations that might make it prudent to modify your direction. You want to set forth what changes should be made, if necessary, to improve the chances of profitability.

Usually, the updates are short and to the point, since they are done simply to make changes or add new information to the original plan. Of course, sometimes you may have important changes that you decide to implement, which you can mention in the update.

I recommend signing the document at the end, dating it, and having it notarized so that there can be no doubt as to when you created it.

4. Suggested Format of a Business Plan

As mentioned, if you wish to write your own business plan, there are many books available on the subject. *Start & Run a Consulting Business*, published by Self-Counsel Press, includes a CD with a template business plan and marketing plan. The CD included with *Turn Your Hobby into a Business — The Right Way* includes a Resources section that lists books and websites for creating a business plan.

The following sections suggest what you should include in a business plan and the order in which it should be presented. To begin, the business plan should have a title page and a table of contents.

4.1 Summary of plan

This is a short summary of what you are going to be doing in your business, which is helpful to anyone who reads the plan. It can be a simple outline of the points you make elsewhere in the document.

4.2 Mission statement (optional)

The mission statement is your opportunity to make a statement about your vision, purpose, management philosophy, and uniqueness, to give others a sense of your integrity and motivation. The mission statement may also express your enthusiasm for the products and/or services you are offering.

4.3 Marketing plan

The marketing plan section is the "meat" of the document. This section should explain what product or service you are offering and how you will exploit the market. This is where you will discuss how you intend to garner sufficient market share to make a profit. You should narrate your market strategy and state why you believe this activity can be profitable. You could include (as an appendix) copies of market information you have researched.

You should also provide a list of major competitors and include their sizes, strengths, weaknesses, pricing strategies, and how your venture is different from theirs. You should highlight any competitive advantages that you have over other similar ventures.

For instance, if you are going into stamp collecting as a business, write about the particular type of stamps you intend to focus on. Provide a history of the auction prices of the stamps to show how they have appreciated in value over the years. Provide statistics or information from industry reports that shows that your particular area is still ripe for investment opportunities.

If you are going to breed dogs, talk about the particular breed you intend to focus on. Provide a history of the prices of these animals, perhaps showing that the prices have gone up over the years. Provide statistics or information from industry reports that justify your belief that you can make a profit in this field.

Discuss what you plan to do to promote the venture. Describe your customer base, your location, and the size of the market. Describe your pricing philosophy. Include the sort of advertising you hope to implement, and which trade shows and seminars you expect to attend. Add anything else that applies to your marketing strategy.

Set forth any weaknesses presented in the market situation or in your particular strategy, and how you anticipate dealing with these weaknesses.

You may want to discuss any licenses or permits you will need to obtain in order to engage in this venture. If applicable, discuss environmental, legal, or governmental factors that could be hurdles.

This central section of a business plan should be the longest part of the document. The more detail you can put in, the better.

4.4 Operational plan

The operational plan will contain information, if applicable, regarding the management structure of your venture — who the key people are; what their duties will be; whether they are employees, independent contractors, or consultants; and what qualifications they have. For instance, if you are operating a vineyard and intend to hire a competent farm manager, talk about it in this section.

If you are going to operate as a sole proprietor, you can simply state that you intend to operate as a sole proprietor and that you will be responsible for day-to-day management, as well as administrative and promotional efforts.

4.5 Financial projections

Most people do not like writing a budget or any other type of financial information. However, this is an important feature of a business plan. You should do your best. If you feel you cannot do this section well on your own, you may want to hire an accountant or CPA to prepare this part of your business plan.

The financial information should show how much money you will need to spend to get the business going; what equipment, inventory, and materials you will need to obtain; and when you expect to make a profit. There should be an indication as to your reasonable estimate of revenue. This is usually very difficult to project. Just do your best, utilizing financial data available to you from industry sources. Preferably, your financial projections should cover a three- to five-year period.

If you hire an accountant or CPA to help prepare the projections, this can further bolster the businesslike nature of the document, although you will still need to spend time developing the figures on your own before you give them to the accountant or CPA.

Most people project operating losses for the start-up phase of the activity, which can be from three to seven years or longer, depending on the particular activity.

Your financial projections of profit should be reasonable, not exaggerated. You may discuss how you anticipate the industry to perform in the next three to five years or so.

4.6 Long-range plan

State your long-term plans; that is, what your vision is for the business five years from now, who your competitors will be, whether the business will have shifted into a new direction, who your customers will be, and how you will reach your customers. If you are optimistic, by all means say why this is the case. If you anticipate changes in market trends, state how you intend to deal with them. If you go over budget, state what changes in operations you might employ in order to reduce costs.

5. Chapter Summary

Writing a business plan is one of the most important things you can do to show that you are operating your activity in a businesslike manner. It will take a certain amount of time, thinking, and research to put your plan together. It is important not only because it helps you generate ideas and put them on paper in a clear and concrete way, but also because it serves as documentary evidence of your profit motive and businesslike manner of operating, which you can show the IRS if you are audited.

Having a written business plan does not guarantee that the IRS will find your venture to be a business rather than a hobby, particularly if you fail to use your plan to help improve profitability. However, the IRS will be impressed that you took the time and trouble to write a business plan or that you paid to have a professional put one together for you. People who engage in hobbies do not have business plans, so a business plan can be very helpful in showing that you are engaged in a business and not a hobby. Also, from a practical standpoint, a business plan helps you focus on certain economic details of your activity, which will in turn help you move closer towards making a profit.

4
OPERATING YOUR BUSINESS

In determining whether your venture is a business or a hobby, the IRS will want to examine the overall manner in which you conduct the day-to-day business. If you operate a business rather than a hobby, you will need to have a different approach to your venture. It is necessary to run your activity with the same vision and zeal that people have in other businesses. This chapter explores what kind of business records to keep, when they come into play, what they are for, and how to use them.

There is a double standard of sorts. People who claim to be operating a business in an activity traditionally thought of as a hobby, such as dog breeding or coin collecting, are sometimes expected to operate in a more businesslike manner than people in conventional areas. For instance, the IRS might allow a fairly loose standard of business records for a mom-and-pop grocery store but not for a dog-breeding activity. The reason is that the mom-and-pop grocery store is clearly not a hobby, but with activities that have some degree of recreation or pleasure, such as dog breeding, the IRS will deny your tax deductions

if you don't have a businesslike manner of operating the venture. The IRS scrutinizes these situations since this is an area in which many people are tempted to abuse the tax laws.

If you conduct your venture in a businesslike manner, the IRS will be more inclined to rule that the activity is a business, but if the venture is conducted in a haphazard way, you will have a hard time proving it is not a hobby. Also, conducting the venture in a businesslike manner will help make the activity profitable.

Remember, your *intention* to be engaged in a business is the entire focus of the hobby loss rule. In order to prove your intention, the best evidence is documentary evidence, as was mentioned in Chapter 1. Maintaining adequate or better-than-adequate business records is the best evidence that you are operating in a businesslike manner.

The adequate type and amount of business records will vary among different types of activities, and there is no absolute standard or requirement. The type and extent of records kept in a dog-breeding activity will be entirely different than those kept by someone pursuing an acting career.

Nobody has perfect business records! Often there are omissions in record keeping, but it is important that you go beyond the shoebox method. It is not enough to keep a file folder in which you throw scraps of paper or receipts, as if you were still a hobbyist.

1. Day-to-Day Business Records

Once you start the venture, you should develop a system for maintaining adequate business records on a regular basis. Maintaining businesslike records is excellent evidence that you are operating in a businesslike manner. The IRS will look at whatever business records you have. Your records can make a good impression or a bad impression, depending on many variables.

Your records should be sufficiently comprehensive to meet the demands of the particular practices of your field. The records should be maintained as is expected in your particular type of business. This will vary depending on the nature of your activity, as you will see in the examples throughout this book.

If you are engaged in horse breeding, for instance, the scope of records will be more extensive than if you are engaged in an Amway distributorship. For example, in horse breeding you would be expected to keep foaling records; records of horses purchased, sold, and those that died; records of veterinary care performed on each horse, and many more records.

Business records involve something above and beyond receipts and other records that you keep for tax return preparation or to substantiate your expenses. Everyone is expected to keep bank records, canceled checks, bills, credit card invoices, cash purchase receipts, airline tickets, restaurant and hotel receipts, and other records needed in order to prepare tax returns.

What the IRS is looking for are records that you utilize to make informed business decisions. The records that most impress the IRS are the type that you can use to analyze how to increase the profitability of the venture. The records should be the kind that can help you analyze past expenses to determine whether any adjustments to those expenses could improve profitability.

The US Tax Court has stated: "The purpose of maintaining books and records is more than to memorialize for tax purposes the existence of the subject transactions; it is to facilitate a means of periodically determining profitability and analyzing expenses such that proper cost saving measures might be implemented in a timely and efficient manner." [*Burger v. Commissioner,* T.C. Memo 1985-523.]

The quality of your records becomes increasingly important if you are not making a net profit after the normal start-up phase for your activity.

You should periodically review your business plan to see if circumstances have changed that justify amending the plan, and to see if certain objectives set forth in the plan have been realized. Every year or two it is advisable to write a supplement to the business plan to set forth appropriate changes. You should keep old and new business plans for possible evidence in the future.

It is quality, not necessarily quantity, of business records that matters. Still, if in doubt, the more documentation you maintain, the better.

2. Importance of Accuracy of Business Records

Records are not considered businesslike unless, in the first place, they are accurate. Inaccurate information, falsified dates, or incorrect numbers erode the credibility of the records and renders them unreliable as business records.

If your business records are inaccurate, you run the risk that your records will be viewed, as one US Tax Court case put it, to be "so fraught with omissions and inconsistencies that it is difficult to imagine how they served any beneficial purpose." [*Daley v. Commissioner,* T.C. Memo 1996-259.]

Often simple inaccuracies, such as discrepancies between the amounts claimed as expenses compared to the amounts shown in canceled checks, are understandable and will not cause any problems. But serious inaccuracies, like falsified records, backdated business plans (or other documents), or highly unrealistic income forecasts will call your credibility into question. Once credibility is lost, the IRS agent will not believe what you have to say, which could seriously imperil your case.

3. Making Changes in Methods of Operation

One of the main hurdles that many taxpayers face in a hobby loss audit is proving they made efforts to change methods of operation. The IRS is always interested in what you are doing to change your methods of operation so as to cut down on costs or to increase your chances of making a profit. In the business world, big companies constantly make changes if profits are hard to achieve, whether it means cutting down on costs by layoffs, changing the focus of the business, or selling off unproductive assets.

If you are claiming losses on your tax returns, the IRS will ask you: "What have you done to make changes in the way you operate the activity?" The IRS will be impressed if you periodically evaluate the overall performance of your venture, and if you make appropriate changes to help increase your chances of making a profit.

Taking a fresh look at operations from time to time, particularly in response to changing circumstances or industry developments, is evidence that you operate as a business rather than a hobby. If you are making a profit, you should keep doing business pretty much the same way, since it is apparently working for you.

Often taxpayers will fail to have documentary evidence of changes they make to enhance operations, which can be a problem in withstanding IRS scrutiny. It is therefore important to accumulate documentary evidence to prove what you have done. For instance, you could generate a memo to the file discussing your analysis of current operations and setting forth ideas on how they may be made more efficient. This usually means figuring out ways of reducing costs.

Some ventures are expensive to conduct and incur sizable costs — most notably, horse breeding, auto racing, aircraft or boat chartering, and collectibles (particularly art, stamps, and coins). The IRS will be impressed if you have used your financial records as tools to help you monitor costs and discover ways of cutting expenses. Cutting down on costs translates into the idea that you are more likely to earn a profit. That's why large companies that are not doing well announce layoffs to reduce costs and help the company move closer to a profitable year.

Selling off unprofitable assets is another way of improving methods of operation. For example, if you are in a horse activity, it could be practical to give away older horses that are no longer productive — to new homes or to animal husbandry programs in colleges — thus reducing your costs of operation. Any practical solution that results in cost savings is evidence that you are operating in a businesslike manner.

However, sometimes it is important to hold onto certain assets that you expect to appreciate in value so that you can sell these assets at a greater price than what the current market would provide.

Adopting new techniques in the face of losses is evidence that you are operating in a business-like manner. Sometimes adopting new techniques can involve significant capital outlays, and if so, you should provide an analysis that states why this expenditure is a businesslike move under the circumstances. For instance, if your citrus farm proves unprofitable, and you learn that avocados or almonds are in high demand, you will need to spend a considerable amount of money to change from one thing to another. You should keep a file on this to document how you came to the decision and why it is economically justifiable to make the capital outlay. Keep copies of market research you conducted, contacts you had with other people in the industry, cost information you obtained from suppliers, emails and correspondence, and other documents related to the project. You will also want to make a revision to your business plan to indicate how this shift in focus will improve the chances of making a profit.

There are other things you can do to cut down on costs. If you are operating a farm or a resort, you can cut down on costs by performing some of the routine labor and repairs personally. If you are conducting a dog-breeding activity, you can save money by grooming your own dogs and by learning to become a professional handler, to help save on costs of hiring others for these duties. Or, if you need to travel in connection with your activity, you could stay at less expensive hotels.

You could try and negotiate better prices or more favorable terms with vendors from whom you buy supplies. You can sometimes defer payments or purchases until a subsequent year, thus reducing costs for the current year. You could also prepay certain expenses for supplies that are to be used in the following year. This could help reduce costs in the following year and increase your chances of making a profit.

In the start-up phase of your activity (usually from five to ten years, depending on the nature of your activity) it may be too early to know whether any changes are needed. It usually takes a period of time to understand if certain things are working or not working to your advantage. You should re-evaluate operations annually to see if other actions are necessary.

4. Improving Your Skills and Expertise

Even if you reach a point where you might be considered an expert in your field, it is important to continue your education in the field and stay up-to-date on the business aspects.

Under the hobby loss rule, the IRS will want to know what you do to keep up with current practices and improve your knowledge in the field. If you are an expert, you are still expected to stay on top of industry developments, and if you are not, it is even more important to do so. Hobbyists do not tend to be serious about keeping up with industry trends.

It is important, in running a business activity, to develop and improve your skills in the given field of involvement. For instance, if you are launching a sideline venture as a photographer, an actor, or a musician, the IRS will want to know what you did to continually improve your skills. Evidence that you have continued your education in the subject matter will help prove that you are engaged in a business rather than a hobby; for example, attending seminars or classes, pursuing other means of enhancing your abilities in the field, keeping on top of market trends, or other strategies.

5. Appraisals of Assets Used in the Activity

Under the hobby loss rule, evidence that certain assets used in the activity have or are expected to appreciate in value helps prove your profit motive. The idea is that if your assets appreciate in value, this could more than offset your losses because an overall profit could result if the assets are sold.

Assets that may appreciate include collectibles such as stamps, coins, antiques, or art; and animals such as dogs, horses, or cattle. If you utilize land in connection with the activity — such as an agricultural farm, livestock farm, or horse farm — appreciation in the value of the property is usually important in showing you could make a profit if the property were sold. If you make improvements to the land used in the activity, this also helps bolster the fact that the property has or is expected to increase in value.

You should have periodic formal appraisals of certain assets to help prove that the property is appreciating in value or that it is expected to appreciate in value. The IRS will not give much stock to your verbal statement that certain assets have appreciated in value. Only a formal appraisal will have an impact, and this often can make or break an audit.

Only use qualified appraisers in your particular field. Let the appraiser know that you wish to substantiate the appreciation in value of the assets in question. For appraisals of land, there are tax guidelines with which a professional appraiser would normally be familiar. The appraisal should indicate that the realty has increased in value as a result of your stewardship over the property (e.g., due to improvements you made) rather than due to general market factors common to all property in the region.

You may want to hold on to certain items until they have reached a certain market value, and periodic appraisals can let you know where you stand. The US Tax Court has ruled that holding onto valuable property (e.g., a stamp collection or a valuable stallion) is justified if you expect to eventually profit when it reaches a higher market value.

6. Written Contracts

It is important to have written contracts for all your business dealings. To my amazement, many people do not have written contracts for any of their transactions, or the contracts are clumsily drafted, or they fail to keep copies.

There are various types of contracts. You might have a lease, a partnership agreement, sales contracts, service contracts, or advertising contracts. Using written contracts, particularly for significant transactions, is evidence of your businesslike manner of operating.

Even if you are selling collectibles at a flea market, you should always issue a sales receipt to the customer, listing the date, a description of the items purchased, the price, and the sales tax. You should add your business name on the top of each receipt. The receipts should be numbered sequentially. You can obtain sales receipts booklets at office supply stores or develop your own customized forms.

For the sale of special items, such as works of art, stamp collections, vintage cars, or animals, you should have a more detailed sales contract. Usually sales of these items are accompanied by assurances that you have marketable title to the property. Sales of important items usually include the seller's warranty that the item is an authentic piece of what it purports to be (e.g., a Van Gogh).

In the sale of animals, customers may want some sort of warranty of soundness of the animal, a statement of fitness for intended use, a statement that the animal is free of infectious disease, a statement as to the animal's pedigree, and statements regarding other pertinent elements. Sometimes you may not wish to provide certain warranties. You may want to sell certain items "as is" with no warranties whatsoever. These are matters to discuss with the customer and to set forth in the sales contract.

Sometimes customers wish to make installment payments on higher priced items. This involves retaining title to the property until it is paid for in full. You always take a risk in selling items to people on an installment basis. It is often very difficult to get the property back if the buyer defaults on payments. If you sell someone something on an installment contract, it is important to enforce its terms. If people owe you money in a business deal, it is considered unbusinesslike if you fail to collect the money due.

Some people generate sham sale contracts because they are desperate to show a profit in case the IRS audits them. It is improper to fabricate paper profits. The IRS is usually suspicious of any "sales" between the taxpayer and friends or family members. You might be asked to explain the circumstances of transactions between yourself and friends or family members. If you have bona fide sales to friends or family members, be sure you actually get paid the amount stated in the contract and that the contract is completely legitimate.

It is important to keep *signed* copies of all contracts, leases, sales agreements, partnership agreements, and so forth, rather than unsigned or draft copies. Of course, simple sales receipts will not have signatures but will simply be issued by you to the customer with a carbon copy retained for your records.

If you have several drafts of a contract that you negotiated with someone, you should keep the earlier drafts as well as the final contract in your files. This will be helpful to show your businesslike approach to negotiating and finalizing particular transactions.

Also, whenever you buy anything for your venture, whether it's office supplies or items for your collection, be sure you get a written sales receipt or contract. This will prove that you have an ownership interest in whatever is involved. If you are collecting art, stamps, coins, antiques, or anything else of value, you will need to compute the amount of profit when you resell the item, and the cost basis can be established by reference to the sales receipt or contract that was issued to you at the time of purchase. Also, the cost basis is important for establishing the amount of depreciation deductions that you might take, particularly on horses, livestock, or other depreciable property. If you are unable to prove your cost basis, the IRS has the right to deny your depreciation deductions. For example, in one case the taxpayer claimed ownership of several exotic farm animals, but she had no record of buying the animals, so the IRS suspected they were gifts she received from her father and denied depreciation deductions. [*Brannon v. Commissioner IRS,* T.C. Memo 2000-76.]

Another reason it is important to keep records of the cost basis of certain items, is that if you are holding onto property that you expect to appreciate in value, the IRS may want to verify the cost basis and compare that to your current appraisal.

7. Keeping a Time Log

If you spend a considerable amount of time on your venture, the IRS will take this to mean you are operating in a businesslike manner. If you devote little time to the venture, the IRS will argue that this is more consistent with a hobby than a business. The US Tax Court looks favorably on individuals who devote themselves "seriously or assiduously" to their business affairs. [*Commissioner v. Widener,* 33 F.2d 833 (3rd Cir. l929).]

While the exact number of hours spent on your activity may vary from month to month due to seasonal requirements, you will want to keep track of the overall amount of time you spend doing the activity.

If you claim to devote a lot of time to the venture, and also have a full-time job, the IRS might not believe you. Often the IRS will question how someone who has a day job can afford to put 20 or 30 hours a week into the hobby-turned-business venture. The IRS will want to know how you can have a full-time job and still have enough time to devote to your venture, or they will argue that the only reason you spend so much time on the activity is that it gives you personal pleasure and is a hobby. The IRS sometimes uses this tactic with retired individuals who spend considerable time on their activity.

In order to prove how much time you devote to the activity, it is important to keep a simple log, calendar, or time sheet that tracks your time on a daily or weekly basis. You could also keep a computer program to corroborate how much time you devote to the venture. The log should show the number of hours per week you spend on the activity, as well as the amount of time spent by your spouse, since the IRS considers a husband-wife team in evaluating the time spent on the activity.

Even if you don't keep a time log, the IRS will still want to know how much time you spend on the activity, and if you are credible, your oral statement could be sufficient. But as previously mentioned, the IRS prefers documents to a taxpayer's self-serving verbal statements. If your overall business records are not businesslike, the fact that you don't keep a time log will do further harm to your case.

The following list includes the typical categories of activity that should go into your time log:

- Consulting with advisers
- Paying bills
- Travel time
- Attending trade shows or seminars
- Keeping business records
- Discussing matters with your partner, adviser, or other consultants
- Implementing or revising business plans
- Reviewing finances or budgets
- Making cost projections
- Speaking with vendors
- Talking to potential customers
- Writing emails
- Supervising others
- Reading trade journals and researching industry information
- Marketing and promotion
- Performing other tasks and decision-making functions

Your time log should be kept as current as possible. A simple form consists of four columns with room to make entries in the following areas:

- Date of the activity
- What you did (using codes makes it easier, see the chart on the next page)
- The amount of time spent doing the activity

- A space for comments (e.g., the name and phone number of an individual to follow up with)

The chart is a simple code system to help you save space and time when completing your time log. You can adapt these codes as you wish. Simply input the code for the type of activity and add the description.

Most people who end up being audited under the hobby loss rule haven't kept adequate time logs and only reconstruct time records in preparation for an audit. IRS revenue agents will usually discount any self-serving records created after the fact. The revenue agent will ask you when you created your time log and if you say you recently created it, it will not look good. The general rule is that time records should be kept contemporaneous with the time period in question. Updating your time log daily is ideal, but weekly would be sufficient.

Some activities require more time than others. A farm requires more time (to attend to animals and crops, conduct repairs, seed, clear land, make improvements, and supervise others) than an activity like collecting stamps or coins. Activities such as classic car refurbishing, dog breeding, writing, and acting can easily take 20 or 30 hours a week.

If you work on the activity only on weekends, evenings, or vacation time, this can be a problem. This pattern makes one look like a hobbyist who spends time on the activity on weekends and evenings when they can enjoy themselves. The IRS might argue that if you were serious about the activity you would spend more time on it, not just weekends or evenings.

If you hire qualified people to help manage your venture, this shows a businesslike concern for the activity and it also enables you to devote your time to certain areas that you know best. Be sure to hire qualified personnel as best as you can manage. The IRS sometimes views hiring family members for no salary as unbusinesslike. Thus, it is important to hire people who are qualified and whom you pay. If you hire a relative, there should be a business basis for doing so, such as the expertise of the individual or the trust you repose in them.

Codes for Time Log

Code Letter	Meaning
A	Attending to books and records of the venture and making disbursements
C	Consultation or meeting
M	Miscellaneous
MRI	Maintenance, repairs, manual labor, cleaning, improvements
P	Planning time, reviewing finances, revising business plans
TT	Travel time
TC	Telephone conversation
S	Supervising others
ST	Attending seminar or trade show
R	Researching the marketplace or the industry; reading journals and industry magazines; researching materials in libraries, on the Internet, or with industry personnel.

Note that in husband-and-wife ventures, both spouses are usually active in the venture, but it is not expected that either of them will get a salary. Their compensation is from the net profits.

Some activities are seasonal. If you are operating a ski resort, you will be putting in time only during certain months. But you will probably need to spend some off-season time marketing and promoting the venture and taking reservations.

8. Travel, Automobile, and Entertainment Expenses

Because travel and entertainment expenses are an important element in tax deductions for most businesses and professions, it is helpful to point out some of the basic rules.

8.1 Travel expenses

There are strict substantiation requirements in connection with travel expenses, set forth in IRS Code section 274(d). You have to keep records of the —

- amount of the expense,
- time of travel,
- place of travel, and
- business purpose of the expense.

The record should consist of an account book, diary, log, or other documentary evidence that establishes each element of the expense.

Sometimes you can deduct the travel costs of your spouse or a partner. For example, Frank Kluckhohn was a newspaper correspondent and writer in Minnesota. Mr. Kluckhohn sent his wife to Australia to gather material that he wanted to use, and did use, in writing a book and an article. He was allowed to deduct the amount expended by Mrs. Kluckhohn in connection with the trip. The court noted that Mr. Kluckhohn did not

profit from the use of the material "but that is not important." [*Kluckhohn v. Commissioner,* 18 T.C. 892 (1952).]

8.2 Automobile expenses

Many people deduct automobile expenses and depreciation. This is one of the biggest and most commonly audited items on tax returns. In order to be deductible, vehicle expenses must be incurred in the pursuit of a trade or business. Expenses incurred in commuting from your home to your day job are non-deductible personal expenses. Similarly, automobile depreciation is permitted as a deduction only if, and to the extent that, the car is used in the pursuit of a trade or business or for the production of income.

It is important to keep good records of all business-related automobile expenses and a daily mileage log showing business miles driven. Ideally, your log should show the date, the beginning and ending odometer readings, the location, the business purpose, and the client. Such detail is hard for people to keep, but it's important to have something in writing in case you're audited. At minimum, make sure you write down the automobile's odometer reading at the beginning and the end of the tax year and have a daily record that you could go back to and use to reconstruct a claimed business mileage tax deduction on your tax return.

8.3 Entertainment expenses

With regard to entertainment expenses, the IRS requires that there is a specific business benefit linked to the entertainment. Section 274(c) of the IRS Code states that:

No deduction otherwise allowable under this chapter shall be allowed for any item —

With respect to an activity which is of a type generally considered to constitute entertainment, amusement, or recreation, unless the taxpayer establishes that the item was directly related to, or, in the case of an item directly preceding or following a substantial and bona fide business discussion (including business meetings at a convention or otherwise), that such item was associated with, the active conduct of the taxpayer's trade or business.

To substantiate entertainment expenses, the IRS requires you to show the —

- amount of each expenditure,

- date of each expenditure,

- name, address, or location of the entertainment,

- specific business reason or benefit of the expense, and

- occupation or other information relating to the person(s) entertained to establish business relationships.

In general, this substantiation rule was designed to encourage taxpayers to maintain adequate written records and documentary evidence of entertainment expenditures. It is important to maintain receipts and other evidence of the expenditures, and to make a notation of the five elements mentioned above on the back of the receipts.

It is recommended that you maintain two types of records to satisfy the substantiation requirements:

1. A summary of expenses (e.g., account book, diary, log, statement of expense, trip sheets, or similar record).

2. Documentary evidence (e.g., receipts or paid bills) with a notation as to the five elements mentioned above.

Expense summaries have greater evidentiary value if they are made at or near the time of an expenditure.

For entertainment that involves travel, it is important to keep a log of the dates of departure and return for each trip away from home, the number of days away that are spent on business, the destination of any travel, the location and type of entertainment, and the place at which the business discussion was conducted.

Taxpayers who cannot substantiate an element, such as cost or time, with adequate records, may substantiate expenses by their own statement (which must be specific and detailed as to each element) plus some corroborative evidence to establish each element.

The key to an entertainment expense, whether it is entertaining people at the Kentucky Derby or at a Super Bowl weekend, is that you should show that the expenditures were tied to or motivated by the intent to secure a business advantage.

9. Chapter Summary

No one has perfect business records or operates in a perfectly businesslike manner. That is humanly impossible. Even Fortune 500 companies are constantly faulted by Federal regulators for inadequacy in record keeping. As long as your overall records are sufficient to help you monitor your successes and failures, and you demonstrate efforts to keep expenses as low as possible, you should be able to prove that your predominant motive is to make a profit.

In operating a sideline business, you are not expected to maintain a sophisticated cost accounting system, but you are expected to keep records that enable you to make informed business decisions as to the activity. The IRS will be impressed if you use your books and records as a means of periodically determining profitability, analyzing expenses, and helping decide on cost saving measures that you can implement in a timely manner. Of course, if you wish to keep elaborate books and records, by all means do so, because it will enhance your argument that you are operating in a businesslike manner.

Operating in a businesslike manner (and therefore having businesslike records) becomes more important if you have a history of losses beyond the start-up years. Continued losses over an extended period of time is a major hurdle in passing a hobby loss audit.

The IRS will want to know if you made changes in the operation in response to changing circumstances, or whether you have sought ways to cut down on costs, in order to improve your ability to make a profit. Whatever you do in this regard, you should maintain a file to prove what efforts you actually made to reduce expenses.

The overall quality of your day-to-day records is important, as is their accuracy. A time log that you keep current will have more value as an item of evidence than a time log that you prepare only in anticipation of an audit.

5
ADVERTISING AND PROMOTION

Under the hobby loss rule it is important to promote your activity by advertising or by using other marketing efforts. The IRS will argue that if you don't advertise, market, or promote your activity you are engaged in a hobby, not a business. Thus, promotion of your product or service is crucial to prove you are engaged in a business.

For many of the activities discussed in this book, if you do not advertise or otherwise promote your venture, the IRS will argue that you are engaged in a hobby because you don't care about selling your product or service.

Advertising is considered to be an effective type of promotion to attract customers or clients. Therefore, it is considered businesslike to advertise, although at times it can be expensive. If you don't engage in advertising, the IRS will want to know what you do to promote (i.e., market) your activity.

There is no concrete definition of what constitutes advertising. Advertising includes any devices that introduce your business name to the public. Advertising consists of anything that provides a promotional linkage to your business or profession.

It is important to determine the right way to advertise or promote your particular venture.

1. Advertising
1.1 Word of mouth

Since advertising usually needs to be repeated and can be expensive in newspapers, in magazines, on TV, and on the radio, many people rely on word-of-mouth advertising as a way of marketing their products or services. Word-of-mouth advertising is an important way to share information with friends, relatives, and colleagues to generate interest in your venture.

With the advent of the Internet, word-of-mouth advertising has taken on a new life. People can use message boards and chat rooms to get the word out for little or no cash investment. Web logs, email newsletters, and chat rooms have become a way of generating interest in products and services.

1.2 Website

Nowadays most small businesses maintain an informative website. This is a useful and affordable means of advertising. Once you have a website, you will need to have Internet traffic. There are Internet resources that, for a modest fee, will help direct people to your site when they conduct searches for certain products or services. Also, you can join with other individuals and organizations to get your site linked to theirs. This is well worth the time and effort.

1.3 Public speaking, organizations, and trade shows

If you are good at public speaking, you can make yourself available as a speaker for various clubs and organizations to talk about your area of expertise.

You could also become involved in the politics of industry organizations. Anyone who wants to can usually get involved with helping the governing boards of organizations, by getting active on committees or by helping to write newsletters. Your participation shows a businesslike concern because you are taking the time to help promote your particular trade.

Attend trade shows, seminars, or industry events to promote your business. Be sure to have plenty of business cards. You could also distribute flyers at trade shows, fairs, seminars, or other suitable venues where there are networking opportunities. Don't be shy about meeting new people and using the occasions as networking opportunities to promote yourself. Ask for business cards from other people. Get to know people who are successful in your field, because they could be mentors from whom you could elicit good advice.

You can think of creative ways to promote your business at events, such as giving away baseball caps, pens, and other items with your business name on them.

1.4 Contact the customer directly

One of the most important ways people market their products or services is by directly contacting people, either as follow-up calls to potential customers or by making cold calls.

Directly contacting old and potential customers is a time-honored way of gaining business. You should maintain an updated list of existing and potential customers, together with phone and address information. Periodically you can send them interesting announcements about what you are doing, what's new, and what you are offering, as well as invitations to receptions where you can showcase your products or services. Of course, keep copies of all letters or emails you send in connection with these solicitation efforts. The IRS will be impressed if you have evidence that you actively solicited customers or clients.

You can also make direct phone calls to existing or potential customers to provide them with information that could be of interest to them regarding your products or services. For instance, if you have a customer who is looking for a particular coin and you have found what he or she wants, you will want to notify that person so as to generate a sale. The same applies no matter what your product or service.

You could also telephone people you have met at seminars or trade shows to remind them of who you are and feel it out a bit. Don't be shy. It's a good way to generate business, and if you have already met someone, the person usually doesn't mind getting a call from you as long as you are courteous and have something interesting to say.

It is a good idea to keep a phone log of these calls, with notations about discussions you had and any follow up that will be required. You can develop a simple form for logging the date, the name of the person you called, and comments.

1.5 Sponsorship of an activity

This section discusses situations in which people have sponsored their own favorite activities as means of advertising their businesses or professions. The sponsorship costs are tax-deductible advertising expenses. This is a creative and legitimate form of advertising that anyone can take advantage of.

While advertising in newspapers or magazines and direct-mail advertising might have limited impact, sponsorship advertising can help reach out to a different group of potential customers.

For example, you might sponsor a local basketball team as a means of advertising. The team would wear your business name or logo on uniforms. In addition, the sponsorship gives you an opportunity to meet potential clients, and entertain existing and potential clients (as well as your employees) at the games.

People who engage in sponsorship advertising clearly enjoy being involved with their favorite activity. The IRS often seeks to argue that these costs are not advertising expenses, but a disguised way of paying for an activity.

It is important, if you are audited, to emphasize the advertising benefits that your sponsorship provides to your business or profession, and that any personal enjoyment you gain from the activity is incidental to the advertising purpose. The IRS may need to be convinced that the sponsorship provides a concrete advertising benefit to your business.

According to numerous market surveys, the public generally has a positive attitude towards sponsorship in sports. The public tends to think that without sponsorship, certain sporting events would not be viable; that sponsors are highly reputable firms, leaders in their industry, dedicated to excellence, and deserving of their business. Sponsorships can help generate or maintain customer good will, which is an important advertising benefit. (See Chapter 21 for more information on sponsoring a sports event.)

Most of the examples in this section and throughout the book are of *self-sponsorship*. This is a type of sponsorship, usually in expensive sports such as auto racing — where the taxpayer "sponsors" his or her own sports activity. The sponsorship costs are considered advertising expenses for promoting his or her own business or profession.

With self-sponsorship, instead of paying sponsorship fees to a third party, you are paying fees to yourself. It comes out as a tax deduction against your main trade or profession. The expenses go toward funding the specific activity or sports team you have assembled.

The test for deductibility is whether you reasonably expect that your sponsorship will provide advertising benefits to your business. The amount of sponsorship fees must be reasonable, considering the size of your business or in relation to your overall advertising budget. The IRS will sometimes argue that the sponsorship expenses are high in comparison to your business income and that your predominant motive is the love of the activity you are sponsoring.

You will need to convince the IRS that your sponsorship has an advertising benefit by enhancing the public's image of your business; by increasing public awareness of your products; or by directly stimulating sales, products, or services. You should prepare records to show that your sponsorship has a valid advertising purpose for your business or profession.

The following case is an example of self-sponsorship.

Example: *Ciaravella v. Commissioner,* **T.C. Memo 1998-31.**

Ron Ciaravella owned and operated the Sarasota/Bradenton International Airport in Florida. He also sold and leased jet aircraft.

His hobby was open-wheeled racing. He drove several times a year in races on a national circuit sponsored by Merrill Lynch and Rolex. He believed that racing could help him build a "dashing, gallant image" that would allow him to meet and ingratiate himself with people interested in buying and leasing high performance aircraft, such as the used Learjets that he marketed. His race car bore the logo of his company as well as his own name, Ron Ciaravella.

Mr. Ciaravella convinced the US Tax Court that his racing activities resulted in contacts that led to the sale and lease of aircraft, including the sale of a Learjet to a Las Vegas construction company for $1.9 million.

The court noted that Mr. Ciaravella got national exposure from his racing and he used this to his advantage. He met several celebrities and other prominent people at the races, and these were the type of people who could be interested in buying or leasing the high performance aircraft he sold.

The previous example provides the following key points:

1. The taxpayer proved that his sponsorship of his own car racing activity provided advertising benefits to his business. The evidence was the sale of a high-priced aircraft to someone he had met as a result of his sponsorship.

2. Evidence of the advertising purpose included the taxpayer's diligence in getting his business name displayed at the races he entered.

3. The taxpayer clearly enjoyed the social aspects of auto racing, but he used these occasions to meet potential customers, and one such contact purchased a jet aircraft from him.

There are many other cases in which people have convinced the US Tax Court that self-sponsorship and sponsorship of others in an auto racing activity constituted deductible advertising expenses for their main businesses. A few examples are summarized below:

• The owner of five pizza restaurants was entitled to deduct his costs as a stock car race driver as advertising expenses. He convinced the court that he used the racing to advertise his pizza restaurants. [*Brallier v. Commissioner,* T.C. Memo 1986-42.]

• Similarly, the owner of a meat processing company was allowed to deduct the costs of sponsoring a race car driver. The taxpayer had his business name displayed on the vehicle, and track announcers referred to his business when announcing his races. Also, the races were frequently attended by local farmers with whom he did business, and he was able to meet with them at these events. [*Hestnes v. Commissioner,* T.C. Memo 1983-727.]

• The owner of a Chevrolet dealership was also a professional auto racer. He deducted the cost of his racing activities as an advertising expense for his dealership. His racing achievements were reported in *Corvette News*, which is distributed to owners of Corvette automobiles. The US Tax Court upheld his deductions, noting that he made a number of sales as the direct result of the racing, and the expenses constituted a relatively small part of his dealership's advertising budget. The taxpayer was already well-known in racing circles and this may have helped attract attention to his sponsorship and enhance the advertising benefit to his business. [*Lang Chevrolet Co. v. Commissioner*, T.C. Memo 1967-212.]

- The owner of a metal buildings company was a car racing enthusiast and he decided to use his racing as a means of advertising his company. Many of the people who attended the races in his area were businessmen and several of them were in the business of erecting or selling metal buildings. The taxpayer made several business contacts as a result of his racing activities, including two that resulted in sales of metal buildings. [*Boomershine v. Commissioner*, T.C. Memo 1987-384.]

1.6 Creative advertising

The following two cases involve taxpayers who deducted the costs of African hunting safaris as advertising expenses. The taxpayers were ardent hunters and this was a passionate interest of theirs. They took back trophies and displayed them in their offices, which generated local publicity about their adventures. This in turn resulted in heightened public good will towards the business.

Example: *Sanitary Farms Dairy, Inc. v. Commissioner*, 25 T.C. 463 (1955).

O. Carlyle Brock was principal owner of Sanitary Farms Dairy, Inc., a large dairy company in Erie, Pennsylvania. He enjoyed fishing and hunting as hobbies. He had been on dozens of African hunting safaris.

A room in the dairy plant was a museum in which Mr. Brock displayed mounted heads and cured skins of the game he had killed, as well as trophies that he put on display. The public was invited to guided tours of the museum and the plant. The museum attracted groups from local schools, clubs, and other organizations. During visits, people were given a pitch regarding the company's dairy products.

Mr. Brock and his advertising director discussed the idea of going on a big game hunt to obtain additional specimens for the museum. They came up with a plan for Mr. Brock to write letters during his trip, which would be published in the local paper, and to have a camera crew take motion pictures which could later be shown to audiences.

Mr. Brock brought back several live animals from this safari and donated them to the local zoo. To the museum he added several specimens that he had killed.

The trip generated considerable publicity and 180,000 people viewed the film of the safari.

Mr. Brock developed the idea of inviting prospective customers and community figures to the plant, and serving them dinners of game he had hunted. He also showed them the safari film.

Mr. Brock's company claimed advertising deductions for the safari costs, film production, taxidermy costs, and dinner costs.

The US Tax Court ruled that the hunting trips, under the circumstances, "provided extremely good advertising at a relatively low cost." The media gave the safaris wide coverage and exploited the films to promote Mr. Brock's dairy business.

The court noted that Mr. Brock clearly enjoyed hunting, but that the trips represented hard work undertaken to promote his dairy business, and not simply recreation.

The previous example provides the following key points:

1. The taxpayer had the clever idea of using his safari trips as a way of advertising his company. He was able to get significant media attention about his trips, which heightened the advertising benefits to his company.

2. He invited the public to visit his museum, which displayed mounted specimens from his expeditions. Visitors were also given a guided tour of his plant and information about its products. This was an effective way of getting captive audiences to listen to information about the company's products. Also, 180,000 people viewed the video of his safaris and the court indicated that this had advertising benefits.

Example: *Brown v. Commissioner*, **446 F.2d 926 (8th Cir. 1971).**

Dana Brown, owner of a coffee company, went on safaris and filmed his adventures. He showed these films at various coffee industry events and at numerous coffee dealer meetings. He also lectured at these meetings, often including information about coffee growing methods and about his company's coffee products.

These films gained Mr. Brown a national reputation as a big game hunter and a coffee expert. His company's coffee sales increased. Some of the film segments were used in TV commercials.

The US Tax Court held that the advertising expenses associated with the safaris were deductible advertising expenses to the company.

The previous example provides the following key points:

1. This case involved a very creative advertising idea. The film of the owner's safaris was used to attract audiences and to entertain people at industry events. The film was then followed by a presentation about the company's coffee products.

2. Also, some of the segments were used in TV advertising for the company, which clearly provided an advertising benefit.

1.7 Socializing as a means of advertising

You can gain business contacts by socializing, networking, or attending functions where people talk about their work and hope to make business contacts. Some people seek to claim the costs of social events as advertising expenses. This can be acceptable, particularly if you place advertisements in the printed program for the events.

In the following case Richard Stasewich claimed an advertising deduction for his activities as an artist. He claimed, unsuccessfully, that his activities as an artist should be tax deductible because they helped advertise his accountancy practice.

Example: *Stasewich v. Commissioner*, **T.C. Memo 1996-302.**

Richard Stasewich argued that his activities as an artist, particularly socializing at art functions, gave him the opportunity to meet potential clients and promote his accounting practice. He argued that his costs were legitimate advertising expenses that he ought to be able to deduct against his accountancy income.

He also argued that most of his accounting clients were acquaintances from the artist community who chose him as their accountant because he was a fellow artist.

The US Tax Court denied his deductions and said: "The mere fact that engaging in an activity affords contact with possible future customers or clients is in and of itself insufficient to justify deducting the cost of the activity as a business expense."

The court said that Mr. Stasewich's activities as an artist gave him social opportunities to meet potential clients, but that there was only a remote relationship between the expenditures and his business.

The previous example provides the following key points:

1. The taxpayer failed to show an advertising link between his activities as an artist and his accountancy practice.

2. The court felt that his activities as an artist were distinctly social or personal.

3. The costs of attending social events are not normally "advertising" expenses, even if you gain business opportunities by attending the functions. In order to take advertising deductions for the cost of social events, it is necessary to show an advertising link such as being listed as a sponsor of the event or having an advertising display in the event's program.

4. The taxpayer could have taken entertainment deductions for those clients whom he entertained at art events. There are strict substantiation requirements for entertainment deductions, as discussed in Chapter 4. Sometimes entertainment expenses overlap with advertising and promotional expenses so that a given promotional activity can function both as a means of advertising and as a means of entertaining business clients.

2. Document Your Marketing Efforts

It is important to keep documentary evidence of any advertising, promoting, marketing, or networking. If you promote your activity through print ads, keep the original of the entire magazine or newspaper instead of just the page on which the ad appears. If you are audited, the IRS will want to see the complete original magazines, newspapers, or other publications (rather than computer-generated copies of your advertisement or the pages ripped out of the publication). You should also retain billing information about your advertisements, together with canceled checks, so you can ensure your ads were published and so you can prove it to the IRS.

If you get a new customer, you might want to ask how he or she heard about you. If the customer heard about you through word of mouth, this is important to note. It is evidence that your word-of-mouth efforts have resulted in something concrete. It is also evidence to support your businesslike approach in conducting the activity. If another person refers a new customer to you, be sure to acknowledge this by sending a letter of thanks and appreciation to the individual who referred the customer.

Of course, any marketing advice you obtain should be documented in some fashion so that you have further evidence of the businesslike manner in which you conduct your activity. If you have consultations with others about how to effectively market your products or services, keep records of the notes you took and the advice you obtained. You may also send a letter that acknowledges the advice you received and thanks the individual for his or her help, noting that you intend to follow the advice he or she gave you (if that is the case).

To further prove your marketing efforts, keep records of all offers you receive, even if they do not result in sales. For instance, if you have an antique auto for sale and you get serious inquiries that talk about price, make a note of these in your files. Evidence of offers is important even if the offers don't result in sales, because it shows that you are actively engaged in marketing your products or services. In some cases, where you might have a large volume of customers, you simply won't have the time to formally keep track of this. In that case, don't worry about it.

Depending on the volume of documents you accumulate, it is usually best to keep them all in one file pertaining to advertising or marketing efforts, as part of your permanent records.

3. Chapter Summary

Advertising today is ubiquitous to the point of even being obnoxious, yet it is so important and effective that it constitutes one of the biggest industries in the country.

There is no end to what you can do to advertise and promote, so focus on what's best for you. There may be some trial and error. Because advertising in traditional media channels can be expensive, you can save money by using word-of-mouth advertising. This is not only economical, but it can also be an important way of generating public awareness about what you are offering.

What you do to promote your business will depend on your field. A writer or an actor will focus on certain areas of networking, while a horse breeder will focus on horse shows and print ads in horse magazines. Maintaining a website and getting links to it has tremendous potential for generating interest in what you are offering.

Attending trade shows is a way of networking, meeting with people who are specifically interested in your field, and making new contacts. You can always follow up with contacts you make by phone, email, or regular mail.

Sponsorship of your favorite activity is an innovative and exciting way of generating local and regional publicity for your business. Sponsorship advertising is growing in importance as businesses, large and small, seek new ways to reach audiences and enhance their images.

Remember, the IRS will want to know if you have taken reasonable steps to promote, market, and advertise your activity. It is important to keep good records of your marketing efforts.

Don't be afraid to declare yourself and show your colors. Be versatile. Interweave your own inner assets and produce synergy — collective energy — in your efforts. Go for it!

6

HOME OFFICE DEDUCTIONS

Millions of people in various occupations and professions maintain a home office that they are entitled to claim for home office deductions. There are certain strict, if not complicated, conditions to be met to qualify for home office deductions. This chapter explores these conditions.

Most people who operate sideline businesses operate out of home offices. They do most of their business at home, on the phone, and out in the field. To rent office space for the activity might be a needless expense.

Under tax law, the space you designate as a home office can be a room or part of a room in your home, workshop, or studio. The room can be a separate structure on your property, such as a guest house, garage, studio, or barn.

You can take the deduction whether you own or rent your home. The larger the space devoted to the home office, the larger the deduction. The amount of the deduction is usually based on the proportion of square footage of the office divided by the square footage of your entire residence, or

the number of rooms used for the business divided by the number of rooms in the house — whichever is more favorable to you.

Whatever percentage of space is involved, you are entitled to deduct that percentage of household expenses (the cost of running your home). That includes a portion of rent if you are renting, or depreciation, mortgage interest, and property taxes if you own your home. Other deductible household expenses include utilities (e.g., electricity, gas, trash removal), homeowner's or renter's insurance, home maintenance and repair costs, condominium association fees, landscaping and gardener costs, snow removal costs, and security system costs.

Part of the deduction may consist of the cost of capital improvements made to the entire residence, recovered through depreciation, to the extent allocable to the portion of the residence used for the home office.

You can also deduct 100 percent of *direct expenses* associated with the home office space itself, such as painting the home office, paying someone to clean it, the costs of a business phone line, and other office expenses and equipment.

Before you decide to take home office deductions, however, you must observe the requirements set forth in section 280A of the IRS Code. Section 280A(c)(5) of the code limits the amount of the home office deduction, generally, to the gross income you generate from your business after reducing that by all other deductible expenses you claim. In other words, if you have gross income of $10,000 from your home office activity, and from that you deduct, say, $5,000 for your overall business expenses, the remainder of $5,000 is your net income. You can deduct home office expenses, in this example, for an amount up to your net income of $5,000.

If your net income is more than zero, then you can take a home office deduction — but the following points need to be observed.

1. Regular and Exclusive Business Use

The home office space must be used *exclusively* as an office and on a *regular basis*. Exclusive use means you must use the space *only* for your business venture. Thus, personal use of the space, even for a short time, could violate the exclusive use test. As a practical matter, the IRS has no way of knowing whether you use the space exclusively for business purposes since it is your own statement on this point that constitutes evidence. At the same time, you don't want to lie to the IRS, since candor and credibility are important if you are audited.

You must use the office on a *regular* basis. The term regular is fairly broad and implies that you use the office on a regular basis given the demands involved in your endeavors. If you rarely

use the home office, it is unlikely to be considered used on a regular basis.

2. Principal Place of Business

Most people qualify for the deduction because their home office is their principal place of business. Your home address might or might not be the mailing address for your business. Either way, it can still be your principal place of business. You should have a separate phone line for your business that is accessible in the home office.

The definition of a home office that qualifies as a *principal place of business* is given as either one of the following:

- Most of your business is done at home.
- Only your administrative work is done at home.

2.1 If you do most of your business at home

Doing most of your business at home could mean you decide to operate a dog-breeding venture in which you will likely use space in your home to do most of your business. Or, if you are an artist, you will create studio space within your home as the principal place of business.

You can have another location where you also conduct the business, or sometimes you will be conducting business while traveling or out in the field. If you do conduct business at other locations, the determination of your principal place of business depends on comparing the —

- relative importance of activities performed at each business location, and
- time spent at each location (i.e., the amount of time spent at the home office compared to the amount of time spent in the other places where you conduct business).

This is known as the *comparative analysis test*, set forth in the Supreme Court's decision, *Soliman v. Commissioner*, ll3 S.Ct. 70l (1993).

2.2 If you only do administrative work at home

Your home office can qualify as your principal place of business even if you only use it for the administrative and managerial activities of your business (assuming there is no other fixed location to conduct these activities). This is known as the *administrative/management activities test*. The home office, under this test, need not be the actual location where you generate most of your business income.

Administrative work means such things as billing customers or clients, keeping books and records, ordering supplies, setting up appointments, forwarding orders, doing research, keeping logs, filing documents, paying invoices, or writing reports.

You can still claim the home office for administrative or managerial activities even if you conduct some *minimal* paperwork at another fixed location of your business. You may also carry on administrative or managerial activities in your car or in a hotel room, as needed, and it won't affect your ability to claim a home office deduction.

For example, a self-employed nightclub singer's time is spent at rehearsal studios or in performances at various venues. She has a small office in her home that she uses exclusively and regularly for the administrative or managerial details of her business. She phones possible venues for gigs, prepares résumés, reviews music arrangements, and keeps books and records. Her home office qualifies as a principal place of business. She uses it for the administrative or managerial activities of her singing venture, and she has no other fixed location where she conducts these administrative or managerial activities.

3. Meeting Clients or Customers at Home

If your home office is *not* your principal place of business, you can still qualify for the home office deduction if you use the home office to meet with customers or clients on a regular basis. For example, if you have an antiques store but you also keep some inventory in your home, you could claim a home office for the purpose of showing items to customers. You can satisfy this test if you meet with customers one or two times a week.

In this case, you can also use the home office for other business purposes, such as paperwork and bookkeeping.

4. Using a Separate Structure for Business

If neither the principal place of business nor the customer-client meeting place apply to you, you could still take a home office deduction if you put the office in a separate structure such as a guest house, garage, studio, or barn. You can use any of these places as a home office even though they are not your principal place of business, and even if you do not meet clients or customers there. This office, like any home office, must be used regularly and exclusively for your business.

For example, if you are an art dealer, your principal place of business might be a commercial space you rent. You may rarely meet customers at your home, but let's say you have a detached garage that you decide to turn into a home office. If you use that space exclusively and regularly for business purposes, the space qualifies for the home office deduction.

5. Storing Inventory or Sample Products at Home

You can also deduct the costs of space within your residence where you store inventory and/or product samples. This applies if you are engaged in selling products, and if you use the storage area on a regular basis. A further requirement is that you do not have an office or studio located outside your home.

The storage space can be anywhere in your house such as a separate room, part of a room, a pantry, or the garage. You can also store other personal things in that space; in other words, the space need not be used exclusively to store your business inventory or product samples.

A deduction for storage space is *not* available if you have an office or studio located outside your home, as you could just as well store your things there.

6. Chapter Summary

If you decide to claim a home office, you might want to take pictures of it, so that if you are audited, you can prove that you actually have one, what it looks like, and its size.

If you qualify for a home office deduction based on one of the situations discussed in this chapter, remember, the office must be used on an *exclusive and regular basis* for the business, and not for anything else. Many people can, in addition to or instead of a home office, take deductions for storage space.

In many of the topics discussed in this book, people might be sustaining net losses rather than making net profits, at least for a period of time. In order to qualify for a home office deduction you have to be making a net profit from the business. If so, you are entitled to take home office deductions, assuming you meet the other qualifications, such as the principal place of business requirement discussed earlier.

7

HOW TO HANDLE AN IRS AUDIT

Each year the IRS audits approximately 1.5 percent of taxpayers. People in hobby-type ventures get audited at a relatively high rate compared to other taxpayers. The principal issue in these audits is whether the losses are deductible as ordinary and necessary business expenses, or whether they are nondeductible hobby losses.

People who have converted a hobby into a business are often selected for audit because they come up high on a "scoring system" that targets returns that show little or no profit from business operations. The IRS gives greater scrutiny to sole proprietorships filing as Schedule C businesses, with gross sales of less than $50,000. That includes most people who have a hobby-turned-business activity.

Tax returns are also selected for audit because they have tax deductions that are high in relation to income, tax items that require proof or an explanation, or tax items that are erroneous. Other returns are randomly selected.

Generally, an audit must be conducted within three years from the time the return was filed. If you have previously been audited and that resulted in a tax deficiency, your chances of being audited by the IRS again are high.

Many people are never audited despite the fact that they sustain losses over an extended number of years. This is due to the fact that the number of returns that have "red flags" exceeds the capacity of the IRS. Since IRS staff is limited, the IRS selects those tax returns that, on preliminary inspection, have high audit potential — returns that are most likely to result in a substantial tax deficiency.

Each district office of the IRS has staff who pour over the computerized selections in order to reduce the number of audit cases to a manageable caseload. Sometimes, instead of a formal audit, the IRS will ask you to explain and support some items or specific matters, and reply by return mail. These queries are usually resolved without a formal audit.

Many books have been written that offer useful guidance on how to handle an IRS audit. This chapter will simply highlight points of special importance for people who are audited on the hobby loss rule. For more information about tax audits see *Tax This!*, another book in the Self-Counsel Press legal series.

1. Election to Postpone an Audit

In any hobby loss audit, you, the taxpayer, have the right to postpone the audit under section l83(d) of the Tax Code. This means that the IRS will come back after an agreed on period of years and audit you at that point in time. You are required to sign a waiver of the statute of limitations for collection. When the time comes, you will be audited for each and every one of those years.

This may or may not be to your advantage. You should carefully consider your particular circumstances. If you are presently not operating in a businesslike manner, perhaps it is best to postpone the audit — and allow them to expand it into future years — because this will give you ample time to organize your activity. Once the audit occurs a few years down the line, you will presumably have taken the trouble to accumulate businesslike records to help prove you are operating in a businesslike manner.

2. Preparing for an Audit

In a hobby loss audit, the main issue is the manner in which you conduct the activity. The revenue agent needs to decide whether you are sincerely engaged in a business activity. If the agent decides that your activity is a hobby, you will be denied the deductions you claimed in connection with the activity. Many revenue agents will take the position that if you have not made a profit within the first few years of the activity, you are not engaged in a business, and you are simply trying to reduce your taxable income with tax deductions from your hobby activity.

In numerous instances, people in the early start-up phase of their venture are audited, and they can lose if they are not operating in a businesslike manner.

If you are selected for audit, you will receive a letter that requests your appearance and asks you to substantiate specific items for a specific year or years. You or your representative should find out what the IRS agent is looking for prior to formally participating in the audit.

Sometimes the letter will ask you to provide documents to explain questionable items, or you might receive an Information Document Request (IDR). This is usually a comprehensive request and can be quite daunting. The IDR normally asks for books and records of various kinds, canceled checks, journals, ledgers, and inventory records. If you are unable to comply with the entire list of requested items, simply do your best.

If you are selected for audit, it does not mean that you have done anything wrong or that you should be alarmed. However, if your tax returns claim significant deductions for your hobby type venture, you should be prepared to prove that the activity is a business, not a hobby.

You will need to prepare for the audit. It is crucial to have your books and records in order before meeting with the revenue agent. When you gather the information you should make sure that the records are complete and in good order, with the arithmetic adding up.

One of the first impressions you will make on the revenue agent will have to do with the appearance of your records. If you have to tidy some records, that will be a useful thing to do. It may take you a significant amount of time to put your documents in order if you use the shoebox method of record keeping.

You will want to organize everything as best you can to help provide a businesslike look to your presentation. You should double check existing records in order to ensure that, for instance, inventory ledgers are complete. If you operate under the auspices of a corporation or LLC, you should make sure that your Minute Book is complete and up to date.

You should only provide those records that are specifically requested. It is important to never give the IRS agent more information (or less) than requested. Always make copies of documents that are given to the IRS (i.e., never give them originals). Depending on how things proceed, you may at a later time find it beneficial to voluntarily offer to provide additional documents that help prove your businesslike manner of operating the venture.

The IRS today is much more respectful to taxpayers in the audit process than in previous years. Many fine dedicated employees spend their careers in the IRS, and on the whole they perform their duties well. Still, the primary function of an IRS auditor is to raise revenue for the government and there is a bureaucratic bias to analyze tax returns with strict scrutiny.

3. Initial Interview

The initial interview is one of the most important aspects of the audit. It is at this point that the auditor gets first impressions and gut instincts by asking you questions to learn about your operation.

It is usually best if you hire an experienced accountant or CPA to attend the audit on your behalf, and for you to stay away. Essentially, IRS audits are adversarial proceedings, although they are usually conducted in an informal atmosphere. Keep in mind that the auditor's main mission is to raise revenue for the government. Your representative will likely be more cool-headed than you could be. A representative can conduct the interview in a more objective and less emotional manner, and better control the flow of information the auditor receives.

If you are present at the audit, you will be expected to give on-the-spot answers to just about any question posed to you, since you are the entrepreneur of the venture. I am not suggesting that you answer questions in a dishonest manner, I am simply pointing out that people can usually respond more fully and intelligently to questions when they have adequate time to consider their answer rather than responding at the spur of the moment.

If your representative goes in your place, certain questions may not be answered on the spot because your representative will not likely know every answer, and will instead have to ask you about it later. Usually it will be necessary to "get back" to the auditor with further information. Your representative can relay questions to you, which allows you to calmly and rationally respond after having time to reflect on the answers.

Also, your representative can shield you from *exposure*, that is, from the risk that the agent will probe into areas that are vulnerable or try to trap you into saying things that can frustrate your purposes or confuse you.

If you are present at the audit, it is important to avoid the pitfall of expressing a passion for your activity (unless, of course, you are treating it as a hobby). A skilled examiner will be able to draw this passion from the taxpayer through conversation. You should avoid saying —

- that you enjoy engaging in the activity,
- that you have always loved the activity,
- that you would do it even if you never made a profit, or
- any other comments that suggest your primary purpose is to conduct a hobby activity.

If you attend the audit, you want to give the best possible initial impression. Be gracious and friendly. Tell the agent that you have brought documents to help answer any questions he or she may have, as well as receipts and other financial information to help substantiate and verify amounts claimed as expenses. Avoid needless commentary or chatter. Answers should be brief and to the point.

Sometimes your personal charisma and credibility, your courtesy, and your ability to say the right things can make a genuine impression. When you speak to an IRS agent, your honesty will go much further than evasive answers.

A good deal of hearsay evidence usually goes into information given to the IRS. If you are present at the audit, your opinions on certain points may be considered even though they are obviously self-serving. The IRS regards a taxpayer's personal statements as inherently self-serving and not nearly as credible as documentary evidence.

Still, if you are attending the audit, your believability can come across, which could be to your advantage. Remember, in a hobby loss audit your main purpose (after verifying and substantiating the amounts you claim as deductions) is to convince the IRS that you are operating a business, not a hobby. It is your *intention in the matter* that is of primary importance. So, if you tell the revenue agent that you sincerely and honestly believe you can make a profit in your venture, this can help win your case *if* the revenue agent believes you.

Remember, it is always important to supplement self-serving remarks with documentary evidence whenever possible. The IRS will want concrete evidence, not just your statement that you conducted market research, for instance, or that you got advice from various industry experts prior to entering the activity.

It always gives a bad impression if you recite facts from memory, particularly if you are equivocal about what you say. If you are asked about certain numbers or the amount of your inventory, reciting figures from memory gives an unbusinesslike impression. You should always refer to charts, tables, or other documentation to provide exact figures if you are asked about them.

Each revenue agent is different. Often, the agent has a sixth sense about things and he or she will follow his or her hunches. Some agents might scrutinize small or seemingly irrelevant details and become argumentative or impatient. Other agents may strive to listen carefully to what you say, seeking to be understanding of your situation. It's always nice if you can strike up a congenial rapport in the beginning.

Keep in mind that it is your job (or your representative's) to educate the revenue agent about your activity, including its dynamics and principles. It is important to explain how you expect to make money in this venture. If you grow and sell Christmas trees, for instance, you will need to make it clear that in order to generate income, it is necessary to wait eight or ten years until the trees can be harvested for sale. Or, if you have a sideline activity as an actor, you may need to explain that you acted in showcase events with no pay, for example, to provide you with important exposure and promotional benefits. Whatever your area of activity, it is important to make sure the revenue agent *understands* the inner workings of that industry.

In some situations it is to your advantage to ask that the audit take place *in the field*, that is, at the location where you conduct your venture. For instance, if you are an artist, you may want to invite the IRS agent to see your studio so that there can be little doubt that you are legitimately engaged in the business of being an artist. The manner in which you store art, display art, and organize sales records will be evident from a guided tour of your studio. The businesslike appearance of your studio, farm, shop, or other work site will make a positive impression on the agent. Sometimes a field audit helps settle concerns of the IRS that the venture might be a hobby, assuming of course that your studio or farm gives the impression of being run in a businesslike manner. However, if your place of operations is in shambles, you will want to *avoid* a field audit.

4. Substantiation

The revenue agent's initial concern is verifying the accuracy of deductions. Bank statements, credit card statements, and receipts must be organized. With business deductions, it is important to show how these expenses relate to business rather than personal activities.

Substantiation of the amounts claimed as deductions is one of the main hurdles that many taxpayers face in an audit. If your books and records are in reasonably good order, this should not be a problem. Unfortunately, for many people it is a problem. There are numerous cases in which people who have hobby type ventures lost their tax deductions simply because they didn't have adequate records to substantiate their expenses.

Substantiation is simply proving that certain expenses were incurred and that they were paid or are in the process of being paid. This is usually shown through canceled checks, cash receipts, and credit card statements that are matched against itemized deductions on your return and supported by underlying invoices.

With cash receipts, there should be a notation on each receipt indicating its business purpose.

Separate substantiation requirements exist for travel, lodging, automotive expenses, and meals away from home.

If you are unable to provide records to verify the accuracy of your deductions, the IRS has authority to estimate the amount of your expenses if —

- you have established entitlement to the expense, and
- there is a basis on which to estimate the amount in question.

The IRS or the US Tax Court should make as "close an approximation as it can, bearing heavily, if it chooses, on the taxpayer whose inexactitude is of his own making." (This is the rule of "indulgence" established by the Court of Appeals for the Second Circuit in *G. M. Cohan v. Commissioner,* also known as the Cohan rule.) [*G.M. Cohan v. Commissioner,* 39 F.2d 540 (2d Cir. 1930).]

If you have had any profit years, it is important to mention this and to prove this. If you had a profit year ten years ago, the only way to prove this would be by some business record or your actual tax return for that year. It is not likely that the IRS will just take your word for it on something so important.

Most people do not hold onto older tax records because they figure the three-year statute of limitations means they can dispense with older records. That is generally correct regarding tax records, but for general business records, that is another matter. Anything that helps show your businesslike manner of operation, including older records, should be kept indefinitely. Thus, if you wanted to prove that ten years ago you had a profit year, you could pull out the appropriate records on that information. If you are audited, these records can be helpful in supporting your case.

5. Questions Presented by the Auditor

Once the substantiation part is over, the next and main hurdle is to convince the IRS that your activity is operated in a businesslike manner. Most entrepreneurs have weaknesses and strengths in how they operate an activity.

The following is a list of questions that are customarily asked by revenue agents in hobby loss audits, as extracted from the IRS *Audit Techniques Guide*:

1. **What research did you conduct into the economics of the activity prior to the commencement of the activity?**

   Ideally, you should be able to show through documents, letters, market studies, and other documented evidence what sort of research and investigation you conducted before deciding to engage in the venture. If you prepared a financial analysis prior to starting the business, it is an important item of evidence.

2. **Have you relied on any experts or advisers?**

   It is helpful if you can show that you consulted experienced individuals in the industry about making money in your particular area. If you have personal expertise, you should provide details about how you became an expert. You should also be prepared to provide evidence of ongoing education on the economics and practical aspects of your particular field. If you sought advice from others experienced in the industry, be sure to have documentation to show this (e.g., notes taken in meetings or seminars, or correspondence).

3. **Can you cite instances where you have chosen to implement your adviser's recommendations?**

   It important to show the IRS agent that you followed the advice given by an adviser. If you did not follow the adviser's advice, give your reasons for not following it.

4. **How did the adviser's recommendations impact the performance of the activity?**

   It is always good if you can prove that as a result of advice taken, your venture actually performed better.

5. **Do you have a business license to conduct this activity?**

   It is crucial to have evidence that you obtained proper licenses and permits for conducting your business and that your property is zoned for this type of venture (or that you have applied for a zoning variance).

6. **Do you have a written business plan?**

   As mentioned in Chapter 3, it is important for your business plan to have a businesslike appearance, proper grammar and spelling, and substance. It should have a realistic income forecast and set forth a time line showing when you expect the activity to become profitable.

   If your business plan has sections that you feel are particularly important, point out these sections to the revenue agent. It is always impressive if your budget or financial forecast is clear, concise, and realistic. You might want to tell the revenue agent how you computed or projected gross receipts for a given year or how you projected costs. If you had a professional prepare your business plan, you should tell the revenue agent.

7. **When was this business plan formalized into writing?**

Even a business plan prepared in anticipation of an audit is better than nothing. It is a formal way of memorializing your business purpose, your strategy, and your honest intention to be engaged in a business rather than a hobby.

8. **If the business plan does not present any form of an economic forecast, when do you foresee the activity becoming profitable?**

If you somewhat adhered to the parameters of writing your business plan, as discussed in Chapter 3, you won't have to answer this question.

9. **What events and circumstances will cause the activity to be profitable in that particular year?**

This is something that involves discussion rather than documentary evidence. You or your representative should be prepared to give a pitch narrating the situations that you hope will produce a profit for your activity.

10. **Why have you not abandoned the activity in light of the history of losses?**

Again, this calls for a narrative answer rather than documentary evidence. You or your representative should inform the revenue agent that you are persisting in the endeavor because you honestly believe you can make a profit at it in the near future, and, if true, that you think you can also recoup past losses. You might want to add that in the future, if you decide that this activity is never likely to generate a net profit, you will abandon it.

11. **What have you done to reduce costs of the activity or change unprofitable methods of operation?**

As you will see throughout this book, it is helpful if you have evidence of what you did after a period of losses to change methods of operation, such as reducing costs of the activity.

12. **Do you have a separate checking account for the venture?**

There should be no evidence of commingling of funds. One of the simplest ways of avoiding commingling is to have a separate bank account for the activity.

6. Best Evidence

Remember that one of the most important features of the hobby loss rule is your intention to make a profit, and objective evidence — documents, documents, documents — is the best evidence of your intention. The IRS will be impressed with the trouble you have gone to in order to keep decent business records. Keep in mind that with every item of evidence, you should emphasize how the particular document helps prove that your sincere intention is to conduct a business rather than a hobby.

As mentioned in Chapter 2, the IRS wants to see business records that you keep in the day-to-day course of your activity, not those that you decide to prepare once you have been notified that you are being audited.

If you have important information that will help explain why you sustained losses, by all means provide that information. For instance, if you claim that market conditions have been volatile, gather articles from various sources that describe the impact on your particular activity. If you experienced unforeseen setbacks such as lawsuits, personal illness, casualties, or other factors, these facts may help explain why losses occurred. Whenever possible, provide documentary evidence to help support your facts.

7. Formal Appraisals of Property

Even if you have no profits from your business, you may still show that an overall profit will result in the future because you expect the venture's assets to appreciate in value, or because they have already appreciated in value. This element can be important in showing that, if you liquidated your assets, you could realize an overall profit. It is important, if applicable to your case, to have evidence of formal appraisals — both of the real property used in the venture and other assets such as inventory.

No revenue agent would be satisfied by a mere verbal statement that your farm or ranch has appreciated in value, or that you expect your collection of stamps to appreciate in value. Rather, what is required is a formal appraisal.

8. If You Are Assessed a Deficiency

Taxpayers, particularly if well represented, will often succeed in convincing the IRS that their activity is a business, not a hobby, despite a history of losses. Those who succeed in audits usually do so because they have good documentary evidence and a persuasive and knowledgeable representative.

If the auditor has decided to assess a deficiency against you, or finds problems with your tax return, the agent has the authority to expand the audit into other tax years that are still within the three-year statute of limitations. If the agent expands your audit into other years, this usually means that he or she has decided to disallow some of your deductions, and feels there is grounds to attack the other returns.

Taxpayers who lose at the audit phase are usually devastated when they learn of the extra taxes that the IRS claims they owe.

You have two main avenues available. As pointed out in IRS Publication 5, "Appeal Rights and Preparation of Protests for Unagreed Cases," you can file an appeal within the IRS bureaucracy. At that point your case is re-evaluated by a different section, and you will often have the opportunity to present new evidence, oral clarification, and witnesses, so you can negotiate an agreed-on settlement figure with the appeals officer.

You can also file a petition in the US Tax Court, which is a complex procedure that usually requires hiring a tax attorney. The US Tax Court is a federal court system that hears petitions from taxpayers who wish to contest deficiencies made against them by the IRS.

More than 90 percent of the cases filed in the US Tax Court are settled between the taxpayer and the government. Settlement negotiations are informal conferences with the government attorneys or accountants who are working on your case. A settlement depends on how good your evidence is.

The judges in the US Tax Court are all highly qualified, experienced experts in tax law, and since there is no jury, the judge makes all decisions in the case. US Tax Court judges are particularly vigilant in ascertaining whether the taxpayer, as witness in the case, is to be believed. Many people have lost cases in the US Tax Court primarily because their testimony was ambiguous, contradictory, and on the whole lacking in credibility.

9. Penalties

Section 6662 imposes an accuracy-related penalty of 20 percent of any portion of an underpayment that is attributable to the taxpayer's negligence. For purposes of the tax law, *underpayment* is the same as *deficiency*. A separate penalty for negligence is imposed by section 6662(a).

In hobby loss cases, the IRS often imposes a negligence penalty in addition to the deficiency assessed. They will justify the penalty on the notion that your tax deductions were attributable to negligence or disregard for rules or regulations. Negligence is defined as a "lack of due care or failure to do that which a reasonable and ordinarily prudent person would do under the circumstances," and is used to determine income tax liability. Negligence includes any failure to make a reasonable attempt to comply with the law.

If the IRS decides to impose a penalty or penalties, it is up to you to provide evidence to show that you reasonably relied on advice given to you by your accountant or attorney.

10. Offers in Compromise Policy of the IRS

The IRS has the authority to compromise or settle your case, particularly if you are unable to pay the full amount of the tax due. A compromise enables you to pay less than the total tax liability due. If collection of the tax would create economic hardship, or exceptional circumstances exist, a compromise may be reached.

A compromise is discretionary on the part of the IRS, and often revenue agents are more interested in sticking to the full amount they claim you owe rather than entertaining a compromise. A compromise is sometimes to the advantage of the IRS because this enables the government to avoid the expense of collection or litigation.

Doubt as to whether the money is collectable and doubt as to liability are the two grounds for entering a compromise. There is no requirement that the taxpayer be insolvent in order to compromise taxes. Many times the basis for a compromise is doubt about the liability rather than inability to pay.

A compromise offer usually must be submitted on Form 656. The compromise may include an installment payment agreement.

The IRS recognizes that people need funds to provide for basic living expenses. In negotiating a compromise, this is a factor. If the offer of compromise is based on inability to pay, a financial statement (Form 433A) should accompany the offer. This form documents your living expenses. The IRS will consider your assets, your future income, the amount collectible from third parties, and assets or income that are outside the country.

Expedited processing can be requested if the taxpayer has a need to resolve a tax liability by a specific date. This is sometimes needed if the taxpayer has a pending business transaction that requires him or her, as a condition to the transaction, to resolve a tax liability.

In order to be binding, the compromise must be accepted by the IRS. The IRS can later set aside a compromise if false information or documentation was supplied with the offer, or if the taxpayer concealed assets or the ability to pay.

11. Chapter Summary

It remains a truism that the taxpayers who succeed in hobby loss audits are those who have prepared well in advance by maintaining proper day-to-day business records. Review Chapter 2 for a discussion of adequate business records. If you have followed a good amount of the advice given there, you will be in a good position to convince the IRS that you are operating your activity in a businesslike manner.

If you are audited, it doesn't mean you have done anything wrong. However, it will be your responsibility to convince the IRS that your activity is a business and not a hobby.

Some people get severe anxiety about being audited. That should not be the case. You should plan for the audit, and hopefully be able to hire a taxpayer representative rather than attend the audit yourself.

Remember, the people who win audits do so because they have businesslike records as evidence that they are engaged in a business rather than a hobby.

PART II
CREATIVE BUSINESSES

8

ACTORS, FILMMAKERS, AND MUSICIANS

This chapter will consider actors, filmmakers, and musicians together, because of similar practical issues involved. The IRS often suspects that people who pursue acting, music, or filmmaking on a part-time basis are really hobbyists or dilettantes.

The IRS will seek to deny your tax deductions if you have ongoing losses, so it is important to understand what you can do to organize your venture in a businesslike manner.

Actors and musicians typically incur similar categories of expenses. Allowable deductions include photo-résumé costs; composites; video résumés; demos; publicity photos; and costs for taping, editing, and copying. These items are needed to show potential employers your skills and versatility.

Actors and musicians may also deduct such expenses as memberships in unions and guilds, and automobile, travel, meal, and hotel costs. Further deductions include telephone, cell phone, answering service, cable TV, and to some extent utilities. Actors and musicians can deduct costs of

lessons, classes, or other training associated with honing their skills.

This chapter discusses another important area of the entertainment business: sponsorship and management agreements with children. If you are a parent who wants to promote your child's singing, dancing, or acting career, you will want to make sure your arrangement with your child is for business and not for pleasure. For more information, see section 4.

1. Actors

Many actors have to struggle, apply for small parts, do some jobs on spec, and work hard with the hopes of eventually gaining recognition. The earlier part of most actors' careers consists of auditioning for roles, working with acting coaches, accumulating credits, and networking. Actors almost always have a day job as they do what they can to develop their career. This is where the IRS comes in concerning the hobby loss rule. The IRS tries to argue that part-time or aspiring actors are engaged in a hobby, not a business, and deny their deductions for acting-related expenses.

Sometimes getting a role depends on being in the right place at the right time. Patience is necessary. Often becoming a successful actor means moving to a city such as New York, Chicago, or Los Angeles. For all struggling actors, things can change at any time.

One of the most daunting challenges for an aspiring actor is getting a good agent. A good agent will have confidence in your skills and your potential, and the ability to get your name, credits, and photos before producers and casting agents.

Actors have many showcasing opportunities to exhibit their skills. This could involve performing without compensation in plays or other shows, or even at the expense of the actor. Many acting coaches host public performances that serve as opportunities for actors to demonstrate their skills, but again, without compensation. Too much emphasis on showcasing and too little on seeking paying jobs, can suggest that you are not conducting the activity in a businesslike manner.

The IRS will try and argue that you are engaged in a hobby if you have a history of losses and no agency representation, or if you take lackluster steps to increase your skills and promote yourself.

The following is an example of how a taxpayer was able to develop his acting career in a way that convinced the US Tax Court that he operated in a businesslike manner.

Example: *Regan v. Commissioner,* **T.C. Memo 1979-340.**

J. Thomas Regan, Balboa Island, California, worked full time as a chemical engineer. He decided to pursue acting. He took acting classes in the evening and obtained an agent to help develop his acting career.

With his agent's help he prepared a photo portfolio, mailed out résumés, and interviewed for various acting roles in movies, TV shows, and commercials. He also joined the Screen Actors Guild.

Initially, he was in a play but received no pay, and was an extra in a Chevrolet commercial, for which he was paid $50.

He deducted the costs of his acting lessons, makeup, wardrobe, photo portfolio, résumés and mailings, Screen Actors Guild dues, and transportation expenses. After five years he was earning more and more acting income, but had no net profit, although he almost broke even one year. He decided to quit his job as a chemical engineer and devote all his attention to acting.

The IRS claimed his acting was a hobby, but the US Tax Court sided with Mr. Regan. What impressed the court was the amount of time he devoted to improving his skills through acting classes, for which he had to commute 50 miles each way. "Although the classes undoubtedly afforded him a certain amount of pleasure or recreation, we think the extensive time which he put into them suggests a serious and studied effort to launch a profitable acting career."

The court also looked favorably on evidence that Mr. Regan had an agent to manage his career, prepared a photo portfolio, mailed out approximately 250 résumés, and attended numerous screenings and interviews.

The court said that the five years of losses was part of the start-up phase, and that "losses during the initial stage of an activity do not necessarily indicate that the activity was not engaged in for profit." Also, Mr. Regan had a dramatic increase in his acting income and came very close to the break-even point the year before he quit his full-time job.

The court did, however, reduce the amount of deductions because Mr. Regan did not adequately substantiate some of them, such as automobile mileage. The court also disallowed deductions for wardrobe expenses. The court said since the clothing could be adapted for personal use, it would be a nondeductible personal expense.

The previous example provides the following key points:

1. Evidence that you have obtained an agent or are diligently seeking one, and that you are actively seeking parts, tends to prove that you are serious about being an actor.

2. It is a sign of professionalism to join unions such as the Screen Actors Guild.

3. It is important to spend significant time and effort sending out résumés, attending auditions, and taking acting classes.

4. The fact that you are earning some income from acting is helpful, and it is even better if you are moving towards a break-even point.

5. Normally, clothing used in acting jobs cannot be deducted as a business expense if the clothing is suitable for personal use. However, expenses for costumes and period clothing are generally deductible if required for a job, and if your contract does not provide reimbursement.

6. The IRS will usually deny deductions for theater and movie tickets or video rentals, even if you claim these are necessary to stay on top of developments in your field.

In contrast to the previous example, the next case involves an actor whose efforts to pursue her acting career were lackluster.

Example: *Kellner v. Commissioner,* **T.C. Memo 1986-524.**

Helen Kellner, New York, New York, did not fare so well in her effort to convince the IRS that she, a retired teacher, was pursuing a career as an actor. She made almost no money as an actor, ($110 for the year in which she was audited), although she appeared in small parts in three films.

She claimed expenses of more than $5,200 that she deducted against her pension, interest, and dividend income. The expenses consisted of books and periodicals, laundry and costume cleaning, postage, entertainment of possible clients and agents, telephone, makeup, wigs, costumes, beautification, photos, résumés and publicity, job hunting transportation, gifts to business associates, research, tapes, and tape recorders. She also claimed the cost of tuition for a theater training course. The theater training course was actually a correspondence course relating to aging actors. In addition, she sought to deduct expenses of a home office.

In the US Tax Court she testified that she religiously bought the weekly trade publications, sent out ten solicitation letters each week, practiced her voice daily, and worked harder to seek roles than she ever worked in teaching.

There was little documentary evidence to corroborate her testimony, and the judge indicated that it did not convince him that she was engaged in the trade or business of acting.

Ms. Kellner claimed that she devoted substantial time to her acting venture, but the judge said that the calendar she submitted was inadequate evidence to show the amount of time expended because there were many gaps, some pages were blank, and it only seemed to show the names and addresses of the people to whom she had sent résumés.

Ms. Kellner testified that almost every year she got the flu and was bedridden for weeks on end, which the judge construed to mean that during these bouts she could not devote much time to her acting venture.

The court said that Ms. Kellner may be "qualified" as an actor, as she had three small roles in films and was listed with several talent or casting agencies. However, she did not have her own agent, she was not a member of an actor's guild, and her manner of conducting her acting activities was disorganized and unbusinesslike.

The court said: "We do not dispute her testimony that actors must be dedicated and must constantly apply for small parts in films to gain recognition. They may make little money at first and then 'make it big.' Moreover, a taxpayer's profit expectation need not be a reasonable one; it is sufficient that the taxpayer has a bona fide objective of realizing a profit. However, the evidence indicates that 'making it big' would be unlikely in the petitioner's case. She has performed in a few films and may have gained some recognition, but she is not taking positive steps to increase her skills or chances for earning a profit. She does not have a manager to increase her chances of financial success, and does not take acting classes."

The previous example provides the following key points:

1. The taxpayer lost mainly because she conducted the activity in an unbusinesslike manner. Also, she did not have a manager and wasn't a member of an actor's guild.

2. It is important to send out résumés and attend casting calls. Lackluster efforts, as in this case, imply that the activity is a hobby.

3. The taxpayer apparently enrolled in a correspondence course, not a real acting class, and this did not help support her case. An aspiring actor should attend reputable acting classes or have a private coach.

4. It can be helpful to maintain a log of your time to support your contention that you are devoting a significant amount of time to acting. The IRS will find this more credible than mere verbal statements as to time expended.

5. The taxpayer claimed personal expenses (e.g., clothing and makeup) as business expenses. Personal expenses are generally nondeductible items even if they are helpful to your career.

6. The court questioned how the taxpayer could devote enough time to her acting career, given her admission that she was bedridden for weeks at a time with the flu.

Someone with a history of past success in the acting profession, but who faces an ongoing slump in his or her career, will still likely be deemed engaged in the acting as a business rather than as a hobby. See the example **Richards v. Commissioner** included on the CD.

2. Filmmakers

Filmmaking is a demanding profession. Numerous universities have excellent departments in film and television studies. They offer degree programs in film and video production with emphasis on individualized courses of study. Obtaining a college degree in this field provides a person with basic tools to launch a career in filmmaking.

Today, filmmaking is only one aspect of the motion picture genre. There are also music videos, DVDs, and movies and documentaries made for TV and cable.

Producers, directors, and others who do creative work in this area usually start somewhere on the bottom, and, after a period of time, they gain public recognition and financial success.

If you claim you are engaged in filmmaking as a business, the IRS will want to know how you qualify for this type of venture, or at least what sort of ongoing efforts you are making to enhance your skills.

In the following case the taxpayer devoted himself full time to what he claimed was a film production venture, but he had no prior experience in the field.

Example: *van Allen v. Commissioner,* T.C. Memo 1983-619.

After retiring, John van Allen, Santa Cruz, California, got involved in aerial movie making, which he pursued under the name, "Sizmark Productions." He had no background in cinematography. He had several projects that he hoped he might sell, but he did very little to actually secure buyers for his films. In a three-year period he claimed about $80,000 in losses.

He started filming a renovation project of the Capital Building in Carson City, Nevada, from the air and the ground, but did not complete this project. He began filming a documentary about the restoration of the Santa Cruz boardwalk, but did not complete this project. He worked on other film projects, including an aerial film of a large fire, some footage of which he sold for only $100 to a local news station. He worked on some short subject films about Monarch butterflies, unusual cloud formations, and the migration of whales from Baja, California. He accumulated about 30,000 feet of film, but did not complete a single project.

In the US Tax Court, Mr. van Allen claimed that his main difficulty was that his Cessna Aircraft had mechanical defects and this made it difficult for him to finish aerial film shots.

In ruling against him, the court said that to begin with, if the defective Cessna was the reason why he didn't complete any film projects, he should have rented a replacement aircraft or taken other businesslike measures so that he could complete his projects.

The US Tax Court noted that Mr. van Allen spent a great deal of time on his filmmaking activity, but that this was consistent with a hobby venture for a retired individual. The court said that he carried on the venture in a haphazard manner and that he failed to keep any businesslike records. (While he kept receipts of expenses incurred in the venture, he had no other records.) Moreover, he had little training in aerial cinematography, and he evidently derived significant personal pleasure from filmmaking. He made no effort to market his films or to ascertain whether any market would exist should he ever complete a film.

The previous example provides the following key points:

1. If you claim to be a filmmaker, you should have some basis for this, such as a college degree in filmmaking or significant apprentice experience.

2. If you decide to initiate a film project without having arranged distribution beforehand, it is important to determine whether there is a market for the work, and to actively market the film at your earliest opportunity.

3. Failure to complete film projects suggests that you are a dilettante rather than a serious filmmaker.

4. Failure to keep adequate books and records of your filmmaking activity suggests that the activity is a hobby.

Example: *Wheeler v. Commissioner,* T.C. Memo 1999-56.

Frank Wheeler, Los Altos Hills, California, was a captain in the US Navy. After retirement he worked for 15 years in the electronics industry, primarily as a consultant. Following that, he decided to engage in a videotape venture.

He installed professional caliber video equipment in his studio, and transferred slides, movies, and prints onto videocassettes. He hoped to sell them via word of mouth. He did very little to market his videos, of which he produced about 75. These were travel, navy, wedding, family, and miscellaneous videos.

He kept a log with details of his video sales, but no other records. He did not maintain a separate bank account for the activity. He incurred more than $155,000 in costs in an 11-year period, primarily for videotape equipment, and he never made a profit from the activity. He did sell some videotapes, but in his best year he had gross receipts of $1,675. He used the losses to offset his retirement income.

In the US Tax Court, Captain Wheeler testified that he had a business plan in his head, and that it seemed a "silly waste of paper to put it down in black and white." The court said that in any case, Captain Wheeler was unable to articulate what his business plan was or how he expected his videotape activity might produce a profit.

The court said that his books and records, while sparse and relatively informal, were adequate, but that there were other problems with

his case. The court noted that despite the losses from the venture, Captain Wheeler spent $75,000 more on equipment, and spent a considerable amount of time learning how to use the new equipment.

The court said that many successful small businesses rely on word of mouth to generate business, but actual efforts to generate word-of-mouth interest need to be made. The court said that Captain Wheeler's business remained meager throughout the years and he did nothing to try and move into the profit column.

The court said that Captain Wheeler produced high quality videos and that he preserved history in these efforts. The court was impressed with Captain Wheeler's expertise in electronics, communications, and business, but nonetheless concluded that the activity was a hobby and not a business.

The overriding factor was the long history of losses, with no change in operating methods. Captain Wheeler gave no indication that, though he was already more than 80 years old, he would give up his videotape activity or make any major change in the way he conducted the venture.

The court said that Captain Wheeler's enjoyment of his work was evident, but not decisive in the court's conclusion.

The previous example provides the following key points:

1. In many hobby loss cases, the main reason the taxpayer loses is that there is a long history of losses with no significant changes in operating methods.

2. The IRS recognizes that retirees may want to pursue new vocations, but retirees often get heightened scrutiny when they claim an activity to be a business.

3. Failure to market your product is evidence that suggests the venture is a hobby, not a business.

4. Evidence that you put more money into a failing venture instead of making changes that might improve profitability, suggests that the activity is a hobby, not a business.

3. Musicians

Many individuals dream of being professional musicians. Regardless of one's individual talent, the path to success can be a struggle, as with the other arts. A musical career may start as a hobby and then develop into a flourishing career while one holds a day job. Often individuals in the music industry will perform various activities in an effort to "make it." Thus, a musician might do studio work (i.e., recording sessions) and perform in local nightclubs as a stepping stone to greater things within the music industry.

The IRS recognizes that musicians often have a poor recordkeeping system or that they have a certain lack of concern for these types of matters. Sometimes musicians are so committed to their work that they spend all their time and energy doing whatever it takes to become a success.

The main element in evaluating whether a musician is engaged in a hobby or a business is the individual's honest intentions. Sometimes this can be shown not so much by neatly organized business records, as by evidence of promotion of yourself and your works, ongoing development of your skills, and exposure and jobs as a musician.

Example: *Bernard Wagner v. Commissioner,* T.C. Memo 1983-606.

Bernard Wagner, St. Louis, Missouri, worked as a CPA. As a hobby, he wrote songs. He had one of his songs published in 1974.

He decided to try and make money as a musician. He established "Bernie Wagner Songs and Productions." He copyrighted his songs and arranged to play his music for producers at a recording studio in St. Louis, and ended up recording several of his songs for the studio. He had a separate checking account for his music activities.

Mr. Wagner hired a producer in Nashville to record some of his songs. He sent copies of the recordings to record companies in an effort to sell them. One record company offered a recording contract, but the parties were not able to agree on terms so negotiations ended.

Mr. Wagner had an attorney draft a management contract with a talented singer he had met. The singer was to perform some of Mr. Wagner's songs and Mr. Wagner would get a 20 percent fee based on the singer's earnings.

He hired four musicians to play with the singer, bought them uniforms and equipment, and paid them for rehearsal time prior to public performances. He also paid them a weekly fee while performing. Mr. Wagner worked with a booking agency to help arrange exposure of the band, which resulted in several gigs at hotels and clubs, and generated income for the band members.

Mr. Wagner did not receive any of the proceeds, however, and also had to pay the booking agency a fee from his own funds. After a few months he dissolved the band (after complaints about their unruly behavior), and he stopped promoting personal appearances of the singer as well.

At one point Mr. Wagner did have one of his songs released on a single, under a contract with Vanguard Records. Mr. Wagner did not receive any money from the sales of that recording.

The US Tax Court said that Mr. Wagner obviously derived great personal pleasure from his music activities, but that his primary motivation was to carry on a business. He worked with a successful music producer and made concerted efforts to promote his projects.

The court said that Mr. Wagner showed businesslike concern in hiring an attorney to draft documents and in relying on the advice of an experienced music producer. The court said that Mr. Wagner's receipts of expenditures were not organized, but that his overall businesslike approach showed that he had a profit motive.

The court said that Mr. Wagner had a viable management contract with the singer who had the potential to become very valuable property, and because of this, Mr. Wagner expected to reap profits. The court noted that the music industry pays extremely large amounts of money to those who succeed and that an opportunity to earn a substantial ultimate profit in this instance suggested that the activity was engaged in for profit.

The previous example provides the following key points:

1. Management contracts must be properly drafted, preferably by an attorney. There should be no oral agreements between manager and artist or else the implication is that the parties are not very businesslike.

2. In this case the taxpayer's business records were inadequate, but he won mainly because he actively promoted his venture in ways that could reap a profit. Still, the more organized your records, the better.

3. The court was impressed that the taxpayer hired a professional producer to produce a recording which he distributed to record companies. The court noted that the taxpayer was in negotiation with a major label, but that he could not agree on the terms, so the deal fell through.

The case of **Suiter v. Commissioner** (included on the CD) involves a retired individual who decided to launch a new career as a musician. He incurred losses and had poor business records, but he convinced the US Tax Court that he had the honest intention of realizing a profit.

Example: *Krebs v. Commissioner,* **T.C. Memo 1992-154.**

David Krebs, New York, New York, was a successful music promoter. He developed his career after leaving the William Morris Agency. He also had a law degree and a business administration degree.

Mr. Krebs was involved in several production and management activities, and had about 30 employees assisting him. He produced several pop musical bands and he launched various other musical projects.

Overall, he was quite successful, although many of his projects failed. One of Mr. Krebs's ventures was promoting his wife Cheryl's music career. He spent substantial sums on promoting her career with a professional band he had hired.

The IRS said that his promotional activities for his wife were not a business. The US Tax Court sided with the Krebs. The court noted that Mrs. Krebs had substantial training and experience as a singer as well as an actor. She had numerous singing and acting credits. She had been represented by agents for many years, but after marrying Mr. Krebs, she wanted him to help establish her as a successful recording artist. Mrs. Krebs devoted her full time to this activity.

After four years, Mr. Krebs and his wife decided to abandon the endeavor because it had not attained the success they had hoped.

The court said that the losses were incurred in the start-up phase of the activity, and therefore were understandable during that period. Also, the court said that their abandonment of the activity once it seemed to be a losing venture is evidence of Mr. Krebs' overall businesslike concern.

The court concluded that Mr. Krebs operated his activity as personal manager of his wife's career with the same professionalism as with his other musical activities.

The previous example provides the following key points:

1. The taxpayer won mainly because he was a professional promoter with a track record of success. Prior experience in a given field is an important element that shows your expertise and suggests that you are serious about making a profit from the activity.

2. The IRS looks with scrutiny on management contracts between spouses, as in this case, or between parents and talented children. It is crucial to have a management contract in writing and to follow the terms of the contract. For management contracts between family members, it is important to have evidence that you did something to investigate the feasibility of making money in the management deal.

3. At times musicians with past success will try and make a comeback. As with other creative fields, a prior history of profits as a musician is evidence that you are a professional, and that you are engaged in a business, not a hobby. However, if you do not promote your music, it can be seen as an unbusinesslike approach. See *McMillan v. Commissioner* on the CD for an example of this type of case.

3.1 Sponsorship and Management Agreements with Children

Some parents seek to promote the talents of a child and enter a management or sponsorship agreement with the child. The agreement sets terms that the parents will pay the costs of developing the child's abilities and receive a percentage of the child's earnings if and when that occurs. The IRS tends to argue that such arrangements are motivated solely by parental affection rather than by the anticipation of economic profit.

A minor's contract needs to have court approval to have full legal validity. The main hurdle is that even if there is a formal contract, parents often provide more funds than called for under the contract, or they don't collect monies due to them, or the contract is simply inadequate to ever generate a profit for the parents. Another problem is that parents sometimes seek to (improperly) deduct personal living expenses paid for the child.

The following case involves a management contract between a taxpayer and her daughter, who was developing a career as a singer.

Example: *Bernardo v. Commissioner,* **T.C. Memo 2004-199.**

Vanessa Bernardo, Mechanicsburg, Pennsylvania, was a manager in a department store. Her daughter, Melissa, studied dance and music from early childhood. After graduating from high school, Melissa attended a dance school in New York and took screenwriting, acting, and modeling classes.

Mrs. Bernardo decided to sponsor her daughter in an effort to further her career as a composer and singer. However, they had only an oral agreement.

Mrs. Bernardo paid the costs of Melissa's efforts to promote her music in Los Angeles area clubs. Melissa performed at various showcase events at nightclubs for exposure to build her reputation, but she did not earn any money for these appearances. Melissa spent considerable time trying to promote her music and make contacts with record company executives. She had a professional CD of her music and was featured on a television show.

Mrs. Bernardo took $35,000 as tax deductions for the costs of promoting Melissa's career.

In the US Tax Court, Melissa testified that under the agreement her mother would be reimbursed for money invested in her career solely from profits Melissa might realize. Mrs. Bernardo testified that she was uncertain as to whether the agreement entitled her to profits after she recouped her costs. She said that in any event, she and Melissa were to renegotiate the agreement and agree to some level of profit participation, if and when she got reimbursed.

In ruling against Mrs. Bernardo, the court said that she was "obviously indifferent as to whether she would earn money from Melissa's career," and that her financial support was motivated by parental affection rather than by the anticipation of economic profit. Thus, the expenditures were in the nature of personal or family expenses and nondeductible.

The court noted that Mrs. Bernardo took no active part in helping to further Melissa's career. Moreover, the court noted that she had "no business plan and no financial projections." The court also said that Mrs. Bernardo had no music industry expertise and no prior experience in backing aspiring recording artists.

The previous example provides the following key points:

1. Many people succeed in taking tax deductions for management or sponsorship agreements in connection with developing their child's career in the arts. This taxpayer lost partly because the agreement was oral rather than written, and because some of the terms were uncertain.

2. The contract should provide not only reimbursement of costs advanced to further the child's career, but also a percentage paid out of the child's earnings, after recoupment of your costs.

3. The contract should *not* provide for personal living expenses of the child, as these are personal family expenses and nondeductible.

4. It is helpful if you have some experience managing an artistic career. Moreover, it is crucial for you to actively participate in managing the child's career (and do more than just write checks).

5. A business plan and financial projections should show how much money needs to be invested in the child's career and how profits might be realized.

Another example of a parental management contract case involving a daughter's ballet career is *Bush v. Commissioner*, which is included on the CD.

4. Chapter Summary

For any creative artists, there can be periods of feast and famine. Income can fluctuate greatly from year to year. If the IRS audits you, it is important to educate the revenue agent about the background and history of your particular artistic endeavors and why you regard your activity as a business rather than a hobby.

It is important to inform the revenue agent, if applicable, that you work in different capacities on different projects. For instance, many actors are also directors or producers, sometimes on the same project.

Explain to the IRS that you are actively promoting yourself; diligently pursuing all leads; working with an agent or seeking an agent; attending auditions; improving your skills by lessons, classes, and training; expanding your credits; and taking what jobs you are offered, even if they are just showcasing opportunities. There is a saying in the entertainment industry, "If you don't promote, something awful happens — nothing!"

You should have written contracts, letters of agreement, or other documentary evidence of your performances, even if they are just showcasing jobs. Be sure to keep all contracts, project agreements, deal memos, and working proposals pertaining to your activities. This is important whether or not you received income from these projects. Also, it is important to be able to substantiate any expenses incurred in pursuing your career.

It is best to refrain from claiming extravagant or inappropriate deductions. Costs of clothing, dry cleaning, makeup, wigs, physical fitness, gym dues, trainer's fees, and theater and movie tickets are not normally deductible. If you are an actor and physical conditioning is required for a particular job, the studio will usually provide the cost.

The IRS is sometimes quite sympathetic to actors and artists who may lack an understanding of bookkeeping and cash flow, but you will still need to show your overall businesslike intention in the matter, and how you expect to make money in your line of work.

ARTISTS AND PHOTOGRAPHERS 9

It is well established that the terms for *trade* and *business* include the arts. The art world is a diverse industry that is to some extent "suspect" by the IRS. Art consists of paintings, sculpture, pottery, rugs, wood carvings, and even jewelry. Photography is considered to be an art form in its own right.

1. Artists

Most artists start out simply with a creative passion for their artistic pursuits, and later decide they want to pursue art for profit. An artist who has obtained an art degree and is ready to set forth into the art world intending to make a profit, will soon learn that it is difficult to find an art gallery to sponsor his or her works and to obtain buyers. It takes a number of years of becoming sufficiently well received in the public eye before an artist will start making a profit.

Truly dedicated artists keep going because they have it in their blood, they know they are good, and they are driven by a solid conviction that they are artists. For many, commercial

success comes sooner or later. In the meantime, those who have not achieved sufficient commercial success to support themselves usually need a day job, and use their free time to develop their artistic career.

The IRS sometimes argues that certain people are pursuing art simply for pleasure or recreation, without the intent of earning a profit. The IRS will deny their tax deductions, especially if there is a history of losses or inadequate marketing efforts. The IRS must be reminded that a history of loss in the art field is more understandable than it is in other fields.

Some people claim that they are art dealers and seek to deduct costs of maintaining and expanding their art collection (including insurance, travel, and other expenses). In evaluating whether an art dealer or gallery is a business rather than a hobby, the IRS considers such factors as whether the gallery is listed in the Yellow Pages, and whether it is operated in the person's home or in a retail storefront with such overhead items as rent, utilities, wages, and insurance.

Freelance art dealers, who may operate without gallery space, will sell artists' works or coordinate which galleries will show particular pieces. They usually work out of their homes and work on a commission basis.

Sometimes gallery owners are experienced artists themselves. The more knowledgeable the gallery owner is about art and the market, the better the business will be. Working knowledge of the industry is a factor that seems to determine the overall strength of a gallery's business. Art galleries have the ability to make unknown artists popular in the art world.

The typical kinds of expenses that are usually deductible by artists include art supplies, art books, studio maintenance costs, telephone, transportation, shipping, gifts, rent, dues, subscriptions, entertainment, and general costs of operating one's art studio.

The IRS has identified various issues that it considers particularly applicable to artists, art dealers, and gallery owners. Among them are unreported income, inventory valuation problems for trades between artists and gallery owners, and bogus sales to family and friends. Another recurring issue involves high travel and entertainment costs.

The IRS believes that many artists are paid in cash, and that there should be receipts or some other form of documentation to support sales. Invoices should be numbered and prepared in duplicate or triplicate. Each invoice should reflect the buyer's name, address, date of sale, amount paid (or, if not fully paid, the terms of installment), sales tax, shipping charges, and framing charges (if that is part of the deal).

The IRS will want to know which galleries have shown your work, where the galleries are located, whether you ever sell directly to customers, what your contractual terms are with the gallery, whether you pay for any of the show expenses or advertising that the gallery incurs, how you record your sales, whether you ever get paid with cash, whether you have ever been commissioned to produce a work of art for a specific purpose, and if so, what the terms were and how you were paid.

In the cases discussed in this chapter, the US Tax Court is usually more impressed by the manner in which the taxpayer seeks to market his or her artwork than the artistic merit of the work.

Most artists who are audited are part time, and they usually operate at a loss for a number of years. Since so many people consider themselves amateur artists, the IRS is understandably concerned that certain people will improperly claim that they are in the trade or business of being an artist.

In the following example the artist had two US Tax Court cases concerning whether he was engaged in art as a business, and in both cases the court ruled that his artistic activity was a hobby.

Example: *Stasewich v. Commissioner,* **T.C. Memo 1996-302 (Stasewich I);** *Stasewich v. Commissioner,* **T.C. Memo 2001-30 (Stasewich II).**

Stasewich I: In Chapter 5 we examined this case in terms of the promotional expenses that were denied. As mentioned, Richard Stasewich, Chicago, Illinois, was a CPA. He also had a long-standing desire to develop his talents as an artist. He hoped his accounting practice would pay the bills while he devoted time to his artistic endeavors. He took substantial deductions in connection with his activities as an artist and he never earned a profit from his art.

In the US Tax Court, his business records consisted of a cash receipts journal and a shoebox full of credit card statements and receipts. The court said that his records were not only limited, but that he also failed to use them to keep track of his activity, to monitor expenses, or to assess the activity's profitability. He had no budget, made no financial projections, and did not maintain a separate checking account for the activity.

Mr. Stasewich did not make any operating changes after sustaining continued losses. "The large unabated expenditures, the absence even at this late date of any concrete business plans to reverse the losses, and the manner in which petitioner conducted his artist activity lead to the conclusion that this was not an activity engaged in for profit."

The court said that he "engaged in the artist activity because of the satisfaction, pride, and prestige it afforded him. Although it is not required that a taxpayer dislike an activity before it will be considered a business and not a hobby, petitioner has shown no evidence of a profit objective with respect to his artist activity."

The court also suggested that Mr. Stasewich inflated his costs to eliminate income tax liability on the income from his accounting business. "This weighs against finding a profit objective because no trade or business exists if the primary purpose of the activity is to generate tax deductions rather than produce an economic profit."

Stasewich II: Mr. Stasewich was again audited, lost, and took his case to the US Tax Court. In this case, Mr. Stasewich had decided to focus on nude drawings. He tried to place some of his drawings with fashion magazines and spent a lot of money on materials, but never secured a large client and never made a profit. He also worked on portraits and installation art displays. He placed ads in the local newspaper to solicit work as a commercial artist of portraits. He painted two portraits that generated about $850 in revenue.

He created four art installations that were displayed in front of his residence. The exhibit got media attention and was the subject of two newspaper articles, but he made no money from the installation works.

He had better records in the second case. He kept a spreadsheet of income and expenses, a cash receipts journal of artwork sales, and receipts for expenses. He obtained a retail sales license and he filed sales and use tax returns with the state. He completed W-2 forms for the art students he employed.

Despite the fact that his books and records were fairly decent, the court was not satisfied with them, and said that his maintenance of these books and records "may represent nothing more than a conscious attention to detail."

He "failed to show that the books and records were kept for the purpose of cutting expenses, increasing profits, and evaluating the overall performance of the operation. He did not maintain a budget for the activity or make any sort of financial projections."

The court noted that his gross receipts as an artist ranged from $266 to $770 annually, while his expenses ranged from $11,279 to $32,544 annually.

The court said that in one year he reported a loss from his artist activity exactly equal to the income as a CPA. "Such an unlikely coincidence indicates that petitioner may be using his artist activity as a device to eliminate Federal income tax on the income from his accounting business. This pattern weighs against finding a profit objective."

The court also noted that since the time of his previous case he had not made any significant changes in the operation of his artistic activity that would create a market for his artwork or allow him to make up for his substantial losses.

The previous example provides the following key points:

1. If as an artist you incur expenses, it is especially important to maintain good books and records. Also, the records should be *utilized* to help you cut expenses, increase profits, and evaluate the overall performance of the venture.

2. The taxpayer's credibility is often important. Here, the taxpayer gave the impression that he had inflated or abused tax deductions, and this seemed to impinge on his overall credibility.

3. It is important to maintain some kind of written budget that will indicate anticipated costs and how much revenue will be needed in order to reach the break-even point.

4. If required, you should obtain business licenses (such as a retail seller's permit and a city business license), and report sales tax. You should always maintain a receipt book for sales of art.

5. It is important to have evidence that you have made conscientious efforts to promote your art.

Full-time artists usually have an easier time with the IRS than those who are part-time artists. Someone engaged full time in an endeavor is less likely to be engaged in a hobby, since so much time and effort is being expended in the activity. Also, many dilettantes and hobbyists engage in art only on a part-time basis, during their leisure time.

See *Waitzkin v. Commissioner* on the CD for a case about a full-time artist with prior success and recognition, who had also inherited wealth.

She convinced the US Tax Court that she was engaged in a business despite extended losses.

There are cases where a full-time artist has lost his or her case. For an example of this see *Rood v. United States* on the CD. In the following case, a full-time artist's activity was deemed a hobby, not a business.

Example: *Porter v. Commissioner*, T.C. Memo 1969-288.

In the 1930s, Lewis Porter, New Canaan, Connecticut, decided that he was not happy working as a lawyer and that he wanted to be an artist instead. He began to study expressionistic painting on a part-time basis under a distinguished teacher. He also spent a year in Paris studying art. Upon returning to Connecticut, he supported himself on an allowance provided by his father, and devoted himself exclusively to painting and continuing studies in art.

He converted a barn on his family's farm into a gallery where he exhibited his paintings. He also invited other artists in the area to show their works. However, he sold no works through the gallery.

He lived the life of the proverbial struggling artist until he inherited a trust fund from his mother's estate. He continued to paint and to study art, but sold only a handful of paintings. He took significant tax deductions against his trust income for artist supplies, studio rental, car expenses, and other costs.

He painted 11 hours a day and produced anywhere from 25 to 172 paintings a year. At the time of his case in the US Tax Court, he had an inventory of 1,000 paintings.

He had an art exhibit at the Denver Art Museum, which resulted in the sale of one drawing for $20, and sold seven paintings to various relatives and friends during a 30-year period.

He made repeated efforts to secure a one-man showing in New York, with the objective of establishing a reputation as an accomplished artist. He made pitches to various galleries, but was unable to secure a showing. He finally was able to arrange an exhibition at a gallery in London, England.

The US Tax Court said that Mr. Porter had no bona fide expectation of making a profit as an artist. The court noted that during a 30-year period Mr. Porter sold only 12 or 13 paintings, mainly to family members and friends. "These facts, along with the long history of his expenditures, the large disproportion between such expenditures and his sporadic receipts, his independent wealth … lead us to conclude" that his activity was a hobby, not a business.

The court added that even though Mr. Porter devoted himself full time to the venture, "We cannot accept his contention that such dedication and accompanying struggles show that his activities did not constitute a hobby or were not undertaken merely for pleasure."

The previous example provides the following key points:

1. A full-time artist is not immune from the argument that the activity is a hobby. In order to withstand IRS scrutiny it is important, among other things, for artists to actively promote or market their artwork.

2. If there is an extended history of losses, as in this case, the implication is that you are subsidizing a losing venture, and that the activity is a hobby rather than a business.

3. If the only sales of art are to friends and relatives, the IRS will tend to regard these as sham sales.

In the following case, the US Tax Court declared the taxpayer to be engaged in a business rather than a hobby, despite the fact that she never derived a profit from her activities. The court believed that she was diligent in making efforts to market her art.

Example: *Churchman v. Commissioner,* 68 T.C. 696 (1977).

Gloria Churchman, Mill Valley, California, occupied herself as an artist for more than 20 years. She mainly painted but also sculpted, designed, drew, and built.

She designed an art gallery and ran it for a year. She sent announcements of her shows to potential buyers from a mailing list she maintained. She visited galleries in San Francisco and New York seeking gallery representation, and she published a book.

She never derived a profit from these activities. When she realized that her works were not selling well, she adopted new techniques. She made posters and worked on books in an effort to produce more salable works for the public. Her records were incomplete, but she at least kept receipts of her costs and a ledger listing what she sold and to whom.

The US Tax Court noted that "the archetypal 'struggling artist' must first achieve public acclaim before her serious work will command a price sufficient to provide her with a profit."

The court ruled in Ms. Churchman's favor. The court said: "It is abundantly clear from her testimony and from the objective evidence that petitioner is a most dedicated artist, craves personal recognition as an artist, and believes that selling her work for a profit represents the attainment of such recognition. Therefore, petitioner intends and expects to make a profit … It seems to us irrelevant whether petitioner intends to make a profit because it symbolizes success in her chosen career or because it is the pathway to material wealth. In either case, the essential fact remains that petitioner does intend to make a profit from her artwork and she sincerely believes that if she continues to paint she will do so."

The previous example provides the following key points:

1. One of your most important assets is your credibility. The court apparently believed the sincerity of the taxpayer's testimony that she was engaged in art to make a profit.

2. The court said that the taxpayer's records were acceptable although incomplete. She kept track of income and disbursements, and had a ledger listing items sold, the buyer's name, and the price. She had a mailing list of potential buyers that she utilized. She had evidence of her efforts to obtain gallery representation, which was accomplished by keeping memos of phone calls and copies of emails and correspondence.

3. The taxpayer changed methods of operation to improve her chances of making a profit. In her case, she switched to making posters instead of drawings and sculptures.

The IRS is familiar with tax schemes in the art world that improperly inflate tax deductions, as you will see in the next example.

Example: *Barr v. Commissioner,* T.C. Memo 1989-69.

Sheldon Barr, Baldwin, New York, studied art in college, and became a lawyer. He had a passion for art, acquired art for his own collection, and studied the art market by attending auctions and galleries.

He decided to acquire rights from various artists and to publish silk-screen prints of their works in book form. He consulted individuals familiar with the field about publishing such a book.

He entered into contracts with three artists, who in turn created silk screen plates that Mr. Barr acquired. Under the contracts, Mr. Barr made a cash down payment and issued a ten-year non-recourse promissory note to the artists.

The artists were to be paid only out of the proceeds from sales. Mr. Barr was not personally liable to pay if sales failed to generate enough revenue to pay back the notes. The artists could only collect from sales.

Mr. Barr claimed depreciation deductions on the silk screens, claiming they had a five-year useful life, and using the full contract price as the cost basis for the depreciation allowance.

These nonrecourse notes were the main reason why he lost his case in the US Tax Court. Tax law limits the amount of loss you can take from activities that involve nonrecourse financing. The court felt that the structure of the financing showed that Mr. Barr was motivated by tax, rather than profit considerations. "It is well settled that nonrecourse obligations whose repayment is remote and contingent will be disregarded for tax purposes."

The notes were made payable solely out of the proceeds, and thus were dependent on public acceptance of the works. Because repayment of the notes was simply too speculative and contingent, the court said it would be improper to claim the face value as the cost basis in computing depreciation deductions. The court said that Mr. Barr's cost basis would be the actual amount of cash paid to the artists under the contracts. But that is only if the silk-screen venture was construed as a bona fide business. The court noted that Mr. Barr did not have any criteria in choosing the artists — such as their reputations or skills. He did little, if anything, to sell the works, either through art galleries or through publicity. He formed the idea of marketing them via mail-order sales, but did not carry out that plan. He made no effort to seek other ways of generating retail sales.

Mr. Barr claimed that he consulted art experts, but offered no proof of this other than his own testimony. The advice he testified he received did not pertain to marketing of the works, their value, or public demand for them.

Mr. Barr argued that the time and effort he expended, the businesslike manner in which he operated, and his expertise in the art field (supplemented by consultation with experts) was proof that he carried on the activity for profit.

The US Tax Court said that Mr. Barr provided no evidence as to the manner in which he carried on the activity other than his testimony.

Mr. Barr testified that he conducted the activity in a businesslike manner, but was not able to present much by way of documentary evidence. He explained that his sales records were lost during the audit of his tax returns. He failed to provide other records concerning his expenses

The previous example provides the following key points:

1. The taxpayer lost mainly because the court believed the inflated depreciation deductions were the taxpayer's principal motivation, and that he was not in a bona fide business.

2. Any kind of venture in which you try to *leverage* nonrecourse notes in order to generate high depreciation deductions will be strictly scrutinized. As in this case, the IRS will disallow the deductions or require you to use a lower cost basis.

3. To market art works as a business, it is important to have a business plan, to decide on marketing techniques (e.g., mail order, Internet, or other means), and to carry them out.

4. Sometimes records get lost, but this is often difficult to explain. When a taxpayer says that records were lost, there is no way of corroborating this. The taxpayer might really be hiding the fact that he or she simply had inadequate records in the first place, as was the implication in this case.

5. If you have consultations with experts about your artistic activities, be sure to document such consultations in specific detail.

2. Photography

Photography is a form of art, but it's also an extremely popular hobby. Most people take pictures while on vacation, at family gatherings, or at parties, and almost everyone considers themselves an amateur photographer. Some enterprising individuals have turned their passion for photography into business ventures.

Tax-deductible expenses include photography equipment, materials, travel costs, attendance at trade shows and seminars, and if applicable, home office deductions. The IRS generally takes the view that photography activities are a hobby unless there is good evidence that the individual is really serious about being in the business of photography.

Example: *Young v. Commissioner, 28 A.F.T.R.2d (RIA) 5442.*

Barbara Young, Baltimore, Maryland, a psychoanalyst, had a passion for photography. Over the years she assembled a book of her pictures and tried to get it published. She incurred significant expenses that she deducted against her income as a therapist.

The IRS denied her deductions and she took her case to US Tax Court. The court held that Dr. Young sincerely and in good faith expected to make a profit, not necessarily an immediate profit, but perhaps over years. The court said that "the odds are strongly against those who expect to make a profit in this field," but nonetheless held that her photography activity was a business.

The court said: "I do not think she played at this as a dilettante. I think she is trying in the best way that she knows how to crash through in this field and to establish this secondary occupation as a profitable one." Dr. Young was able to write off her photography costs.

The previous example provides the following key points:

1. It is well understood that making money in photography is an elusive matter, although some people might abuse the tax laws by declaring themselves to be in the trade or business of photography when they really are hobbyists. In this case, the court was impressed by the taxpayer's sincere expectation that she should make money.

2. One of the most important things is your credibility as a taxpayer. It is important to come across as honest and candid, and to show that you have the honest hope and expectation of making a profit in this type of venture.

Example: *Snyder v. United States,* 674 F.2d 1359 (10th Cir. 1982).

Paul Snyder, an attorney in Boulder, Colorado, was an amateur photographer for many years. He took pictures primarily of his family.

He decided to get into commercial photography and bought sophisticated photography equipment. He devoted 30 hours a week to taking pictures of the Colorado high country. He hoped to publish and sell a book containing his pictures. He kept detailed records of technical data regarding his photographs.

After a year he had approximately 3,000 slides, and began to send letters to publishers soliciting their interest in his book. He received replies from six or eight publishers who expressed interest, and he went to New York to discuss the book with some of them. He also traveled to San Francisco, at the expense of a publisher, to discuss the book with an editor. He was encouraged by the publishers he met, but none of them offered him a contract.

Mr. Snyder deducted significant expenses associated with his commercial photography venture against his law practice income. The IRS argued that he was not in the trade or business of "nature photography" because he had not yet produced a book of his works.

The US Tax Court said that the fact that Mr. Snyder had not yet produced a book did not, in itself, imply he was engaged in a hobby. "As a policy matter, such a position would have an unwarranted and undesirable chilling effect on budding authors who are serious in pursuing a writing career."

The court concluded that Mr. Snyder was motivated by a good faith expectation of profit, and that he was entitled to deduct ordinary and necessary expenses related to his photography activities.

The previous example provides the following key points:

1. The taxpayer was able to show that several publishers expressed interest in his photography book and that he pursued these leads.

2. The taxpayer promptly started to market his project once he gathered a sufficient number of pictures to put into a book.

3. The taxpayer purchased commercial photo equipment, which bolstered his claim that he was engaged in a business and not a hobby.

4. As with any creative field, if you have not finished a particular work, it has little to do with the question of whether you are engaged in a hobby or a business. However, in some situations creative people have been denied deductions because they seemed to be endlessly working on unfinished projects.

In the following case the court ruled against a taxi driver who claimed he was a freelance photographer, taking pictures as he saw interesting things during his driving.

Example: *Burns v. Commissioner,* T.C. Memo 1993-532.

Atwood Burns, a taxi driver in Park Forest, Illinois, claimed to have a side business as a photographer. He had previously worked as a photographer. At the time his case came to the US Tax Court, he said he was in the start-up phase of his own freelance venture.

He claimed deductions for expenses related to his activities as a photographer, including rent on his apartment. As a result of his deductions he paid no taxes for two years.

Mr. Burns said that he always kept a camera with him while driving a taxi, and that he was "hoping some day" to take a picture worth selling for thousands of dollars. If he came across an interesting scene during the day, he would take a picture and develop it in his darkroom that night.

When he took pictures for individuals he did not charge a fee. He said this was a way to create business goodwill and position himself for more lucrative photography jobs in the future.

The US Tax Court held that his activity was a hobby, not a business. The court concluded that Mr. Burns did not have an honest expectation to make a profit in this area. The court felt that Mr. Burns gave little concern to the question of whether or how he might make a profit as a photographer.

The previous example provides the following key points:

1. It is important in a photography venture to determine how you can make money from the activity. It is also important to charge money for your work. Prices should be established and charged, except when it is appropriate to give away work as promotional or advertising efforts.

2. It is important in a photography venture to keep adequate business records as evidence of your concern for the economics of the project, particularly if you have a history of losses.

3. The court, in this case, may have been influenced by the idea that the taxpayer simply kept a camera in his taxi with the vague hope of someday snapping a brilliant shot that he could market. It seemed perhaps highly implausible to the judge. Still, the hobby loss rule allows you to select an area that is highly speculative as long as you have an honest expectation of eventually making a profit. However, along with this is the requirement that you must conduct the venture in a businesslike manner.

For any deductions taken for business purposes, the nature of the expense should be established at the time it is incurred, such as for travel costs. For an example of this see *Stephens v. Commissioner* on the CD.

In the following case, the US Tax Court ruled against an individual who claimed she took pictures at weddings and other functions as a business.

Example: *Windisch v. Commissioner,* **T.C. Memo 1996-369.**

Deborah Joyce Windisch, Soquel, California, worked full time as an account clerk for a health services agency and part time as a telephone bill collector. In her limited free time she took photos of weddings, family reunions, graduations, rock bands, and musicians, and claimed she was in it as a business.

Ms. Windisch did not have formal training in photography and did not maintain a darkroom. She had the quality of her photos analyzed and critiqued. She joined the Professional Photographers of California and another professional group.

She did not advertise, but relied on flyers and word of mouth to promote her activity. Most of her customers were coworkers.

She incurred losses over a period of several years and claimed on average $20,000 in deductions each year, which helped offset her day job income.

While she kept meticulous records, the US Tax Court said that she did not use her records to help evaluate costs or the overall performance of her operation.

The court said that she made no changes to how she operated her activity in an effort to make a profit. She generally did photography for coworkers, friends, and relatives, indicating that personal, rather than business considerations, influenced the manner in which she carried on the photography activity.

The court said she used the activity as a means of deducting personal expenses and the cost of social activities. The court concluded that she carried on the activity because of the personal satisfaction it afforded and that it constituted a hobby. The court said that while her activity had some "trappings" of a business, they were insufficient to prove that the activity was carried on for profit.

The previous example provides the following key points:

1. The main reason why the taxpayer lost was that the activity seemed more social in nature. She only took photos of family, friends, and coworkers. The court felt that her motivation was simply the personal satisfaction the activity afforded her.

2. The court seemed influenced by the fact that the taxpayer did not have formal training in photography or maintain a darkroom. Of course, nowadays, with digital photography, many professional photographers do not maintain darkrooms anymore.

3. In recent years the US Tax Court has repeatedly said that in operating a venture in a businesslike manner, it is important to *utilize* business records to evaluate the economics of the project and to help decide if you should make any changes in operations.

In the following case, the US Tax Court was impressed by the taxpayer's diligent efforts to market her photographic works and to seek out a niche market for hand-tinted photographs.

Example: *Hughes v. Commissioner,* **T.C. Memo 1995-202.**

Cynthia Hughes, Tallahassee, Florida, worked as a secretary. Dissatisfied with the job, she quit and decided to conduct a full-time venture involving hand tinting of photographs. She used oil-based paints and fiber-based paper to add color to black and white photos. This technique, popular in the early days of photography, fell out of favor as color film came into vogue. Now, tinting survives as a specialty or novelty service.

She provided services to photography studios. Ms. Hughes' father owned a photography studio and her mother was a photographic artist. However, Ms. Hughes had no formal training in the art of photography. She informally studied how to paint photos and then took an art class at a college. She operated out of two rooms in her home. She lived primarily off her savings and earnings from temporary jobs until her money gave way and she started a full-time job at a law firm.

She maintained a mailing list of photography studios and sent fliers to them announcing her services. She advertised in a national photographers' magazine on one occasion, but she was unable to develop more than a handful of local studios as clients. She kept records of her transactions, noting the type of photo, the date of the order, the date she finished the item, and the amount charged. She only had two profitable years in a ten-year period. In other years her gross receipts ranged from a high of $4,586 to a low of $68.

She claimed office and utility expenses, telephone, car expenses, meals, education, postage, travel, and office supplies.

The US Tax Court held that Ms. Hughes had an honest intention of engaging in the trade of hand-tinting photographs. "The activity does not have the earmarks of a hobby. Petitioner was not occasionally selling photographs that she had painted to amuse herself. Rather, she filled orders that arose from her solicitations. She dedicated her spare time to the activity, hoping to get out of the professional rut into which she had fallen."

The court, however, limited the amount of her deductions, saying that Ms. Hughes apparently had been "overly liberal" in the amounts she claimed as business expenses. The court also disallowed her home office deductions because of the limitations imposed on home office deductions under section 280A(c)(5). (For a discussion about home office deductions, see Chapter 6.)

The court denied other deductions because Ms. Hughes was not able to substantiate the amounts or the business purposes involved.

The previous example provides the following key points:

1. Full-time photographers are more likely to convince the IRS that they are operating a trade, not a hobby, than part-time photographers.

2. In this case the court modified the amount of the taxpayer's deductions because some of her expenses were personal, not business, in nature. It is important to substantiate the amounts and purpose of expenditures or else you run the risk that they will be denied.

3. There are many elements showing a businesslike manner of operating her venture. The court was impressed with her dedication, her earnest marketing efforts, and her artistic technique.

3. Chapter Summary

With artists, the IRS recognizes — or is supposed to recognize — that losses are more understandable than in other fields because a struggling artist must first achieve public recognition before the art will generate good prices.

To be a professional artist or photographer does not mean that art or photography has to be your sole or even principal occupation, but it must constitute a recurring activity that you conscientiously pursue for gain.

If you are skilled in teaching art or photography, it is helpful to obtain a teaching position, at least part-time, to bolster your credentials and to help support the fact that you are an expert in your field.

The business of being an artist or photographer, like other occupations, requires that you keep adequate books and records if you wish to take tax deductions against your other sources of income.

You should have records showing your efforts to promote and market your works. Keep a file with promotional material, news articles, critical reviews, and other information about your exhibitions, art shows, and lectures you have given. It is also helpful if you maintain a time log showing how much time you put into working on and promoting your artwork or photography.

If you are audited, it could be important to have the revenue agent visit your studio and any art galleries displaying your work. A professional artist's studio is usually an impressive site, fully equipped with tools of the trade and storage space, and imparts the impression that the person is serious about being an artist.

A big area of contention with the IRS involves writers who claim deductions for their writing expenses. Most writers have a passionate interest in their writing. Many writers become successful after a period of years in which they struggle to earn any kind of income. With the IRS, the problem is that the activity may seem to be one engaged in for pleasure or recreation. The IRS must be reminded that profits may not be immediately forthcoming in this, or any other, creative field. Many writers have to struggle in their early years, or throughout their lives. This does not mean that serious writers do not intend to profit from their activities. It only means that their lot is a difficult one.

1. Conduct Your Writing Venture in a Businesslike Manner

Being a professional writer does not require writing to be a person's sole or even principal occupation, but it must constitute a recurring activity that the person conscientiously pursues for gain. Writers who have not yet achieved sufficient commercial success to support themselves usually have a day job, and deduct expenses of the writing activity against their wages or salary. They usually work on their writing in the evenings and on weekends.

Maintaining a full-time job in addition to your writing venture is a positive factor reflecting your motivation. It shows that you are making efforts to be responsible about earning a living while devoting time to developing your writing career.

If the IRS audits you, and there is little or no income realized from your writing in recent years, the question of motive becomes acute. The IRS will want to see objective evidence that you have the honest intention of being engaged in writing for profit, or else the IRS will deny your tax deductions.

The problem is compounded by the notorious fact that writers are extremely poor at business. Record keeping is usually the farthest thing from their minds. Still, the business of being a writer, like other trades, requires that a person carry on the activity in a businesslike manner if he or she wishes to take tax deductions against his or her other sources of income. The examples in this chapter will help underscore what the busy writer can do to withstand IRS scrutiny.

The expenses of writers include: writing tools; computers; office equipment and furniture; costs of developing work; deductions related to a home office (see Chapter 6); fees paid to publishers, publicists, lawyers, and accountants; advertising costs; travel expenses incurred in researching and writing a book; travel expenses to attend promotional events or writers' conferences; subscriptions; membership dues; photocopy costs; costs of research materials; and secretarial expenses.

Expenses that are inherently personal are usually disallowed even if they are important to your research. In the following case, the writer sought to deduct the costs of visiting prostitutes in Nevada as part of the research for his book.

Example: *Vitale v. Commissioner,* T.C. Memo 1999-131.

Ralph Vitale, Arlington, Virginia, was an experienced writer. He had worked for the Department of the Treasury, writing reports and analyses, and was given an outstanding rating for his writing skills. He also edited the Treasury's in-house newsletter.

As he approached retirement he wanted to develop writing as a second career, and decided to write a book about two men who travel cross-country to patronize a brothel in Nevada. He wrote a basic storyline, which he copyrighted.

For research, he visited numerous legal brothels in Nevada and acted as a customer for prostitutes in order to authenticate his story and develop characters for the book. He kept a detailed diary of the brothels he visited, the prostitutes he met, and the amount of cash he paid each one, as well as general notes about the house rules of each brothel, the manner in which he negotiated a price, his dialogue with the prostitutes, and the clothing they wore. He spent about three days per month on average meeting with prostitutes at the brothels.

He finished a manuscript called *Searchlight, Nevada*, and after consulting *Writer's Market* he submitted the book for publication with Northwest Publishing, Inc. He paid a fee of $4,375 to publish 10,000 copies of his book, which was one-fourth of the publisher's total cost. He entered into a royalty agreement with the publisher. The book was released and distributed to several major bookstores.

He also actively participated in the promotion of the book. He mailed about 60 complimentary copies of the book, along with individualized letters, to bookstores, newspapers, magazines, and hotels. He worked with a marketing expert at Northwest Publishing to get his book stocked by distributors and to set up book signings at major bookstores. He worked closely with the public relations department to ensure that his book was widely advertised and readily available in bookstores. He helped write the press release on the book.

Mr. Vitale did not make a profit with this book. About four months after the book was distributed, the publisher filed for bankruptcy. He filed a claim with the Bankruptcy Court for $17,854 for unpaid royalties and breach of contract. Mr. Vitale secured the return of his rights to the book and began soliciting other publishers to have his book published a second time. He rewrote his manuscript in an effort to make it more salable to the public, and thus, more attractive to prospective publishers. He sent letters to literary agents, soliciting their interest in his book. He received several responses to submit his manuscript for review. He was contacted by a Hollywood script agent who expressed interest in using the book for a television movie or feature film.

As business-related expenses, Mr. Vitale deducted the amounts he paid to the prostitutes, among other expenses.

The US Tax Court said that Mr. Vitale was clearly engaged in the business of writing. The court allowed him to deduct expenses associated with the development and publication of his work, but not the "interview" payments to the prostitutes. The court said these were "inherently personal" in nature. The allowable deductions were for advertising, office and travel expenses, as well as amounts paid for supplies and utilities, and to his publisher.

The court said that he conducted the activity in a businesslike manner and that he kept good records of his expenses, including a contemporaneous journal to substantiate cash expenditures (payments to the prostitutes) and a journal of his interviews with the prostitutes. The court was impressed with the fact that after his publisher went bankrupt, he did not abandon his writing, but sought the return of his copyright of the book and diligently searched for a new publisher.

The previous example provides the following key points:

1. In the business of writing (or any other business), deductions are generally not allowed for inherently personal expenses, even if they are necessary to carry forward your work. The IRS considers the following to be "inherently personal," and hence nondeductible: television sets, VCRs, tickets to concerts or the theater, personal valets, clothing, child care, and other items (such as the costs of prostitutes in this case).

2. If you are traveling to do research, keep adequate notes to substantiate what you researched. There are special substantiation requirements for travel-related expenses, which were discussed in Chapter 4.

3. It is important to actively market your work, either through a literary agent or directly with publishers. If, as in this case, your publisher goes bankrupt, arrange to get your copyright back and then seek another publisher.

4. In this case the taxpayer had a bachelor's degree in marketing and advertising, which suggested that he had some familiarity with the business side of his writing activity.

Sometimes writers will change from one genre to another, such as from technical writing to writing a novel as in the previous example, and then not attain immediate success in the new genre. At times the IRS will argue that you are not qualified to switch to the new genre, and that your new area of writing is a hobby.

Example: *Howard v. Commissioner,* **T.C. Memo 1981-250.**

Upon graduating from college, Eleanor Howard, New York, New York, worked as a writer for 20th Century Fox. After moving to New York, she supported herself by writing profile articles of celebrities which were published in various magazines. She also wrote and published two books and a short story.

In New York she met and married Jack Howard, president of the Scripps Company, which owned Scripps-Howard Newspapers and various radio and television stations. After marrying Mr. Howard, she was no longer solely dependent on writing to support herself and she turned to more speculative writing projects.

Mrs. Howard wrote a few magazine articles, but mainly focused on writing plays — an entirely new genre for her — and sent them to agents and producers. She also joined various writers' organizations, including the American Society of Journalists and Authors.

She deducted rent for an office that she used two to four hours a day for writing, plus utilities, insurance, dues to professional organizations, and other costs.

Mrs. Howard made no money from her writings during the years for which the IRS audited her. The IRS claimed that her writing was a hobby and disallowed the tax deductions. The IRS argued that she was no longer dependent on her writing because she was supported by a wealthy husband, and that in any event she was writing plays, and had no experience in that genre.

The US Tax Court sided with Mrs. Howard. The court said that Mrs. Howard had been a recognized professional writer for decades and that her experience enabled her to switch genres.

The court noted that she pursued her writing in a businesslike manner, maintained accurate records, and marketed her finished works in a reasonable manner. Also, she devoted a substantial amount of time and effort to her writing.

The court said that whether a taxpayer needs the money or has independent means, the test is the same — the intention to make a profit. It is irrelevant whether a writer intends to make a profit because it symbolizes success in his or her chosen career, or because it is the pathway to material wealth.

The previous example provides the following key points:

1. If you have experience as a professional writer, you are very likely qualified to switch from one genre to another.

2. If you are engaged in writing as a business, it is important to actively market your work, either with a literary agent, publishers, or through other marketing channels (e.g., self-publishing through the Internet).

3. From a business standpoint, it is useful for writers to periodically attend writers' seminars and to join writers' organizations to improve their skills and keep on top of industry developments.

4. It is important to show that you consistently devote a significant amount of time to writing. It is helpful to keep a current log or diary of your time, for this constitutes objective evidence of the amount of time spent on the activity.

Evidence that you have made reasonable efforts to market your work is an important ingredient in proving that you are engaged in the business of writing, even in the absence of profits.

Example: *Kalbfleisch v. Commissioner,* **T.C. Memo 1991-61.**

Gary Kalbfleisch, Long Beach, California, worked in the aerospace industry as a technical writer of manuals, proposals, and contracts, and he edited the writing of other workers.

In his spare time he wrote short stories (a different genre for him) because he believed that there was a market for them. He issued a catalog of his stories, but he had no plan for circulating it and he did not sell any of his stories.

He also published a newsletter of his views on the political scene. He consigned copies to newsstands and offered subscriptions by mail. The newsletter grew to include articles by several other writers. However, he earned less than $100 in revenue over a five-year period.

He did not consult advisers or experts to determine whether there was a need or market for his short stories or the work he was generating for the political opinion pamphlet.

The US Tax Court held that his activity was "sporadic" and "nothing more than a hobby." The court said that Mr. Kalbfleisch did not seek any expert advice on how to start or maintain such a business, and made no serious effort to analyze the economic viability of his activity. There was no evidence as to the amount of time he spent in the writing activity. The court said that he made no projections of income or expenses, and that he had no marketing plan. He merely hoped that somehow word of his short stories and political tracts would get to the public and that the public would buy his works in sufficient quantity to enable him to make a profit.

While he had writing skills, they were mainly in the technical fields, and the court said that there was no evidence he could contribute anything in the personal reading or political arenas that could be marketable.

The previous example provides the following key points:

1. Again, in switching from one genre to another, it is important to justify the shift based on your overall writing experience and abilities.

2. If you are unable to market your work on your own, seek advice from experts. (For another example of bad marketing practices, see *Sherman v. Commissioner* included on the CD.)

3. If you are not making a profit, prepare projections of income and expenses, and seek other means to analyze how the activity can be made profitable.

4. It is important to consistently apply yourself to the writing venture rather than to engage in it sporadically, as in this case.

The IRS gets especially concerned if a writer has failed to produce a finished manuscript, suggesting the unending process of a dilettante, as you will see in the example *Clark v. Commissioner*, included on the CD. This is compounded if the taxpayer has no prior experience in the business of writing.

In the following case the taxpayer, who was an experienced writer, failed to convince the US Tax Court that his writing activity was a business.

Example: *Nauman v. Commissioner,* T.C. Memo 1998-217.

St. Elmo Nauman, Jr., El Toro, California, worked full time for the asylum office of the Immigration and Naturalization Service, and taught philosophy and religion part time at Chapman University. He was an ordained minister with the United Church of Christ, and served as a chaplain for the US Navy.

There was no question that Mr. Nauman was an experienced writer. Mr. Nauman worked for a publishing company developing manuscripts for publication. Also, he had published three reference works (i.e., *The New Dictionary of Existentialism*, *Dictionary of American Philosophy*, and *Exorcism Through the Ages*). He also wrote papers on philosophy, religion, politics, and logic, but none of them were published. He only submitted one of the papers for publication and it was not accepted.

Mr. Nauman claimed he had a sideline business as a writer and took depreciation deductions for his personal library of 6,400 books, with a purported purchase price of $160,000, as well as deductions for office equipment and computers.

The US Tax Court held that his writing was for "mere personal enjoyment." The decision hinged primarily on the finding that he did not maintain any books and records, that he submitted only one manuscript for publication, and that he earned no income from his writing activity.

In addition, the court said that he did nothing to improve his chances of making money at writing, had no business plan, and did not even investigate the basic factors that affect profitability.

The previous example provides the following key points:

1. This experienced and talented writer's activity was deemed a hobby mainly because of the failure to have any plan for making money with the writing, as well as the absence of records, and lack of sincere marketing efforts.

2. It is always important to maintain adequate records that document what you did to market your writing.

3. In this case the taxpayer sought to depreciate the cost of his personal library. Even in situations where a writer is clearly engaged in writing as a business rather than a hobby, deductions for the purchase of books will usually be limited to those books actually used for research in one's writing project.

Some writers need to travel in order to do research for their books. Travel expenses can sometimes be tricky to justify, particularly if the travel has elements of personal pleasure or if the amounts deducted seem excessive compared to the income generated from the writing. The CD includes a case involving a celebrity who tried to deduct travel and dining expenses in connection with his book project. (See **Dreicer v. Commissioner**.)

In the following example, the taxpayer wanted to write a travel guide, but had little experience as a writer, much less as a travel writer.

Example: *Lesher v. Commissioner,* **T.C. Memo 1987-345.**

Sarah Lesher, North Haven, Connecticut, quit her job as a computer programmer for Yale University School of Medicine. She obtained writers' guidelines for submissions for an upcoming revision of *Backpacker's Africa*.

Ms. Lesher had very little writing experience. She did not consult experts on how to collect information for writing about travel. She studied books about Africa and traveled to Africa for research purposes. She maintained a diary of her travels.

A new edition of *Backpacker's Africa* was completed before she submitted any materials to the publisher. She then took on a new job as a computer programmer, and worked on a novel based on her travel adventures. She never submitted her manuscript to any publisher or literary agent.

The US Tax Court said that she was not engaged in the business of writing because she had no experience writing, she failed to conduct research or consult any experts on how to write a book about travel, and she did not obtain any commitments for the publication or sale of her travel writing. The court concluded that her writing endeavors were a hobby.

The previous example provides the following key points:

1. It is important to have some sort of background in writing if you are planning on engaging in writing as a business, or at least to consult with experts about writing and marketing your work.

2. Perhaps the chief distinction between writing as a hobby and writing as a business is that serious writers are expected to actively market their work with the help of a literary agent or directly with publishers. Failure to market your writing suggests a hobby.

3. The IRS is aware that some people who claim to be travel writers are in fact simply seeking to deduct the costs of personal travel as business expenses.

Even in situations where you succeed in getting your writing published, a recurring problem involves travel expenses for seminars and/or research that exceed the amount you earn for the writing project.

Example: *Miller v. Commissioner,* T.C. Memo 1998-463.

Nancy Miller, Akron, Ohio, decided to write about travel and related subjects. Previously she had worked as a secretary and office manager for a travel agency. She joined several travel writers' organizations and wrote numerous articles that were published in about three dozen publications. She received compensation ranging from $20 to more than $300 for each article.

Ms. Miller and her husband purchased an RV and a travel trailer and used them for some of the trips, deducting the costs from their gross income. On the trips Ms. Miller took pictures that she sometimes submitted with her articles. Some publishers paid a higher fee for articles that included photos.

Ms. Miller took an "education seminar" cruise in Europe that was hosted by travel writing and photography experts. During the two-week cruise there were five and a half hours of formal instruction. She took 900 photos during the cruise and she published one article related to the cruise, for which she was paid $150. The cost of the cruise, one-half of which she claimed as a business deduction, was $12,067. Ms. Miller also deducted other travel expenses in connection with her research.

Her writing activity resulted in a net loss of about $64,000 during a six-year period. She maintained detailed records of her expenses and used a separate bank account for her writing activity.

The US Tax Court said that even though her writing activity was conducted with continuity and regularity, the activity was a hobby.

The court said that she failed to consider whether she could make a profit on any of her travel writings. "In fact, the income-producing potential of a particular trip seemed to be of little concern to Ms. Miller. It appeared that she would first decide on a destination and spend whatever was necessary to travel there, regardless of the amount of income that she could objectively expect to earn from the sale of articles resulting from the trip."

The court noted that Ms. Miller had not planned on writing any articles about certain trips, but upon returning she had decided to deduct the costs because she had taken photos or interviewed various people.

The court concluded that the Millers enjoyed traveling and did so frequently, and that they were motivated primarily by recreation and pleasure. The court said: "Where the possibility of profit is small (given all the other factors) and the possibility of gratification is substantial, it is clear that the latter possibility constitutes the primary motivation for the activity."

The previous example provides the following key points:

1. Travel writers often face hurdles with the IRS because of the notion that travel, particularly to foreign destinations or on cruises, involves personal pleasure and recreation.

2. Travel expenses should not exceed the income that might be generated from writing about the trip.

3. Only a portion of the costs for seminars on cruise ships are tax deductible. Section 274(h) of the IRS Code limits the deductions for conventions, seminars, or other meetings on cruise ships. The meeting must be related to your trade or business, the cruise ship must be registered in the United States (most ships are not), and the ports of call must all be in the United States. This means there are no deductions for a European cruise even though it might include an important seminar that pertains to your trade or business.

As mentioned in Chapter 1, the hobby loss rule recognizes a start-up phase, which is the idea that it may take a number of years until you can make a profit with a new venture. If you are a writer in the start-up phase, your chances of withstanding IRS scrutiny are much better than if you have gone on for many years without making a profit.

Example: *Dickson v. Commissioner*, **T.C. Memo 1986-182.**

Willie Dickson, Upland, California, wrote a college thesis on career planning, and later he became an engineer. In his free time he decided to develop and market books on career planning, such as "How to Get a Job." Mr. Dickson planned to self-publish and to market his materials through mail orders. He obtained a business license, designed and purchased business stationery with his logo: "Dickson's Innovative Enterprises," purchased office furniture and equipment, test-marketed some of his bowling aid materials for a book titled "Over 101 Ways to Improve Your Bowling," and contacted printing houses concerning the cost and method of publication.

The IRS audited him in the first year of the activity and denied his deductions, claiming his writing activity was a hobby even though it was in the early start-up phase. However, the US Tax Court reversed the IRS decision, noting that Mr. Dickson spent a considerable amount of time on the book projects and that he was carrying on the venture in a businesslike manner, while diligently seeking to market his materials. Also, the court said that Mr. Dickson was in the early start-up phase of the activity, and it is understandable that losses would occur in the formative stage.

The previous example provides the following key points:

1. If the IRS audits you in the first few years of a new venture it is important to emphasize that you are in the start-up phase of the activity, which could explain it if you have not yet made a profit.

2. At the same time, even in the start-up phase it is important to operate the activity in a businesslike manner.

3. If you are going to self-publish, it is important to have a plan for marketing your work. In this case the court was impressed by the fact that the taxpayer obtained a business license, designed a logo, contacted printing houses, and took other steps to move his project forward in a businesslike manner.

Writers with past success are more likely to

withstand IRS scrutiny than writers who are novices with little track record. See **Richards v. Commissioner** on the CD for an example of a successful writer who convinced the US Tax Court that his writing activity was a business despite many years of not selling anything new.

There are many situations that involve quirky sorts of writing in which the taxpayer is hard pressed to prove a profit motive, as you will see in the next case.

Example: *Callahan v. Commissioner,* **T.C. Memo 1996-65.**

Myrna Callahan, Plaquemine, Louisiana, worked at various jobs. Her hobby was entering sweepstakes and using refund and rebate coupons. She developed a method for improving one's chances of winning sweepstakes contests. She also developed various strategies to help maximize the savings available from product coupons and rebate offers.

She decided to write two booklets: *Mrs. M.'s Quick & Easy Refund & Rebate System* and *Mrs. M.'s Winning Sweepstakes System.* She placed an advertisement for these in a coupon booklet and made inquiries with several publishers. She was unable to get the works published, but several people did respond to her advertisement.

She then self-published these booklets under a name and logo of her own design and offered them for sale at $10 per copy. She generated publicity for them in the local print and broadcast media, and attended a number of autograph parties at local bookstores, libraries, and clubs. She had her booklets listed in various databases. She wrote to published authors for marketing advice. She generated sales of only a few hundred dollars during a six-year period, and claimed close to $100,000 in expenses, which helped offset her salary and her husband's.

The IRS said her activity was a hobby and denied her tax deductions. The US Tax Court agreed with the IRS. The court said she did not carry on the activity in a businesslike manner. She did not maintain any type of records or accounts and she was unable to explain the purpose of the numerous expenses she claimed in connection with her writing activity. The court said that her "shoebox method" of record keeping was inconsistent with a business. Also, she failed to provide evidence of the amount of time expended in the activity.

The court said that Ms. Callahan was not a professional writer. She claimed that she had prior experience writing for a political candidate and that she had many pieces published in various newspapers, but she failed to submit into evidence any of her purportedly published material.

The court said: "We are not required to accept petitioner's self-serving and uncorroborated testimony, particularly where other and better evidence to prove the point in question is available." The court concluded that "refunding and rebating, and entering sweepstakes, have long been hobbies that petitioner enjoys."

The previous example provides the following key points:

1. If you have little experience as a writer, it will be difficult to claim that you are engaged in the business of writing.

2. Haphazard record keeping is consistent with a hobby and not a business.

3. It can be worthwhile to self-publish books or other writings. However, in this case, the taxpayer failed to generate more than a handful of sales, thus giving the impression that she was not serious about making money from her writings.

In the case *Taylor v. Commissioner* (included

on the CD), the taxpayer disseminated his religious writings for free, which gave the impression that he was engaged in a hobby and not a business.

Some people decide to self-publish booklets and seek to market them with some degree of diligence. They might not make money, but their sincere efforts will enable them to withstand IRS scrutiny, as in the case of *Crymes v. Commissioner* (included on the CD).

2. Research Projects by Educators and Scientists

2.1 Special rules for educators

A number of US Tax Court cases have denied deductions to teachers and professors who claimed they were engaged in research projects. These cases generally held that the individuals failed to undertake the research with a profit motive.

Often educators are motivated to write about their research and ideas — not to make money, but due to the "publish or perish" principle that permeates colleges and universities. It can take considerable time to develop an academic work, and further time and effort to get it published in a suitable academic journal. Usually there is no expectation of profit, but simply the privilege and prestige of getting the research published in a good journal.

A special rule for educators has been established in recognition of this academic custom. (This special rule for educators is set forth in Rev. Rul. 63-275, 1963-2 C.B. 85.) This rule entitles educators to deduct the costs of their research, including travel expenses, even though they might not expect to realize a profit from the publication of their research. The rationale is that these expenditures are necessary to maintain their professional standing, to be eligible for prospective salaried research appointments, or to retain their academic job.

Research often involves travel to places where research materials are available. For example, an archaeology professor on sabbatical will want to visit a site and conduct research, publish a paper about it, and deduct the expenses of the expedition. (Remember, with any travel-related expenditures, it is important to observe the substantiation requirements that were discussed in Chapter 4.)

2.2 Scientific research

Sometimes scientists hope to eventually publish their findings, but that may take many years of research during which losses are generated. In conducting a research project, it is important to have evidence of a profit-making motive for the research project. Evidence would include correspondence with a publisher or literary agent about the project, or with journals that intend to publish the research.

If you have distinguished yourself in a particular field, and you are working in a systematic manner on research, you may justify the lack of current income on the grounds that the research is going forward in a timely manner and, when completed, you expect to publish your findings and achieve a new level of success.

Example: *Stahnke v. Commissioner,* **T.C. Memo 1980-369.**

Herbert Stahnke, Tempe, Arizona, was a professor of zoology at Arizona State University, and the recipient of numerous awards and honors for his contribution to science.

Professor Stahnke had a lifelong interest in venomous animals, which was the topic of his doctoral thesis. Over the years he published more than 100 articles in scientific journals on scorpions and snakes. He developed a lifesaving scorpion antivenin that his laboratory distributed, and he discovered that the use of morphine to ease the pain of scorpion victims substantially increases the toxicity of the venom.

After retiring from his position at the university, he moved his laboratory to his home so he could continue research without commuting to the campus. He purchased laboratory equipment and worked on several research projects concerning scorpions. He also was a consultant to medical doctors and hospitals, but did not charge a fee. He published various pamphlets and tried to sell them to clubs and organizations. The National Park Service purchased a quantity of his pamphlets and sold them to the public. Professor Stahnke made 50 cents on each pamphlet sold.

During retirement he received modest fees for some of his lectures, and some income from his various writings that were sold by Arizona State University, but overall he reported a net loss that he deducted against his pension.

The IRS claimed that his activities of writing, researching, lecturing, and consulting, constituted a hobby. The IRS said that Professor Stahnke was merely continuing his lifelong interest in the research of venomous animals. Professor Stahnke argued that while his efforts had not proved profitable up to that time, his hard work would be rewarded with substantial income if his research proved successful.

The US Tax Court said that Professor Stahnke was regarded as an expert in the field of venomous animals, that he had notable successes in his past research, that he devoted a substantial amount of time to his research, and that he conducted his research in a systematic manner. Although he made no profits, the court said that if profits ever did result, they would occur only after years of diligent research. The court concluded that his activities were engaged in for profit, and

that he was entitled to deduct his laboratory costs and other expenses in connection with his writing, consulting, lecturing, and research.

The previous example provides the following key points:

1. With research projects, it can easily take a number of years to develop and test scientific findings. Thus, publication of the findings, and eventual financial rewards, may not occur for many years. This needs to be explained to the IRS in the event of an audit.

2. People engaged in research projects do not necessarily expect to make money from the publication of their findings, but to make money as a result of new opportunities that come as a result of their research.

3. Chapter Summary

Sometimes it is hard to distinguish why one taxpayer would win and another would lose when there is a similar set of facts. The sincerity of your demeanor during an audit, coupled with how well organized your records are, can clearly make a difference.

The IRS understands that practically all writers have day jobs, and that this is what makes it so appealing for them to deduct various costs that are claimed in connection with their writing venture. The IRS will tend to view your tax deductions with skepticism unless you can offer some evidence showing that you are serious about seeking to make money in your endeavor.

The most important thing that distinguishes a dilettante from a professional writer is the effort made to actually market work. The IRS wants to see evidence that you are seeking representation with literary agents or publishers, that you are making plans for self-publication, or that you are seeking funds from organizations that might help distribute the work. The IRS will also tend to regard your writing as a hobby if you are endlessly revising manuscripts rather than completing projects.

Serious writers usually have some previous experience or qualifications. Thus, it is helpful to have a resume that lists your experience as a writer.

It is important for you to join literary organizations to learn more about the industry, to consult with experts on the dynamics of making money in your particular writing genre, and to attend writing seminars.

PART III
AGRICULTURAL AND ANIMAL BUSINESSES

11

TREE FARMING AND GREENHOUSES

1. Tree Farming

The IRS analyzes tree farming and other types of farming under the hobby loss rule, and there are several US Tax Court cases on the subject that will be explored in this chapter. Sometimes the IRS will say that the taxpayer's main motive for cultivating a tree farm is the pleasure derived from the beauty and serenity of the farm setting.

A tree farmer does not always expect to make money in the short term, because the better quality trees (which garner higher prices) take many (between 50 and 60) years before they are mature enough to harvest for timber or other uses. Old growth trees are more valuable for lumber because they have a greater stability of strength, and thereby provide the best quality hardwood.

There are other types of tree farming in addition to cultivating trees for timber, including Christmas trees, which take a relatively short period of time to grow.

The land used in the venture is an important consideration, and regardless of location you can expect the land and expanded tree growth to appreciate in value over time. Some farmers who cultivate crops also devote a few acres to cultivating trees because this turns unproductive land into productive land.

Many timber farms were formerly wilderness areas that have come into private hands. It is always important when raising trees to have fire precautions. Most farms have some sort of fire protection, such as a lake, and many people buy used fire trucks to keep on hand in case of an emergency.

People who are serious about operating a tree farm must become familiar with forest management practices and consult with experienced people in the industry. Each state has a Department of Natural Resources with a forestry division, and you can obtain useful literature from them. It is important to learn how to maximize the growth potential of your tree farm. Some states offer government subsidies or other programs that help offset the costs of tree farming.

There are numerous woodland owners' associations, all of which host conferences. They offer useful lectures and opportunities to meet others in the field. See the Resources section on the CD for the websites of these associations.

In the following case the taxpayer was in the start-up phase of his venture when the IRS audited him.

Example: *Clark v. Commissioner,* T.C. Memo 1969-241.

Harold Clark, Annapolis, Maryland, was a bricklayer and mason by trade. While working in Northern California he saw a specimen of Oregon myrtle — a tree which is native to the West and often used as an ornamental tree. Its leaves, known as California bay laurel leaves, are sold commercially as a spice. Mr. Clark became fascinated by the qualities of the tree and its possibilities.

After an injury, he was unable to work full time. He decided to raise Oregon myrtles as a side business, and to sell the seedlings as well as the bay leaves. He gathered a large quantity of seeds in the woods in Northern California and took them to his home in Maryland. He sought advice from various experts about cultivating these seeds.

Mr. Clark planted about 6,000 seeds in his backyard. Three hundred of them came up, and he transplanted those into cans. He hoped to sell them to nurseries as ornamental trees. He left seeds at various arboretums with the hope that he could stimulate their interest in the trees.

However, his first crop soon withered due to a drought. The next year another crop of new trees died because he put too much fertilizer on them.

He bought about 15,000 new seeds from a vendor who gathered them in California and planted a third crop, but that one also failed. He soon discovered that his backyard was contaminated by oil and gas from a nearby filling station.

The IRS denied his tax deductions because it said there was no established market for the seedlings, and there was a significant risk associated with growing these trees in Maryland.

The US Tax Court did not agree with the IRS and said it was a commercially feasible activity, "albeit fraught with difficulties and limitations." The court said Mr. Clark was in the start-up phase of the venture, and during that time he had discovered the difficulties and limitations and had dealt with them. Also, the court noted that since Mr. Clark was able to work as a bricklayer only part-time due to his injury, his main activity was growing the Oregon myrtles.

The court said that Mr. Clark "assiduously investigated the botanical possibilities and problems involved in growing Oregon myrtle but, because his efforts at propagation were unsuccessful, made little effort to sell the production." The court said that there is no requirement that an immediate profit be realized, "nor does the expectation of profit need to be reasonable, although the prospect of an eventual profit has a bearing on the taxpayer's state of mind."

The court said that Mr. Clark was believable as a witness and that he had an honest expectation of eventually making a profit.

The previous example provides the following key points:

1. A basic tenet of tax law is that people are engaged in a business, rather than a hobby, so long as they have an *honest intention* of carrying on the activity as a business. People may choose a highly speculative venture,

as in this case. It is not necessary that your expectation of profit be reasonable. A business is judged not on the reasonableness of the activity, but on the sincere intention of the taxpayer to make a profit.

2. Prior to starting a tree venture, it is important to investigate the commercial aspects of the particular species, primarily whether there is a market for the trees and how to grow them.

3. In this case, the taxpayer was allowed to deduct a portion of rent on the property on which he cultivated the trees, based on a proportion of square footage used.

4. The IRS sometimes audits people in the early start-up phase of an activity. It is important to inform the IRS during the time of audit that you are in the start-up phase because losses are customary in many types of tree-related ventures during this phase.

However, even in the early start-up phase, it is important to have facts showing an overall businesslike approach to the venture. A number of US Tax Court cases have ruled against taxpayers in the early start-up phase of their venture, primarily because they failed to conduct the activity in a businesslike manner.

It is helpful to show why losses occurred. In a tree-farming venture, environmental setbacks such as weather or disease can cause losses, but so can marketplace setbacks, such as an event like the Great Depression. For an example of this see *Montgomery v. Commissioner* on the CD.

Some people are unlucky enough to get audited on multiple occasions, as you will see in the following case. The US Tax Court ruled, for the third time, that the taxpayer's tree farm was a hobby.

Example: *Mitchell v. Commissioner,* **T.C. Memo 2006-145.**

Austin Mitchell's family owned and operated a farm in Salem, Missouri, for more than 100 years. This was the third US Tax Court case that ruled Mr. Mitchell's farming activity was a hobby, not a business.

Mr. Mitchell grew up on the farm, became a lawyer and an accountant, and returned to live there in 1991 when his mother took ill. After her death, he inherited the farm and continued living there and managing it.

Mr. Mitchell spent a huge amount of time working on the farm, in addition to his law practice. He converted ten acres of uphill pasture to timber (white oak and black walnut). He worked on weed control. He cleared multiflora rose and native thistle, did work to facilitate tree growth, and took on other hard physical labor.

The farm had trees in various stages of maturity that he sold for lumber. He made a profit in one year from the sale of mature timber. Mr. Mitchell also sought to make money selling hay.

In the US Tax Court the evidence indicated that timber from the new walnut trees would take 30 years to harvest, and timber from his white oak trees would take 50 to 70 years to harvest.

Mr. Mitchell testified that he had selectively harvested some white oak trees and generated $7,500 in revenue. He had consulted with a logging expert to advise him of trees he could cut. He also said that he could harvest walnuts from the trees in about five years, and that this could provide a cash crop.

For the period covered by the third, most current case, the court decided against Mr. Mitchell. The court said that although he made a small profit in one year (1999), and the losses in the other years were fairly small, he still had losses every year since 1991, which was a long time to be generating losses, unless it was a hobby activity.

The court also said that "the lack of a separate bank account for petitioner's farming activity, coupled with the lack of complete and accurate books and records, tends to show that petitioner did not carry on the farming activity in a businesslike manner."

The court also faulted Mr. Mitchell for not having a written business plan.

The court said that Mr. Mitchell failed to advertise his farming activity in an attempt to increase its profitability. The court felt that he derived personal and recreational benefits from the farm, even though he worked about 50 hours a week as a lawyer and accountant, while also conducting most of the manual labor on the farm himself.

The court also noted that Mr. Mitchell did not seek expert advice on how to operate his farm profitably, but only talked about farming with farmer acquaintances and neighbors.

The court noted that Mr. and Mrs. Mitchell resided on the farm, and that "they derived personal and recreational benefits from the situs of the farming activity. Petitioner devoted regular and substantial time and effort to the farming activity, although he continued to work an average of more than 50 hours per week as a lawyer and accountant. Petitioner did not explain how the work he performed on the family farm related to making it profitable."

The previous example provides the following key points:

1. The taxpayer was audited on three occasions for different tax periods. He lost each audit, went to US Tax Court each time, and lost all three cases.

2. The court apparently believed that the taxpayer's primary motivation in the farming activity was pleasure and recreation, despite the fact that the taxpayer put a lot of hard labor into the improvements he made.

3. It is important to have a separate checking account, a written business plan, and reasonably well-organized overall records when conducting a tree farm. The court ruled that the taxpayer did not conduct the activity in a businesslike manner.

4. The court was influenced by the fact that the taxpayer had a long history of losses, although there was one profitable year.

5. It is important to change methods of operation if you continue to operate a farming venture after losing an audit. Usually, an IRS auditor will indicate specific reasons why the determination was against your claim of conducting a business. This will enable you to examine what sort of meaningful changes you might make in how you operate the activity.

Note: In an IRS audit the government can examine the entire history of an operation in terms of how the taxpayer was performing his or her activity, even though the earlier years might be beyond the statute of limitations.

In the following case, the taxpayer convinced the US Tax Court that his pecan farm was operated in a businesslike manner despite ten years of losses and a lack of adequate records.

Example: *Cole v. Commissioner,* **T.C. Memo 1992-51.**

Dr. James Cole, Houston, Texas, was a dentist. He acquired an 80-acre farm from his father, with 355 pecan trees. He decided to expand the pecan operation and attended a one-week course on pecan management at the Texas A&M University. Dr. Cole bought an additional 80 acres adjacent to the farm. He planted 334 new pecan trees on the old acreage and 779 trees on the new acreage.

He hired irrigation specialists who designed and installed the irrigation system for the trees. He also acquired various pieces of equipment necessary for the proper care of the trees.

He joined The Texas Pecan Growers Association and attended the annual meetings. He read various periodicals about pecans. He consulted various experts concerning planting techniques and the proper varieties to plant.

He had experts visit his farm to instruct him on weed control and proper techniques for pruning, watering, and fertilizing the trees. He received expert advice on measures to prevent soil erosion.

He did not prepare any cost or income projections in connection with the pecan operation.

Dr. Cole employed a farm manager who was responsible for conducting the annual harvest, and for hiring workers to gather and sell the pecans.

There were problems that interfered with full production. One year, microscopic worms in the soil caused a reduction in yield. Dr. Cole had to spend a lot of money for chemicals to treat the problem.

Another year there was a lack of fertilization and water, resulting in the tops of some trees dying out. It would take three to four years of intensive management to bring these trees back into production. He implemented a program that included weed control, worm control, and fertilization to bring these trees back to productivity.

In several other years there were droughts and late spring freezes that affected productivity.

One year some younger trees suffered from "sun scald," which is a sunburn of the trees' bark due to sun exposure on cold, clear days in late fall and early winter. It takes approximately two years for pecan trees to recover from sun scald.

Dr. Cole had losses during a ten-year period. The IRS contended that the trees merely had sentimental value to Dr. Cole and that he engaged in the activity for pleasure.

The US Tax Court noted that Dr. Cole did not maintain a formal set of books for the farm, and had very few records of production. He had no written agreement with the farm manager. His records consisted simply of canceled checks reflecting expenses. He did not prepare a projection of income and expenses.

However, the court said that Dr. Cole worked diligently to educate himself on pecan horticulture, and he bought equipment necessary for the pecan operation. Dr. Cole also worked on the farm to help reduce expenses.

The court said that pecan trees normally begin to produce after 5 years, with yields gradually increasing until the tree reaches maturity between 10 and 12 years. It takes approximately 12 years to recover the expenses of establishing a pecan orchard.

The court noted that Dr. Cole devoted extensive time and effort to the pecan operation. No appraisal of the property was offered into evidence, but the court said that it is likely that Dr. Cole expected the farm would appreciate in value, and that the farm might eventually be sold for a profit.

The court concluded that he operated the farm with an actual and honest objective of making a profit. The court said "pecan farming is by its very nature an uncertain venture. In this light, petitioner's activities are best viewed as a long-term investment, and thus the lack of current profits is not compelling."

The previous example provides the following key points:

1. In this case it is interesting that the taxpayer won despite the lack of records such as a business plan, cost projections, or proper production records. The court felt that the taxpayer operated the pecan farm, overall, in a businesslike manner, despite the lack of formal records.

2. In growing and harvesting pecan trees, the trees do not reach maximum production until about 10 or 12 years, which indicates that the first ten years or so are the start-up phase where no profits will be realized.

3. It is important to educate yourself on the details of tree farming and to consult with experts in the field. This enables you to approach the activity in as businesslike a manner as possible.

4. Another element in this case was that there were many setbacks due to disease, fertilizer problems, drought, and sun scald. The court believed that the taxpayer and his farm manager handled these unanticipated situations competently, and that these setbacks helped explain why there was still no profit after ten years.

Timber farmers who engage in the venture on a large scale are more likely to be considered a business than smaller operations. In the following case, the taxpayer had a large and very professionally-run timber farm. The IRS claimed his farm was a hobby, but the US Tax Court sided with the taxpayer.

Example: *Kurzet v. Commissioner,* **T.C. Memo 1997-54.**

Stanley Kurzet, Park City, Utah, was a successful inventor and businessman. He owned a timber farm near Coos Bay, Oregon. The entire region consisted primarily of commercial timber properties.

Mr. Kurzet had no prior experience in timber farming. He did, however, consult forestry experts to teach him move about the timber industry and to aid him in inspecting the property before he bought the farm. The forestry experts advised Mr. Kurzet about the soil and terrain, the expected growth rate of the trees, and the water resources on the timber farm. Mr. Kurzet also independently studied industry sources relating to tree growth and management.

The farm had Douglas fir, spruce, and other trees that were on average 30 to 40 years old. These trees could be harvested by commercial foresters once every 35 to 60 years. Mr. Kurzet calculated the value of the standing timber on the farm and believed he could make a profit selling harvested timber to commercial loggers.

He made various improvements to the farm, including eliminating poisonous plants that could affect the trees. He improved the roads on the farm to provide ready access for cutting and harvesting, which he hoped to do on short notice, thereby taking advantage of favorable prices in a fluctuating market.

He designed and performed much of the work done to improve the farm. He even helped operate heavy equipment used for improving the roads. He purchased timber-farm equipment and sought to get lower prices by buying used equipment at auctions. He personally fixed some of the equipment to make it operational.

He hired two experienced workers who worked and lived on the farm. Mr. Kurzet visited the farm four or five times a year, and stayed several weeks on the farm during each visit.

Kurzet had a water reservoir constructed to provide a source of water for fighting forest fires, which posed a major threat in the region. He purchased a used fire truck to be used in the event of a fire.

Mr. Kurzet conducted ongoing consultations with experts about how to manage the farm. He often checked the market price for cut timber and evaluated whether any of the timber on his farm should be cut and sold.

For several years, the market prices of timber fell dramatically. Mr. Kurzet decided not to sell any timber until market prices improved because the cost of harvesting the trees would exceed what he could sell them for. Also, he decided to postpone cutting many of the older trees, because once they reach 60 years of age, their market value increases by about 30 percent. During a ten-year period, the volume of trees nearly doubled.

He had a formal appraisal showing that the value of the timber was $2.1 million. His purchase price of the farm had been just $569,000.

The US Tax Court found that Mr. Kurzet operated a business despite the fact that he had not sold any timber. The court said that Mr. Kurzet conducted the activity in a businesslike manner, hired competent people to manage the farm, made significant improvements to the property, and put in long hours working on the farm when he was there. The court noted that the volume of his timber was increasing substantially, as was its fair market value. The court said that in the timber business, individual trees are typically harvested only once every 50 to 60 years.

The court said that Mr. Kurzet was "creative and innovative in attempting to improve the timber farm and eventually to realize substantial overall net profits there from at the time the trees are cut and sold."

The court also said that Mr. Kurzet didn't use the farm for personal entertainment or recreation. There were no recreational amenities or activities on the farm, "no tennis court, no putting green, no swimming pool, no horses, no lake, no boating, no fishing, no recreational or resort facilities."

The previous example provides the following key points:

1. The taxpayer had excellent facts that convinced the court that his timber farm was a business. The court was impressed that the taxpayer consulted forestry experts, worked diligently to expand the volume of tree growth, designed and planned improvements, personally operated heavy equipment, and worked to improve and maintain the access roads to the trees.

2. In certain cases a great deal of money needs to be put into tree farms to keep them going until the trees can be harvested. In some cases it can take decades. It is usually wealthier taxpayers who end up operating the larger tree farms.

3. The IRS sometimes tries to argue that individuals are motivated solely by tax benefits and the sheer enjoyment of owning tree farms. However, the mere fact that a taxpayer has a substantial income from other sources does not foreclose a profit motive.

2. Greenhouses

There are thousands of greenhouse farmers in the US, many of them "mom and pop" operations that are a favorite target of the IRS.

It is important to investigate the competition in your region and focus on a particular crop. You should determine how you will market your crops, what zoning and environmental regulations apply in your area, and what the costs of shipment will be. You might want to focus on specialty crops, such as certain flowers that are unique to the trade. Some people focus on niche markets, such as Easter lilies.

In the following case, the US Tax Court held that a taxpayer's greenhouse, in which he cultivated tomatoes, was a hobby.

Example: *Brown v. Commissioner,* **T.C. Memo 1989-645.**

Ronald Brown, Chehalis, Washington, owned a nursing home. He decided to build a greenhouse to grow vine-ripened tomatoes and later sell them. He did not know anything about growing tomatoes, but consulted an agronomist who agreed to serve as a consultant.

Mr. Brown entered into a contract, paying the consultant $8,000 a year to help develop the soils, implement a fertilizing program, take tissue culture samples, and provide advice on growing vegetables in the greenhouse.

Mr. Brown's stepson, Kim, was also involved. Kim and the consultant contacted various sources to obtain information on how best to grow vegetables in greenhouses.

Mr. Brown obtained a building permit for the greenhouse and had it built. He began paying Kim a monthly salary of $1,750 for his work in the greenhouse. Mr. Brown ended up spending nearly $200,000 in a two-year period on building materials, fees, equipment, utility services, and salaries.

In the first year of operation the tomato crop failed due to bacteria in the water. A chlorinator and an iron removal system were installed to alleviate further problems with the bacteria. However, soon afterwards another tomato crop was lost, this time due to ethylene poisoning emitted from the propane heaters. To eliminate that problem, electric heaters were installed. Soon afterwards the tomatoes started growing properly.

Kim marketed the tomatoes to local grocery stores. He entered an agreement with Safeway stores in Seattle that guaranteed them the entire crop of tomatoes that could be produced the following year, for 78 cents per pound.

Kim calculated that given the price offered by Safeway, they could generate a decent return within five years if they built four greenhouses, reduced their operating costs, and lost no crops during that five-year period.

However, Mr. Brown was not willing to fund the additional greenhouses, and decided to liquidate the remaining produce and terminate the venture. Mr. Brown spent very little time on the project. All day-to-day decisions were left to Kim.

The US Tax Court said that Mr. Brown's motive in entering the activity was not to make a profit, but to provide his previously unemployed stepson, Kim, with an opportunity to establish a business of his own. Mr. Brown's only participation in the venture was funding it.

The court noted that Mr. Brown failed to keep any business records. "Petitioner was an experienced and successful businessman. It is difficult to believe that an individual with his business experience would fail to keep adequate records of an activity from which he planned to make a profit."

The previous example provides the following key points:

1. It is perfectly acceptable to hire family members to work in your venture. However, in this case it appeared that the taxpayer's principal motive was to pay his stepson, who was otherwise unemployed, a salary for working in the greenhouse.

2. The court felt that the taxpayer's failure to spend much time on the greenhouse venture was evidence that he was not serious about conducting a business.

3. The taxpayer abandoned the venture after he realized he could not make a profit unless he spent more money and expanded from one to four greenhouses. The court, however, apparently failed to give this due consideration. Normally, ceasing operations when the taxpayer determines it will not be profitable is important evidence of a profit objective.

4. The court did not seem to take into consideration the setbacks that occurred due to the two crop failures, which were due to unforeseen problems that were subsequently corrected. Ordinarily, setbacks are evidence that helps explain why there were losses.

The following is a situation where the taxpayer operated a small nursery venture, which the US Tax Court said was a hobby and not a business.

Example: *Gagnon v. Commissioner,* **T.C. Memo 1996-430.**

George Gagnon, Des Moines, Washington, was an employee at Costco, and his wife worked as a secretary. Mr. Gagnon decided that he could make money by starting a nursery business. He got a business license, using the name "Gull Cottage Nursery," and started raising potted tulips and daffodils.

Mr. Gagnon was not a horticulturist and had no experience in the nursery business, but he clearly enjoyed working with plants. He made no financial study of the business, other than figuring he could sell potted plants for $4 each to grocery stores, and that his cost would be $1.47 per plant. He read handbooks on how to cultivate bulbs. He decided that he would need to plant 5,000 pots to make a profit. He also bought bushes and trees from wholesale dealers, and held them for sale on his property while they matured. He sold hundreds of plants, but incurred several years of losses.

He did not have a separate checking account for the activity. However, he kept records of income and expenses in journals. He deducted car expenses, cable TV fees, telephone charges, utilities, taxes, repairs on his property, automobile club dues, tools, and the local newspaper.

The US Tax Court said that when all the costs that Mr. Gagnon associated with his venture were considered, "the venture could never produce a profit, and there could not have been an actual and honest objective of a profit." The court said that even if he produced 5,000 pots of tulips a year, he still would not be able to make a profit.

Also, the court noted that many of the deductions were for personal expenses, and that even if Mr. Gagnon had conducted the nursery in a businesslike manner, he should have allocated some of these expenses (e.g., utilities and car expenses) between the nursery activity and personal expenses.

The previous example provides the following key points:

1. It is important to ascertain how many plants need to be developed and how many need to be sold in order to make a profit. In this case, the taxpayer failed to make a basic cost analysis before starting the venture. The court said that even if the taxpayer produced plants from all 5,000 bulbs, and sold all of them, he still could not possibly make a profit given his

costs and the amount for which he could sell the plants.

2. The court was also influenced by what apparently was an abuse of tax deductions. For instance, the court noted that the taxpayer deducted all his car expenses, rather than allocating only the usage attributable to running his nursery. Also, the taxpayer deducted all repairs to his home, whereas only a small portion of the property was used for the nursery.

3. Another element that worked against the taxpayer was the lack of a separate checking account. In many instances, that in itself would not make or break a case. There are numerous cases where the taxpayers lost even though they did have separate checking accounts.

3. Chapter Summary

Before starting to run a tree farm or greenhouse, it is important to confer with experts for guidance on the aspects of growing specific trees or plants.

Whether a small or large operation, it is important to consider the amount of time needed before particular species of trees will be mature enough to be cut for timber or other purposes. Since it may take decades before any trees are mature enough to be profitably harvested, no revenue can be anticipated for an extended period of time. This makes the situation an appealing target for the IRS. The IRS may argue that the tree farm is not a business, but a tax shelter for the individual taxpayer.

In the event of an audit, it is important to educate the revenue agent about the unique aspects of your business; for example, why it is economically important to wait until trees are older before they can be harvested profitably. Keep abreast of market conditions, as market prices for timber are often in flux.

The value of a timber farm often appreciates significantly as tree growth increases, so it is important to have periodic appraisals of the property and to keep these appraisals as part of your permanent records.

There are numerous university extension courses on the science of greenhouse production, and taking a course is strongly recommended if you are inexperienced in this area. You could also consult your state's Agricultural Development Board or Horticulture Council.

12
AGRICULTURAL FARMING

1. Family Farms

Farming is a lifestyle that takes tremendous dedication and focus. All aspects of a farmer's life are usually centered on the farm. Many farmers grew up on farms. Many of them inherited their family farms and are attempting to run them in a businesslike manner.

The IRS regards farming — of all kinds, whether agricultural, timber, or livestock — to fall under the hobby loss rule. It may seem counterintuitive that farmers would be considered part of the hobby loss rule, because farming has been an essential way of making a living for millennia.

This chapter will focus on small family farms, most of which do not make a profit. Most farmers on small farms have day jobs that provide their principal source of income, and they attend to farm activities in the evenings, on weekends, and in other free time.

To operate a farm in a businesslike manner it is crucial to be familiar, or have a farm manager who is familiar, with numerous issues including soil quality and the nature of your particular crops, and to know about growing, harvesting, gathering, sorting, processing, packing, and shipping.

Uncertainty as to prices, yields, government policies, and foreign markets means that there are certain risks in any farm operation. Some risks can be managed by yield and revenue insurance, futures and options, contracting sales and purchases, crop diversification, or debt-level management. Weather always poses a risk to crops. A drought can have catastrophic results for the farming community. Even a brief period of frost can destroy a good portion of a crop.

Government programs addressing farm risk management have played a helpful role in US farm policy in recent years. More than 200 million acres are now covered by crop insurance, and government insurance subsidies are expected to average more than $2 billion annually during the next few years.

About 10 percent of farms go out of business every year, which is comparable to exit rates for nonfarm small businesses in the US. The probability of exit is higher for recent entrants than for older, more established farms.

Many people enjoy some recreational elements as part of their working farm. It is important that any recreational elements, if present, are insignificant to your overall purpose of operating a working farm. In the following case the taxpayer enjoyed some recreational elements on his farm, but still convinced the US Tax Court that his farm was a business.

Example: *Wise v. Commissioner,* **T.C. Memo 1957-83.**

W. Clark Wise, Cleveland, Ohio, was part owner of an automobile sales agency. When growing up, he helped operate his father's 500-acre farm. Later, he decided to buy a run-down 42-acre farm with tillable ground.

He remodeled the house and rented it. He re-roofed the barn, improved the outbuildings, and repaired fences. He learned that there were problems with the soil, so he began fertilizing it to bring it to its full crop-producing capacity.

He purchased a tractor, a farm truck, a mowing machine, seed, and other farm equipment. He planted wheat, corn, and oats. He also purchased and sold cattle.

Mr. Wise used part of his farm property for occasional pheasant hunting.

Mr. Wise spent a substantial amount of time working on the farm in addition to his work at his automotive business. He planted, cultivated, and harvested crops for sale every year. However, his farm sustained losses for a number of years. He kept accurate but minimal records of farm expenses and income.

The IRS denied his tax deductions, saying that the farm was a hobby. The US Tax Court reversed the decision. The court said that the failure of the farm to show a profit was due largely to its size and the poor condition of its soil, and that Mr. Wise was working diligently to improve that.

The court said, "it is clear that he has conducted the operation with an object to rehabilitate his farm for the purpose of bringing it eventually to the point where income will exceed the expense of doing business."

The court found it significant that, except for occasional hunting, Mr. Wise and his family and friends did not use the farm for recreation. "It might, of course, be argued that petitioner in laboring on the farm derives recreational enjoyment therefrom, but, if so, there would be no inconsistency with its operation as a business for profit for such is not uncommonly the case with respect to many businesses and their proprietors where there is no question but that the operation is a business and not a mere hobby."

The previous example provides the following key points:

1. Rehabilitating a run-down farm and restoring it to a working farm is evidence that you are intent on operating the farm in a businesslike manner.

2. In this case the taxpayer owned a working farm and regularly planted, harvested, and sold crops. He did what he could to improve the quality of the soil, but still did not make a profit. His records were minimal, yet he was able to convince the US Tax Court that he had an honest expectation of eventually making money in this venture.

3. The taxpayer enjoyed occasional hunting on the farm property. However, the court found this recreational element to be insignificant.

The IRS regards gentleman farming to be a hobby. *Gentleman farming* means farming mainly for pleasure rather than profit. An example of this is the case ***Remuzzi v. Commissioner*** (included on the CD). The court felt that Dr. Remuzzi was not interested in operating his farm profitably.

In the following case the taxpayer moved her father onto her farm to give him something to do and claimed that the farm was a business venture. However, the US Tax Court disagreed.

Example: *Takahashi v. Commissioner,* 87 T.C. 126 (1986).

Gloria Takahashi, Hacienda Heights, California, was a science teacher. She also owned a 40-acre grape farm in Fresno, California. The farm was originally owned by her grandfather and had remained in the family. She bought it from her uncle.

She wanted to provide her father with steady employment and old-age security, so she asked him to operate and manage the farm. They had a verbal understanding that they would share costs, that Mrs. Takahashi would receive farm income to the extent of her costs, and that her father would receive any remaining income. They agreed that regardless of the profitability of the farm, her father would receive income sufficient to support himself and his wife.

All farm losses were to be allocated to Mrs. Takahashi. The farm incurred net losses for many years, and Mrs. Takahashi deducted these losses against her salary as a teacher and her husband's salary.

The US Tax Court said that the farm was not used for personal pleasure or recreation, but nonetheless "it seems self-evident" that Mrs. Takahashi did not operate the farm for profit, since under the agreement, any net profit would have gone to her father.

A letter written by Mrs. Takahashi to the IRS was introduced into evidence, and it stated: "My intent is not to make money but to have a tax shelter and mostly help my folks, whose income is solely from this small farm." The court said, "this letter, standing alone, is an admission by petitioner that she engaged in the operation of the farm primarily to provide her parents with a steady income and to obtain tax deductions rather than to make an economic profit."

The previous example provides the following key points:

1. The taxpayer's primary motivation for running the farm was apparently to give her father something to do and a place to live.

2. The absence of a written agreement between the taxpayer and her father concerning his management of the farm was evidence of a lack of businesslike concern for the activity.

3. The terms of the verbal agreement between the taxpayer and her father made it impossible for the taxpayer to ever make a profit, since he was to get all profits after she recouped her costs.

There are many people who invite their parents to come live on their farm to give them something enjoyable to do. In the previous case the taxpayer lost in such a situation. However, in the next case the taxpayer won in a similar set of facts. This case involved a working farm owned by a famous boxing champion.

Example: *Frazier v. Commissioner,* T.C. Memo 1985-61.

Joseph Frazier, a famous professional boxer who lived in Lafayette Hills, Pennsylvania, was raised on a ten-acre farm in South Carolina, where his parents farmed the property. Mr. Frazier decided to buy a 365-acre farm near his childhood farm. Mr. Frazier moved his mother onto the farm, as well as his sister and her family. They lived on the farm rent free.

He hired two full-time managers who were paid salaries, as well as several field hands. Mr. Frazier's mother worked on the property and assisted in most aspects of the farm operations. Mr. Frazier had an oral agreement whereby he would share any farm profits equally with his mother, but that he alone would bear tax liabilities and be responsible for farm losses.

Mr. Frazier visited the farm only a few weeks each year, during which time he mended fences, repaired barns and corrals, fixed up the houses on the property, and worked in the fields.

In the US Tax Court Mr. Frazier testified that he considered this to be a working farm. There was no evidence of the farm being used for recreational or resort purposes.

A bookkeeper professionally maintained financial records, together with detailed payroll records.

Crops consisted of vegetables, corn, wheat, and soybeans. However, the soil was mostly clay, covered by a thin layer of topsoil, which resulted in low yields. The farm managers were unable to market the crops successfully, and the farm realized only $9,000 income in a five-year period.

Before buying the farm, Mr. Frazier did not obtain soil studies or consult with farm experts to determine whether the farm could be operated profitably.

Mr. Frazier decided that due to rising beef prices, it might be profitable to raise cattle in addition to planting crops, so he bought 60 head of cattle. A setback soon occurred when a rare parasite disease took the lives of most of the herd.

He also decided to develop a recreational facility on part of the farm for duck hunters, as public interest in the farm was heightened due to Mr. Frazier's celebrity status. He hoped to make money from fees charged to hunters. To develop the duck preserve it was necessary to flood a portion of the land to attract ducks. However, there was difficulty developing a canal system to secure a sufficient supply of water, and Mr. Frazier abandoned the idea due to excessive costs.

Evidence indicated that the farm appreciated in value from $175,000 to $400,000 in a period of ten years.

The court said that Mr. Frazier conducted the farm in a "relatively" businesslike manner. He made efforts to change methods of operation in order to make a profit by planting different crops, attempting to raise cattle, and attempting to develop a duck preserve. He sought advice from a neighboring farmer who was successful.

The court said that much of the losses were due to events beyond Mr. Frazier's control. The court said that Mr. Frazier and other witnesses were highly credible and forthright in their testimony.

The court said that clearly Mr. Frazier wanted to improve his mother's life by having her live on the farm, and wanted to give her an opportunity to share in farm profits. "Profit motive is not negated simply because a taxpayer derives a sense of satisfaction in providing for relatives, friends, or loved ones. The fact that petitioner's mother and some of his other relatives lived on the farm doesn't establish that the farm was not operated with an intent to make a profit."

The court noted that there were substantial losses over many years, but that under the facts of this case the period of time over which Mr. Frazier incurred losses was not unduly long and did not, in any event, negate his intent to make a profit.

The court said that "if losses, or even repeated losses, were the only criterion by which farming is to be judged a business, then a large proportion of the farmers of the country would be outside the pale."

The court concluded that "the losses more accurately are explained in terms of an inefficient farming operation, and hindsight should not cause us to substitute our judgment for that of a taxpayer who, with his funds, 'gave it a try.'"

The previous example provides the following key points:

1. The taxpayer won even though there was a significant history of losses, and despite the fact that his mother obviously enjoyed living on the farm and helping in its operation.

2. Hiring of professional farm managers helps support your contention that the farm is operated as a business.

3. It is usually important, prior to buying a farm, to obtain soil studies to determine whether anything needs to be done to optimize crop productivity. However, in this case, the court was sympathetic to the taxpayer's "inefficient farming operation."

4. The taxpayer had businesslike records that were maintained by a professional bookkeeper.

5. The court was impressed by the fact that the taxpayer diversified; he tried to raise and sell cattle and he tried to develop the duck preserve as ways of generating income, but due to circumstances beyond his control, these efforts failed.

There are numerous cases, such as the next one, where the taxpayer has failed to show any businesslike concern in operating a farm. The implication in this and other cases like it is that the taxpayer's main motivation is to have a tax shelter.

Example: *Schirmer v. Commissioner,* **89 T.C.** 277 (1987).

Dolphus and Mary Schirmer bought a 554-acre farm in Paraloma, Arkansas. They did not live on the farm, but lived in Tulsa, Oklahoma, where Mr. Schirmer was a mechanical engineer. Mr. Schirmer, who had experience with farming since childhood, visited the farm two or three days a month. Other family members visited the farm four to six times a year.

Mr. Schirmer did not plant crops or lease the farm to others. He had no analysis of how much income could be derived from the farm. He never hired a farm manager.

He had income from the farm one year of about $8,200, for the sale of timber that grew wild on the property. Otherwise, there was no income from the farm, no separate checking account, and little by way of books or records. No crops were ever planted.

Mr. Schirmer did consult with farming officials as to what crops were most suitable for his farm; however, he failed to implement plans they recommended. The farm sustained losses for many years.

The US Tax Court said that this farm was a hobby and not a business. The court pointed out that Mr. Schirmer did nothing to actually run the farm as a farm. Rather, it appeared that the farm was a tax shelter and a place where he and his family could get away for pleasure.

The previous example provides the following key points:

1. Failure to spend much time working on the farm, and failure to plant crops, shows a lack of business concern about the activity.

2. It is important to consult farming authorities about making a profit and about choosing crops that are best suited to the land. Failure to follow their advice, unless there is good reason, indicates an unbusinesslike manner of operating the venture.

A citrus farm can take ten years before the trees reach full production. Nonetheless, the IRS has denied tax deductions for people in the start-up phase because the activity was not conducted in a businesslike manner. In the following case, the amount of time spent on the farm activity was also an important issue. Often people will say they devote a significant amount of time to the venture on a consistent basis, but they might fail to maintain logs or other evidence to back this up.

Example: *Bangs v. Commissioner,* T.C. Memo 2006-83.

Larry Bangs, Valley Center, California, was very successful in real estate investing and in the fiber-glass business. As he approached retirement, he and his wife purchased a 40-acre farm in California. They decided to grow lemons after an agricultural adviser suggested that lemons were fairly hardy and could thrive with little water.

Mr. Bangs planted lemon trees and made some improvements to the property, including building a warehouse, a ripening room, water pumps, and a 6,000-square foot residence.

Mr. Bangs said that he spent 60 to 80 hours a week on the lemon farming activity, but there was no log or other record to corroborate this claim. The US Tax Court said it did not believe

Mr. Bangs' testimony about devoting so much time to the venture.

The only financial records for the farming activity consisted of stacks of receipts. There were no separate bank accounts or records of income and expenses.

In operating the farm, Mr. Bangs harvested lemons too early, so they were not marketable. There was a water retention problem, but he did nothing to overcome it or to correct the quality of the soil.

The court said: "Based on all the circumstances, we find that petitioners have not shown they conducted their lemon farming activity with the primary, predominant, or principal purpose of realizing an economic profit independent of tax savings."

The previous example provides the following key points:

1. Exaggerated claims of the amount of time spent in the venture will be viewed with suspicion. As mentioned in Chapter 4, you should document the amount of time spent on the activity with logs, diaries, calendars, or other records. In this case the taxpayer claimed he worked 60 to 80 hours a week on his citrus farm, but the court said this was not believable given his other activities. There was also no documentary evidence, such as a log, to support the taxpayer's claim.

2. If there are problems with the venture (such as the soil problem in this example), measures should be taken to resolve them. It is important to get proper agricultural advice on the timing of harvesting; otherwise, the implication is that the activity is not run in a businesslike manner.

2. Chapter Summary

The IRS takes the position that many wealthy individuals invest in farms solely to obtain tax losses that they utilize to offset their taxable income, and that for them a farm is simply an enjoyable place to get away.

In order to withstand IRS scrutiny, particularly if the farm produces no profits, it is important to operate the farm much like any other business, with adequate books and records.

It is important to conduct some type of market research before starting the farm, to enable you to forecast, the best you can, expenses and revenue. A written business plan is helpful evidence to support your intention to be engaged in a business, rather than a hobby (see Chapter 3).

It is always important to get professional advice on how to operate the farm profitably, unless you yourself are an expert in farming. If you have no prior experience in farming and if you do not consult professionals about the economics involved, the IRS will take the view that the activity is a hobby.

If you have lost crops due to drought, poor soil, or other circumstances, you should keep documentary evidence of what happened, such as a report prepared by an agricultural adviser or farm manager, or information from news reports. If there are losses due to unexpected adverse market conditions, you should also document these facts to help explain why there were losses.

If you are not making profits, it is always a good idea to make changes to your operation to help move it towards being profitable. That can mean diversifying the farm, cutting down on costs, or other measures that have been discussed in this book.

For information on livestock farming, see the CD-ROM included with this book.

13
DOG BREEDING

According to the American Pet Product Manufacturers Association, 63 percent of all US households own a pet. Because there is such a great demand for dogs — and since they do not usually live much more than 15 years or so — there is a continual buying, selling, and breeding of these animals.

Many individuals decide to breed dogs and sell the litters, not as a hobby, but as a business. These are usually small ventures conducted in a person's home. Other larger-scale breeders build kennels on their property or open pet shops in order to engage in the retail end of the business.

Dog breeding, whether as a hobby or a business, is a labor-intensive activity. If it is a business, there are certain requirements that do not apply to a hobby activity. For example, as a business, you would need to enter dogs into dog shows, and obtain breeding permits and a kennel license, as well as actively seek buyers for your puppies.

This chapter will focus on dog breeding because there are many cases on the subject, but the rules apply just as well to cat breeding. Generally speaking, it is more difficult to make a profit selling cats than dogs. Many people wish to adopt cats at animal shelters, which is usually a free (or very inexpensive) process. The cost of pedigreed cats of various popular breeds is fairly low, so it can be difficult to make a profit breeding them.

Dog breeders usually make money if they focus on higher-priced pedigreed animals that have significant popularity. In order to sell your dogs for a decent price you have to show them at dog shows. This is an important way of gaining recognition; dogs that are successful in shows attract customers interested in obtaining stud services or purchasing puppies.

The IRS targets dog breeding because people rarely make money on a litter. Even if you reduce costs by learning to do some things yourself, such as giving inoculations, it is hard to make a profit. If you focus on breeding top quality show dogs and sell show prospects or show-quality older dogs, you are likely to garner higher prices. A lot depends on demonstrating that your dogs win in the show ring on a consistent basis.

Before starting, you should confirm that there is a demand for the breed you intend to produce. Calculate medical, food, and breeding expenses to determine if you can make a profit. Of course, you should also determine if you are able to put in the significant amount of time the venture will take out of your daily routine.

Marketing your litter involves advertising in newspapers, trade magazines, or online. You have the ethical duty to screen potential owners to ensure your animals are sold to caring, responsible individuals.

1. Successful Dog-Breeding Cases

Many dog breeders have been successful in the US Tax Court, even though they have had a history of losses. The following is a model case in which the taxpayer did everything right and convinced the US Tax Court to rule in his favor.

Example: *Keanini v. Commissioner,* 94 T.C. 41 (1990).

Samuel Keanini, Honolulu, Hawaii, and his wife, converted their love of poodles into a breeding business called "Pua's Poodles." They attended a three-month seminar on how to manage a new business. They built a kennel at their home and started breeding poodles, as well as grooming dogs. They acquired quality breeding stock and entered into written co-ownership agreements with other dog owners. Under these agreements they shared the costs of purchasing and breeding various dogs, and shared in the litters.

They hired professional dog handlers to show their poodles at dog shows, kept records of their breeding stock, and won some national championship titles that substantially increased the value of their breeding stock.

They also provided dog-grooming services and served as an approved animal quarantine station. (Animals brought to Hawaii must be placed in a kennel at an approved quarantine station for 120 days.) They used written contracts for the dogs they held in quarantine. At times they hired part-time dog groomers. They advertised the breeding operation in the Yellow Pages, local newspapers, and national dog magazines.

Mr. Keanini worked full time with the Honolulu Police Department and part time in the breeding operation; his wife devoted full-time hours to the dog activity.

They had a separate checking account for the activity, and prepared monthly and quarterly income and expense statements for the venture. They kept a daily log of mileage and expenses in using their car in the activity.

They implemented cost-saving practices such as purchasing supplies for the grooming operation from wholesalers. The co-ownership agreements enabled them to reduce the cost of acquiring breeding stock.

They sustained losses for a period of five years, but these losses decreased steadily each year until in the sixth year they realized a small profit of $1,201.

The IRS claimed that Mr. and Mrs. Keanini were engaged in a hobby. They took their case to the US Tax Court, which ruled in their favor. This case serves as a model of how to properly operate a dog-breeding venture.

The previous example provides the following key points:

1. Note that the taxpayers operated their breeding activity out of their home. They conducted the activity in a very business-like manner and they were resourceful.

They obtained all permits and licenses associated with the breeding venture and complied with animal health inspection requirements. They made additional money by boarding dogs that were under quarantine. They found ways of reducing costs, used written agreements, and advertised.

2. Often breeding and grooming are carried on in a single integrated business because the same customer that purchases a puppy also needs grooming services and dog care products.

3. The taxpayers were not familiar with how to run a small business, so they took a course on the subject before starting their breeding venture. It is important to do what you can to confer with successful breeders in the industry to get tips on how you might make money in dog breeding, or to otherwise educate yourself on the economics of the field.

4. It is important to hire professional dog handlers to show your best dogs at competitions. The goodwill derived from winning prizes enhances your reputation and serves to bolster the prices of your animals.

5. It is smart to share costs by entering into co-ownership agreements with other dog owners. Under these agreements you share the costs of purchasing and breeding various dogs, and share in the litters.

6. Some breeders build large kennels and make extra money by boarding dogs and cats or, as in this case, operating as a quarantine station under state law.

If you are new to dog breeding, it is important to educate yourself before you start your venture. The court was impressed by the taxpayers' efforts in the case *Larson v. Commissioner* (included on the CD) to educate themselves about how to make a profit in dog breeding.

The following taxpayer changed his methods of operation in order to make his business profitable.

Example: *Sasso v. Commissioner,* **T.C. Memo 1961-216.**

Leonard Sasso, Pittsburgh, Pennsylvania, was in the coal business. For many years his passion was bird hunting, for which he used hunting dogs. At one point he decided to start raising bird dogs for profit. He discussed the venture with different trainers whom he had met. He was advised that he could make a profit if he could get good dogs.

He purchased a male and a female dog of proven ability. He proceeded to breed them, and in about three years had 55 to 60 dogs.

Mr. Sasso hired an experienced trainer, but the trainer did not produce any well-trained dogs. About a dozen of the dogs died in an outbreak of distemper and hepatitis.

He then moved all the remaining dogs to a farm he owned and built a kennel following instructions obtained from the head veterinarian at Penn State University. He maintained an employee at the farm to feed and exercise the dogs.

He visited the dogs several times a week and used some of them in hunting. The dogs he considered good prospects were sent to trainers who were paid a monthly fee for each dog. Mr. Sasso only registered the dogs he thought were good enough to enter trials. In the fall he hunted with some of the dogs and also helped train some of the younger ones.

During a ten-year period he incurred losses, which he deducted from his principal business income. The expenses included wages, food, medicine, kennel improvements, fees for trainers, travel expenses, and membership and subscription fees.

The US Tax Court ruled that Mr. Sasso was engaged in the dog-breeding business. The court said that Mr. Sasso was very familiar with bird dogs, having utilized them for hunting for more than 40 years. Mr. Sasso conferred with numerous trainers concerning the chances of making a profit from such a venture and was advised that this was definitely feasible. He purchased breeding stock of proven quality, and hired an experienced trainer. He changed methods of operation after several dogs died, and constructed kennels following the instructions of an experienced veterinarian. The court said "the foregoing facts clearly demonstrate that the kennel was established and operated as a business."

The previous example provides the following key points:

1. It is important to consult with experts as to the feasibility of making money in dog breeding prior to embarking on the venture.

2. It is important to focus on bloodlines of proven quality.

3. It is a good idea to change methods of operation if you have a history of losses, in order to improve the chances of making a profit.

4. In this case, the court regarded the taxpayer's construction of kennels for boarding his animals as evidence of his businesslike purpose in the endeavor.

In a security-conscious era, there are people who breed and sell security dogs, which are not pets, but dangerous and difficult animals.

Example: *Sampson v. Commissioner,* **T.C. Memo 1982-276.**

Sherman Sampson, Mt. Hope, Kansas, worked in undercover drug enforcement, and was involved in several business ventures.

He had trained dogs for his personal use and decided to raise guard dogs as a sideline business; however, he did not conduct research or undergo training for such an activity. He focused on breeding and raising wolfdogs, a crossbreed of wolves and German shepherds, which are said to be excellent guard dogs. He soon had about 18 wolfdogs and spent an hour per day on the activity. He employed a trainer for several months. He sold several of the dogs.

He built a "dog tight" chain link fence on his property, but the dogs regularly tore through it and attacked and killed cattle on neighboring farms. Some neighbors shot and killed some of the trespassing dogs. Mr. Sampson had to reimburse neighbors for the loss of cattle.

He decided the dog-breeding venture was not economically sustainable and abandoned it after two years.

He kept records indicating his purchase of breeding stock and canceled checks, but maintained no other records.

The US Tax Court said that he conducted the activity in a generally businesslike manner, particularly with regard to his decision to terminate the activity. Also, the court said that his losses were during the start-up phase and this was understandable for a new venture. "Thus we have an abbreviated string of losses, which all occurred at the inception of the activity." Since Mr. Sampson was quick to withdraw from the activity in the face of adverse economic signals, the court said that he carried on the security-dog activity for profit and was entitled to the tax deductions claimed.

The court also said that the breeding of wolf-dogs did not seem to have features of personal pleasure or recreation because the dogs were unorthodox and uncongenial.

The previous example provides the following key points:

1. The taxpayer in this example was only in the start-up phase and decided to abandon the venture after two years because he did not see how he could make a profit. Usually people will wait beyond the start-up phase before deciding that it is time to terminate an unprofitable venture. In any event, terminating an unprofitable venture is evidence of an overall business purpose.

2. Breeding of guard dogs will usually be regarded as a business venture because it is hard to characterize raising these dogs as pleasurable or recreational in nature, because they are not pets.

3. Breeding of guard dogs requires specialized training in order to ready these animals for their intended purpose. It is imperative that proper boundaries around the kennel be maintained to prevent the dogs from endangering other animals in the vicinity and to protect yourself from liability.

2. Unsuccessful Dog-Breeding Cases

The next case is about a taxpayer who lost his case because of the impression given that his love of outdoor activities was his primary motivation in operating a dog-breeding activity.

Example: *Benz v. Commissioner,* 63 T.C. 375 (1974).

Francis Benz, Andover, Massachusetts, owned a metallurgical business. He enjoyed bird hunting and decided to purchase a few pointers with the aim of developing champion studs. He used a DBA ("doing business as" name) but did not register the name with the American Kennel Club, so he did not have a registered kennel. He did, however, register several of his dogs individually. He entered some of his dogs in field trials and shows, and earned some points. He boarded most of the dogs with a trainer.

Over the years he sold only a few dogs, and incurred sizable losses that he deducted against his substantial income.

The US Tax Court said that the activity had overwhelming elements of a hobby rather than a business. The court said that Mr. Benz had an interest in outdoor activities from an early age, and that he derived great pleasure from visiting his dogs and participating in trial shows.

The court said that Mr. Benz did not conduct the activity in a businesslike manner. He failed to register his kennel with the American Kennel Club. He failed to conduct more than a cursory investigation of the potential of making a profit in this field. Also, the court said that Mr. Benz had substantial outside income that afforded him the means of engaging in the dog activity despite its history of losses.

The previous example provides the following key points:

1. The taxpayer did not conduct even a preliminary investigation of the economics of dog breeding before starting out.

2. It is important to make sure that your kennel name or DBA name is registered with the American Kennel Club, otherwise this gives the impression that you are not operating in a businesslike manner.

3. In this example there were strong elements of personal pleasure and recreation. This led to the conclusion that the dog-breeding venture was a hobby, not a business.

If you have an obvious lack of concern for the profitability of your dog-breeding venture, the court will rule against you. This is what happened in the case **Ballich v. Commissioner**, which is included on the CD.

In the following case, the taxpayer failed to convince the US Tax Court that he was engaged in dog breeding as a business, despite lots of businesslike evidence. The court got the impression that the taxpayer's main motivation was personal pleasure and recreation.

Example: *Smith v. Commissioner,* T.C. Memo 1997-503.

Dr. David Smith, Los Gatos, California, was a surgeon. He and his wife raised standard poodles as a hobby, and built a kennel at their home to care for a growing number of dogs.

They consulted with dog breeders and researched the subject of dog breeding. Dr. Smith attended veterinarian seminars for dog breeders.

They decided to convert their hobby interest into a business. They focused on breeding Portuguese water dogs (a rare breed) with hopes of commanding high prices. They operated under the name "Dacher Kennel" and spent thousands of dollars advertising in national dog-breeding magazines. They hired professional dog handlers, and had about 30 dogs.

They roughly estimated that they could earn $30,000 to $50,000 in gross receipts per year. However, they did not prepare formal cost projections and did not consult with economic advisers. They had a separate checking account for the venture, and kept a book of receipts and expenses.

The Smiths achieved their goal of breeding high-quality dogs. One dog won 21 best-of-breed competitions. However, they incurred losses of $218,000 during the three-year period considered.

They claimed the losses were due primarily to the high cost of dog boarding and handling.

The US Tax Court said that while they kept accurate books and records, the business records were inadequate. "The lack of detailed records as to which dogs were or were not profitable is an indication that the dog-breeding activity was not carried on for profit."

The court said that the Smiths advertised in national magazines, but did not advertise in any local outlets, which could reach customers who were close enough to come look at the dogs.

While they did meet with breeders, attend seminars, and study dog breeding, they did not seek advice on the economic aspects of the venture.

The court said that Dr. Smith testified that the value of his dogs had increased as a result of awards achieved, but he offered no formal appraisal into evidence.

Dr. Smith argued that the losses were typical for the start-up phase of any profit-making activity. However, the court said that about 90 percent of the expenses were for dog boarding and handling, with these costs likely to grow with the size of their dog stock, and yet there was no effort being made to reduce these costs.

The court concluded that Dr. and Mrs. Smith derived substantial personal pleasure from the time they spent with their dogs and that their activity was not carried on for profit.

The previous example provides the following key points:

1. If your dogs win championship titles or other awards, this helps establish your reputation and helps increase the value of your animals. A formal appraisal is important to prove that your best dogs have increased in value as a result of your care. Valuable dogs should be insured.

2. It is also important to seek advice from experts on how to improve operations so as to make a profit. It is important to keep looking at ways you could reduce costs and move closer to making a profit. This may mean building your own kennels, thus cutting down on boarding costs.

3. It is important to advertise in local media, instead of or in addition to national magazines, on the logic that local ads will be seen by customers close enough to come look at the dogs.

4. It is important to prepare some sort of budget or break-even analysis to show the profit potential of the activity. This should be done prior to starting the venture.

5. In this example, the court faulted the tax-payer for not keeping specific records on which dogs were doing well in the shows. It is important to keep individual records that track the progress of each of your show dogs.

3. Pet Stores

Some people decide to open up full-fledged pet stores. In addition to selling pets, they often have pet grooming services. The IRS at times contends that certain pet stores are nothing more than the owner's hobby, as seen in the following case.

Example: *Ranciato v. Commissioner,* T.C. Memo 1996-67.

Anthony Ranciato, New Haven, Connecticut, was an electrician and real estate agent. He also owned a pet store that sold fish, birds, and other animals and supplies. He worked evenings and weekends in the store.

His business records consisted of receipts, canceled checks, ledgers, and some (but not all) invoices. He had no inventory records, and the records he had were very disorganized. Mr. Ranciato's mother, who did most of the work in the store, operated the store for 26 years without pay.

His store incurred 20 years of losses. He made no effort to change methods of operation in order to increase profitability. He conducted almost no advertising for the store.

The US Tax Court said that Mr. Ranciato's "inattentive business practices" and "haphazard and incomplete" records were compounded by his failure to advertise to any significant extent. He kept no record of the store's inventory, even though it was supposed to be a retail establishment. The court said that he never investigated what might affect his store's profitability.

The court said that since his mother received no salary for her work, it must have been a pleasurable pastime for her, and one "could only assume that she reaped personal pleasure from her full-time efforts."

Mr. Ranciato testified that his store made profits in its early years, but was unable to provide evidence to back up his claim. The court said that his testimony was inconsistent and vague.

The court noted that Mr. Ranciato did not change methods of operation or seek a ways to reduce the number of animals that got sick. The court faulted him for not obtaining expert advice to help improve the store's performance.

The court said that his principal source of income enabled Mr. Ranciato to finance the store, and the store losses allowed him to significantly reduce his income taxes. "If petitioner were truly profit motivated, we expect that the store's recurring losses would have persuaded him to change his business practices. Instead, petitioner continued to spend more money and incur additional losses ... We infer that he kept the store open because he and his mother received benefits from operating it independent of its ability to earn a profit."

The previous example provides the following key points:

1. A pet store must be operated in a business-like manner, or else the implication is, as in this case, that the venture is a hobby.

2. The taxpayer had inadequate records. He did not have an inventory, and the records he did have were disorganized, which led the court to conclude that he did not operate in a businesslike manner.

3. The impression was that the taxpayer was motivated to have a shop that his mother could occupy her time with. The evidence indicated that his mother took great pleasure in working at the shop, for no pay.

4. With a pet shop, as with any other venture, it is important to advertise or otherwise promote your business, and to change methods of operation (if appropriate) to help improve your chances of making a profit.

4. Chapter Summary

From the IRS's standpoint, dog breeding is high on the list of hobbies; if you are not making a profit, you will have the burden of proof to convince the revenue agent that you are operating a business and not a hobby.

It is important to research your particular breed before starting the venture and to calculate the costs, the risks, and the potential revenue involved. Remember to stay on top of marketing trends and to learn as much as you can about making money with your particular breed.

If you want to operate a breeding kennel in your home, be sure your property is zoned for the number of dogs on your premises and that you have the proper permits to operate. Sometimes it is necessary to apply for a zoning variance, a commercial (retail) license, and dog licenses. Some states require a kennel license in order to breed above a certain number of dogs. Failure to comply with these requirements is not only unbusiness-like, but can also get you into trouble with licensing authorities.

Whether you are operating from home or a retail storefront, it is important to advertise, particularly in local newspapers, and to maintain complete books and records. If your current methods of operation are not working, make changes in order to improve your chances of making a profit.

Commercial fishing is a very big industry through-out the world. Often fishing is seasonal, and weather is an obstacle that can prevent boats from getting to the fish. There are also a host of national and international fishing regulations that impose administrative burdens on people who go into fishing as a business.

It is necessary to have at least one experienced fisher on your team, to develop your own skills in the particular area of fishing you are involved in, and to have proper fishing equipment.

The IRS tends to scrutinize tax returns where people claim they operate a part-time fishing venture, since fishing is a quintessential American hobby. Thus, in situations where people are really interested in fishing as a business rather than a hobby, it is important to operate in a businesslike manner.

1. Unsuccessful Commercial Fishing Case

Devoting enough time to your fishing venture to prove that you are operating in a businesslike manner is important, as you will see in the following case.

Example: *Edwards v. Commissioner,* T.C. Memo 1990-70.

Everette Edwards, Jr., Apex, North Carolina, was part owner of a lumber supply company. He was an avid fisherman and boater. Initially he used his boat for recreational fishing purposes. He decided to form a commercial fishing venture, which he called "Evan Commercial Fishing," after a friend suggested he could sell his excess fish to a local fish market.

He had never operated a commercial fishing venture before and knew little about its business aspects. He consulted with several commercial fishermen about income potential and obtained a commercial fishing license.

Mr. Edwards engaged in the activity only on weekends. He did not figure out how he could make a profit with the limited time he put into it. He did not calculate operating costs or the break-even point.

He installed sophisticated fishing equipment on his boat. He hired one or two crew members, whose payment was contingent on the proceeds from the sales of fish. He obtained liability insurance for his crew. He caught a lot of fish on the weekends, and sold what he could, but never made a profit.

He also entered some fishing tournaments, hoping to win large amounts of prize money; he did win a third place prize of $8,000 one year. All told, he incurred a loss of approximately $113,000 during an eight-year period, which included boat repair costs.

The US Tax Court said he sold fish in a haphazard, casual manner rather than systematically. The court said that instead of devoting his time entirely to commercial fishing, Mr. Edwards appeared more interested in entering fishing tournaments.

He fished on average 30 times per year, on the weekends only, and in one year he fished on only 4 occasions. Mr. Edwards said this was because his boat had engine problems requiring substantial repairs, but the court said that it was difficult to believe that the majority of the year was used to repair the engine.

The court said that prior to entering the venture, Mr. Edwards made no attempt to analyze the costs, risks, and returns of running the operation or even to calculate a break-even point.

The court faulted him for not preparing for the venture with an extensive study of accepted business practices in his field. For the first three years he did not realize that the normal method of commercial fishing was bottom-fishing. "If petitioner had done any research prior to starting his operation, he would have already followed these practices."

The court said that Mr. Edwards has always enjoyed fishing and that he derived a great deal of pleasure from the activity. He made quite a few friends from his fishing activity and these friends worked as his crew for little or no pay. The court said that his primary motive was to engage in a recreational activity rather than a business.

The previous example provides the following key points:

1. It is important to investigate the profit potential of a commercial fishing venture before starting it. In order to make a profit, you will need to devote substantial time to the venture.

2. Failure to observe accepted methods of commercial fishing suggest that you are not concerned with operating in a business-like manner.

3. Utilizing friends as a fishing crew, with little or no pay, tends to suggest a hobby venture.

4. Entering fishing tournaments is a way to supplement income you derive from commercial fishing. However, in this case, the entering of tournaments was perceived as a strictly recreational element. It is important to make a cost analysis to see how much it will cost to enter tournaments and what prize money is available.

2. Successful Commercial Fishing Case

In the following case, the taxpayer was successful at winning his case because he was able to prove that he was engaged in the fishing venture for profit.

Example: *Lamb v. Commissioner,* T.C. Memo 1996-166.

Derril Lamb, Jr., Bowdoinham, Maine, had a successful lumber and building supply business, and was passionate about fishing. He learned how to harpoon tuna from experienced fishermen. He acquired significant expertise in his own right. He successfully harpooned tuna ranging from 175 pounds to 980 pounds.

Due to the significant rise in tuna prices, he decided to purchase a boat and rigged it as a commercial fishing boat. He obtained a Federal Fisheries permit to harpoon Atlantic bluefin tuna. In the first season (June 15 to September 30) he fished on 15 days and was accompanied by a fishing mate who was to receive one-third of any fish caught. He caught one tuna weighing 294 pounds and sold it for $1,250. The next season he did not catch any tuna.

Mr. Lamb had a separate bank account for his fishing activity. He maintained a log recording the weather and tide conditions on fishing days, as well as the loran coordinates of each tuna he spotted so that he could return to that location in the future.

He took depreciation deductions on the boat and incurred other expenses that resulted in losses of about $81,000.

The IRS claimed he did not spend enough time at the venture — 15 fishing trips in his first season and 12 in his second season. However, in the US Tax Court Mr. Lamb testified that there were usually only 15 to 20 days per season when the weather made it worthwhile to go out to sea.

Mr. Lamb also said that his eyesight, which is vital to success in fishing, deteriorated due to diabetic retinopathy, and that this explained why he caught only one fish in two years.

The court said that Mr. Lamb never used the boat for recreational purposes, that tuna was in great demand, and that Mr. Lamb had become an expert in catching tuna. The court said that Mr. Lamb "was a fisherman whose purpose was to earn money from the sale of tuna," and that his activity was engaged in for profit.

The previous example provides the following key points:

1. Learning advanced skills, such as how to harpoon large fish, is evidence that you are qualified to engage in a commercial fishing venture.

2. In this case the taxpayer decided to focus on tuna because of favorable market conditions, which suggested a businesslike motive. He also obtained a federal permit authorizing him to engage in this activity.

3. Maintaining a separate checking account for a fishing venture is evidence of a businesslike motive.

4. It is important to be able to explain why setbacks happened in a particular fishing season. In this case, it was due to a deteriorating eye condition on the part of the taxpayer. Of course, if such a condition does not improve, the taxpayer should abandon the venture as a business.

3. Chapter Summary

As with other activities covered by the hobby loss rule, fishing as a business presents unique challenges. The key is to operate in a businesslike manner if you are claiming to be fishing as a part-time business venture.

It is important to determine how you can make money converting your fishing hobby into a business. If there is a realistic plan, then you have a businesslike reason to proceed. It is always important, in the business of fishing, to observe accepted methods of commercial fishing to show that you are operating in a businesslike manner. As with other hobby loss areas, it is important to devote enough time and effort to the activity, and to hire qualified personnel, as needed, to assist in the operations.

To read about animal businesses such as horse breeding and racing, and dog breeding, please see the CD-ROM included with this book.

PART IV
AUTOMOBILE, AIRCRAFT, AND BOAT BUSINESSES

15
CLASSIC CAR RESTORATION

Many people take great pride in acquiring and fixing up vintage cars. There is a significant market out there for people who want to sell vintage cars; people who love vintage cars need to buy them from someone, either a dealer or a private party. Thus, it is not surprising that many people get involved in the business of buying, refurbishing, and selling classic cars.

Classic cars nowadays means any car as recent as the 1970s (the "gas guzzlers"), and the older the car, the more *classic* it may be considered. Restoration of classic cars can be an expensive and time-consuming process. The most elaborate restoration recreates the original car in every detail, including operational ability. Prices can be high for those in mint condition; however, the costs of refurbishment can eclipse the resale value even when a car is restored to mint condition, so it is difficult to make a profit unless you are mindful of restoration costs.

The IRS regards automobile restoration as an activity with all the trappings of a hobby, so if you don't operate in a businesslike manner, and if you don't make a profit over a period of time, the IRS may deny your tax write-offs for the venture.

Restoring classic cars involves a considerable amount of time and effort. You must first learn about the market conditions — which classic cars are popular, how much they are selling for, and how you see yourself making money in the activity.

You will need to figure out how much to budget to buy the cars, and to hire specialized mechanics and body workers. If you are experienced as a mechanic, you can help reduce costs by conducting some of the mechanical restoration yourself. The IRS is always impressed with efforts made to reduce operating costs.

Marketing is what distinguishes a hobby from a business in this field. It is crucial to market your vintage cars once you have finished restoring them. Nowadays, marketing is easier than ever because of the Internet; however, some diligence in seeking buyers is necessary if you are operating a business rather than a hobby. A hobbyist is more likely to work on the cars endlessly, rather than bring projects to a close to sell the cars.

You can put ads in trade publications, you can use word-of-mouth advertising on classic car club websites and at car shows, you can have your own website, or you can send mailings to a list of potential customers.

Nowadays there are several big classic car dealerships in different states. You can sell directly to these dealers at a wholesale price. There are classic car auctions as well, but you should always put in a reserve or minimum bid so as to avoid a financial blunder.

1. Restoration

The IRS will usually be concerned if your restoration expenses rise significantly, which can easily happen given the high costs involved. For some restorations, the costs could well exceed what you are able to sell the car for, which would suggest to the IRS that you are not operating in a businesslike manner. Thus, it is important to prepare some sort of economic analysis or budget to help you figure out an approximate break-even point. If you are mindful of restoration costs, and shop for deals, you can end up selling your cars at a considerably higher price than you paid for them, even after deducting your refurbishment costs.

If you engage in classic car refurbishing as a business, rather than a hobby, you should take all the necessary steps to ensure you are operating the activity in a businesslike manner.

In the following case, the court felt that the taxpayer was engaged in his business for personal pleasure.

Example: *Peterson v. Commissioner,* T.C. Memo 1987-508.

James Peterson, Mill Valley, California, was an insurance salesman and his wife worked as a nursing

supervisor. He'd had an interest in cars all his life. He decided to purchase and restore cars commonly referred to as "gas guzzlers" and "muscle cars."

He was very knowledgeable about older vehicles, although he had no training as a mechanic. He joined a vintage car club and became involved with a group of people who specialized in selling special-interest vehicles.

He subscribed to magazines on special interest cars and used these resources to help decide on pricing for his vehicles. He advertised in these magazines, as well as in his local newspaper. He attended classic car auctions and kept abreast of the market for vintage vehicles.

He searched around and found a skilled mechanic that he hired on a contract basis. For body restoration, he used a company 100 miles away because it offered him a competitive price for the work.

During a five-year period he sold two cars for a profit, and one at a loss. Thereafter, he simply held onto three classic vehicles that he claimed would appreciate in value — including an Austin-Healey, which had been his personal automobile.

In the US Tax Court, Mr. Peterson said he wanted to build his inventory so that he could retire from the insurance business, hire employees, and open a showroom for vintage cars.

The court said that Mr. Peterson's evidence consisted almost entirely of self-serving and uncorroborated statements that he intended to restore the cars and sell them at a profit. The court said that Mr. Peterson did not maintain adequate books and records and that he did not have a separate bank account for the venture.

The court noted that Mr. Peterson did sell one of his cars, but that "the occasional sale of an item does not constitute an ongoing business."

The court dismissed Mr. Peterson's argument that he expected his vehicles to appreciate in value and that he wanted to eventually open a showroom. "The mere fact that petitioner owned several vehicles which might or might not appreciate in value over time does not sustain petitioner's contention that he engaged in the activity for profit. He enjoyed old automobiles, he took pleasure in acquiring, holding, and selling them, but he did not do it with the bona fide objective of a profit."

The previous example provides the following key points:

1. The taxpayer claimed that he wanted to develop an inventory of restored cars, retire from his insurance job, and open a classic car dealership. However, the court did not believe his testimony on this point and he had no documentary evidence to support this goal. The court got the impression that the taxpayer's principal motivation was personal pleasure and recreation.

2. The personal testimony of a taxpayer on any issue is inherently self-serving. It is always important to have corroborating evidence of important issues. For instance, if you claim a restored car has significantly appreciated in value, you should have a written appraisal to support this claim.

3. In a restoration venture, it is important to be a member of vintage car organizations and to spend time reading trade journals. It is important to have a business plan, a budget, a separate checking account, and other evidence that you are operating in a businesslike manner.

The taxpayer in the case *Smith v. Commissioner* (included on the CD) said his car refurbishing venture was a hobby, which helped him lose his case.

If your business records are inadequate, or if you keep them in a haphazard manner, this will give the impression that you are engaged in a hobby rather than a business, as in the following case.

Example: *Crawford v. Commissioner,* **T.C. Memo 1993-192.**

Dr. Lynn Crawford, Dallas, Texas, decided to start a car and truck restoration activity in addition to his medical practice. He felt that restoring older cars could be lucrative.

He grew up working on cars and learned how to do metal work and welding. He also had experience working on electronic ignitions.

On weekends, he worked on his own cars as well as those owned by others. At times he employed workers to assist in the restoration activity. He kept the cars at his parents' home, a five-hour drive away.

He did not make a profit from the activity in any of the years in issue. The only records he kept consisted of spiral notebooks with various entries. He did not keep a record of the cars purchased to restore and he did not have the titles put in his name.

In the US Tax Court, Dr. Crawford testified that he kept an inventory of parts he used, but not of the cars being restored. However, he failed to produce even the parts inventory. He also failed to substantiate the deductions he claimed in connection with the activity. Dr. Crawford claimed that he made a profit one year, but did not have records to prove this.

The court said that Dr. Crawford failed to conduct the activity in a businesslike manner and denied his deductions. The court also said that he kept the cars at his parents' home, which required him to drive five hours each way. Locating the restoration activity so far away from his medical practice made little business sense, and the court said that the location chosen was for his personal convenience in visiting his parents, not for the profitability of the activity.

The court added that Dr. Crawford never investigated the feasibility of making a profit in this activity and never prepared a budget.

The previous example provides the following key points:

1. It is important to maintain records of cars that you purchase for restoration, including their acquisition costs and an itemized list of refurbishment costs. Also, it is important that the vehicle titles be properly held in your name or that of your business entity.

2. If you are working on cars yourself, it is important to keep them at a location convenient to you. In this case, the taxpayer kept the cars at his parents' house, which was a five-hour drive away. The court said that this made no business sense, particularly given the taxpayer's busy medical practice.

3. It is important to investigate the feasibility of making a profit in this type of activity before starting it, and to prepare some type of budget to help you see what costs to anticipate.

1.1 Depreciation of restoration costs

Expenses of restoring or improving automobiles are usually capitalized rather than qualified as current deductions. That means the costs are treated as depreciation deductions rather than deducted in the year in which they are incurred. A capital expense differs from a deductible expense because the anticipated benefit of the expense extends beyond the tax year.

Usually capital expenditures materially enhance the value, or substantially extend the useful life of the property in question.

Some items of restoration might be considered ordinary repairs, which are deductible in the year incurred. Ordinary repairs are considered to be repairs that do not materially add to the value of the car or appreciably prolong its life, but keep it in an efficient operating condition.

An interesting case is **Harrah's Club v. United States**, which is included on the CD. This case involved the question of whether the Harrah's Club of Reno could take depreciation deductions for the costs of refurbishing classic cars put on display in its National Automobile Museum (The Harrah Collection).

1.2 Restoration of vintage cars for rent

People in many cities are in the business of renting vintage cars for weddings, parties, and other festive occasions. Renting a refurbished classic car to customers is an alternative to selling it outright. However, as seen in the following case, it can be difficult to promote a vintage car's rental activity, much less make a profit.

Example: *Lockwood v. Commissioner,* T.C. Memo 1989-519.

Frank Lockwood, Barrington, Illinois, became interested in restoring an antique Rolls Royce. For this purpose, he bought a 1938 Phantom III that had been utilized in the television series *The Beverly Hillbillies*.

He paid $25,000 for the car. His plan was to rent the car as a limousine once it was refurbished. A Rolls Royce mechanic quoted an estimate of $15,000 for restoration of the engine and for painting at a body shop. The repairs took two years. Extensive problems were discovered while the car was in the shop, and Mr. Lockwood ended up paying $120,000 for the restoration. He also installed a console with a television, stereo, and bar, at an additional $13,000.

Mr. Lockwood's attorney drafted an operating agreement with a car rental agency in Chicago. The agency agreed to maintain the car, provide drivers, take care of all advertising, and split rental receipts with Mr. Lockwood 50/50.

In the initial year of operation, there was only one rental customer, who paid $500. Then, the rental agency decided not to renew its operating agreement with Mr. Lockwood. Following the collapse of the rental agreement, Mr. Lockwood took the car home and parked it in his garage.

He contacted a number of individuals to try and arrange rentals, including a friend who managed a Hilton Hotel. He spoke to acquaintances about the availability of the car for rent and put up a small sign at the local supermarket. He managed to rent the car seven times. Mr. Lockwood served as chauffeur. He never advertised in newspapers or in the Yellow Pages. He did not have a separate checking account or phone line for his rental activity.

He attempted to sell the car for $150,000 to $175,000, but at the time of his trial still owned it.

The US Tax Court held that his antique car rental venture was not engaged in for profit. Mr. Lockwood did not prepare for the activity by studying accepted business practices or consulting an expert. He investigated the costs of acquiring and restoring the vintage Rolls Royce, but there was little evidence that he investigated the rental market for antique cars.

The court said that there was very little market for such car rentals, evidenced by the fact that Mr. Lockwood was unable to secure a new rental agreement after the initial one collapsed.

"At a minimum, petitioner's failure to obtain another rental agreement demonstrates that he failed to adequately investigate the demand for antique automobile rentals in Chicago, Illinois."

The court also noted that Mr. Lockwood had no experience in this field and did little to consult with experienced individuals about the business. Also, the court said that Mr. Lockwood did not spend a significant amount of time trying to arrange rentals.

The court noted that the unexpectedly high costs of restoring the car were not attributable to "unforeseen circumstances," but "these costs are directly attributable to petitioner's failure to evaluate the condition of the Rolls Royce and to concern himself with the relationship between costs and the potential income that might be generated. This conduct indicates that petitioner did not engage in this activity in a businesslike manner."

The court noted that Mr. Lockwood had significant income from an investment in a shopping mall and that the losses from the activity generated substantial tax benefits.

The previous example provides the following key points:

1. It is important to investigate the market conditions for antique car rentals before plunging into the venture.

2. In this case the court said that the taxpayer should have spent more time soliciting potential customers.

3. It is important for any business to have a separate phone number, a separate checking account, and a listing in the Yellow Pages under the appropriate heading.

4. The court criticized the taxpayer because he did not advertise his car rental activity in the local newspaper. For most business

ventures, it is important to engage in some type of advertising and promotion to show a businesslike concern for the success of your venture.

1.3 Restoration for vintage car races

Another venture involves restoration of cars for vintage car races, in which it is possible to win significant amounts of money. Of course, with vintage car races, the top speeds are quite a bit lower than in modern race car competitions.

In the following case the taxpayer was not able to show how he could possibly make a profit, even if he won first prize in a major race.

Example: *Dunkel v. Commissioner,* T.C. Memo 1991-336.

Dr. James Dunkel, a dentist in Rockford, Illinois, raced Indianapolis 500-type formula racing cars for a number of years as a hobby, but he was forced to quit racing due to injuries.

He then decided to restore antique cars as a business. His plan was to enter his 1927 Nash in the Great American Race, which is a cross-country event for older vintage cars. The grand prize was $100,000.

He paid the $5,000 entry fee. He obtained about $35,000 of sponsorship money from local individuals and businesses, and used the money to help restore the car for the race. He also provided $27,000 from his own funds, which he claimed as a tax deduction.

He had an agreement with his sponsors in which they were to receive 60 percent of any prize money; 20 percent would go to his partner, 10 percent would go to his ex-wife, and Dr. Dunkel would end up with only 10 percent.

Dr. Dunkel had a separate checking account for his vintage car venture. However, he did not maintain written records of expenses, as required in the sponsorship agreement, and he did not prepare any documentation relating to restoration of the 1927 Nash.

Dr. Dunkel had never driven a vintage car more than 200 miles and this race was between Los Angeles and New York. He finished 21st in the race and won no prize money.

The US Tax Court said his activity was not engaged in for profit. The court noted that under the sponsorship agreement Dr. Dunkel would receive only 10 percent of any prize money, so that even if he had won the top prize of $100,000, he could not have earned more than $10,000. And as mentioned, he spent $27,000 of his own funds towards the restoration. "We find it incredible that a person who insists he has a profit objective would contribute almost three times as much money to an activity than the activity can produce if all goes according to plan."

The court noted that while Dr. Dunkel did maintain a separate checking account, he did not maintain any other business records that would normally be kept in a business venture. Further, he did not maintain records that he had agreed to maintain for the sponsors. Finally, the court noted that Dr. Dunkel had no experience in preparing for or participating in vintage auto races. The court concluded that his interest in competing in the race was purely recreational.

The previous example provides the following key points:

1. While it is possible to win a significant sum in classic car races, you must determine if the activity will result in a profit after considering costs.

2. The taxpayer in this case was able to obtain significant sponsorship support from

local merchants, but he still had to contribute his own money to the venture, and his sponsorship agreements left him with only 10 percent of the money he might win. This completely hindered his ability to make a profit.

3. The taxpayer failed to keep the records required under his sponsorship agreement, which the court said was evidence of his unbusinesslike approach to the activity.

2. Chapter Summary

The IRS will strictly scrutinize anything to do with classic cars, because it is well known that these cars are usually the source of tremendous personal pleasure and recreation. If you claim that you are in classic car refurbishing as a business, but you don't make any profit, you will need to prove to the IRS that you are operating in a businesslike manner.

It is important to keep refurbishment costs realistic so that you can make a profit. Sometimes it is necessary to be satisfied with less than mint restoration so that you are able to make a profit. If you strive to restore vehicles to mint condition, be sure you can do this in a way that will still be cost effective.

As with the other ventures examined in this book, it is important to have a separate checking account, a separate phone line, a listing in the White Pages and Yellow Pages, business cards, business stationery, and proper business licenses.

16
AUTOMOBILE RACING

Automobile racing is a big sport that has many different classifications. There is motorcycle, truck, and vintage car racing, as well as drag racing and high-end NASCAR racing. People who race can earn money — sometimes very substantial sums — and many professional race car drivers earn a very comfortable living in this sport.

1. Ways to Make Money as a Race Car Driver

For car racers, there are several ways of making money, such as:

- **By winning or finishing in a race.** Most races pay cash to the winner and place finishers of a race. However, amateur races usually have little or nothing by way of cash prizes. The IRS has contested many race car owners and drivers on the grounds that car racing is inherently recreational, and that you can't make a profit even if you win a number of races. The main obstacle is showing that the potential for purses exceeds the high cost of racing. You have to show that there are opportunities to win enough prize money to make a profit.

- **By accumulating points in division and national races.** Just as with other sports, you can accumulate points over a racing season, and this can result in monetary awards from the relevant race car association.

- **By contingency awards.** You can get "in kind" booty (for example racing parts or supplies) from companies whose logo you agree to display on your racing vehicle. For low-end racers, this amounts to little of value; however, sponsors will sometimes pay a cash bonus to winners and place finishers who are displaying their advertising logo.

- **By sponsorship fees.** Race car advertising generates about a billion dollars in revenue that car racers use to pay for their ventures. Millions of people make up the consumer audiences of race car events so commercial advertising has inevitably imploded into this sport.

Race car drivers usually own their own vehicles, and since maintenance and other costs are high, it is helpful for the race car owner to obtain sponsorship funds. This helps to defray costs, thus making it more likely that you will make a profit. The money from the sponsor constitutes income in addition to whatever you win in the races entered, and the sponsor deducts the costs as advertising deductions.

Many people engage in self-sponsorship of their own race car activities. The topic of self-sponsorship of sports activities is discussed in Chapter 5 as well as in section 3. of this chapter.

2. Racing for Profit

In this chapter, the main focus will be on race car drivers who claim they are engaged in racing for profit. They often seek sponsors to help defray the costs of racing. The IRS takes the view that many race car drivers are simply engaged in a hobby, particularly if they are competing only at the amateur level, and that they are simply using the sport as a way of generating tax breaks. Evidence that you have obtained, or that you have diligently sought to obtain sponsors helps prove that your activity is a business, not a hobby.

If you are competing in the lower end of the racing spectrum, it will be hard to get sponsors to pay much for the advertising benefit they might get out of being your sponsor. Still, it is important to make efforts in this direction in order to show a businesslike manner of conducting your racing activity.

There are professional firms that collect a commission by soliciting sponsors for race car drivers. Enterprising race car drivers will sometimes solicit sponsors themselves by visiting business establishments, sending solicitations in the mail, and networking.

Sponsorship fees can be high or low, depending on the qualifications and reputation of the race car driver. Professional race car drivers can earn very substantial fees from their advertising sponsors. Others, in amateur racing, usually get nominal fees from small business sponsors.

2.1 Motorcycle racing

Many people decide to engage in motorcycle racing as a way of making money. But, as shown in the following case, there is very little profit potential in this venture at the amateur level. It is at the professional level that riders stand a chance of winning good money.

Example: *Zimmermann v. Commissioner,* **T.C. Memo 1976-123.**

Philip Zimmermann, Bethany, Connecticut, was a police officer, and spent many of his weekends participating in motorcycle racing. He never won prize money or other income from the activity during the three-year period for which he was audited. He claimed deductions for depreciation, a trailer hitch, tools, a license, and entry fees.

He did not make a study of the profit potential of motorcycle racing, and did not try to relate his expenses to his potential income. The races he entered offered prizes as low as $10 for fourth place and as high as $1,500 for first place. Some of the races offered no prize money. Mr. Zimmermann continued entering races and continued to accumulate expenses for entry fees, repairs, and other expenses. However, even if he won all the races he entered, there was no evidence that he could have earned enough to cover his expenses, much less make a profit.

The US Tax Court said that "the most realistic inference is that racing was mainly a form of recreation or amusement," and that the expenses were not deductible.

The previous example provides the following key points:

1. Before starting any racing venture, make a study of the profit potential. How many races would you have to win or place in to generate a profit or break-even point? If the arithmetic simply does not show a profit potential, your activity is more likely a hobby than a business.

2. The taxpayer in this case lost because he was unable to show how he might make money in motorcycle racing at his amateur level.

It is a general truism in sports that unless you have attained professional status, you are not likely to be eligible to compete where the real money is. This is true with motorcycle racing. You can become a pro if you can pass the qualifying tests. There are numerous motorcycle races sponsored by the American Motorcyclist Association Pro Racing.

In the following case, the US Tax Court ruled in favor of a motorcycle racer because he attained professional status, so he stood a chance of winning large purses.

Example: *Canale v. Commissioner,* **T.C. Memo 1989-619.**

Wayne Canale, Naperville, Illinois, was a motorcycle mechanic. Friends encouraged him to try motorcycle racing because he was a talented rider and there was the possibility of making some money.

He investigated various types of racing, such as dirt track and motocross, and decided the bigger purses were in road racing. Mr. Canale felt he had sufficient skills to be competitive in this field.

He learned from the American Motorcycle Association that it would take a few years of racing at the amateur novice level before he could earn enough points to qualify for professional races, where the purses were attractive.

For two years, he raced on the weekends. The next year he did not race at all, but instead worked full time as a mechanic. The next year he entered races again, and finally, after about six years from the start of the activity, he attained professional status. He was eligible for ten professional races each year. He entered four or more races per season.

He had four racing motorcycles and a van and trailer to transport them to the racetrack. He entered a 200-mile race at Daytona in which he finished 20th in the race. He entered other races as well. He entered the Daytona race another year, which then had a first prize of $20,000, but he finished 29th.

Mr. Canale also tried to gain sponsorships to help make money. He wrote several letters seeking sponsorship, but never acquired a sponsor.

During a seven-year period he earned only $3,500 in purses, and needless to say, did not make a profit. He decided to stop racing at that point.

The US Tax Court noted that Mr. Canale stood a chance of making a profit if he had won the Daytona race. Thus, "there was a practical possibility that petitioner could win enough money in a year to exceed his expenses."

The court noted that he diligently progressed to the professional level, and after a number of races at that level, he decided to quit racing because he felt he was not sufficiently competitive to win what he had hoped. His decision to leave racing at that point was evidence that he entered racing with a profit objective, so the court upheld his tax deductions.

The court ruled in his favor even though his business records were inadequate. He never consulted with business advisers regarding racing. His attorney told him he should be better organized and have a separate checking account for the activity.

He kept a mileage log for his van and retained all receipts, but nothing by way of financial analysis, budget, or business plan. The court said that in a racing venture such as this it was not necessary to keep a separate bank account or complex accounting records.

The previous example provides the following key points:

1. The taxpayer won primarily because he had attained professional status and was eligible to earn large purses in motorcycle racing, making it more likely that he could make a profit. As with any sport, if you are good enough you can eventually qualify for professional status.

2. Deciding to abandon an unprofitable venture is evidence of your overall business motivation.

3. The taxpayer won even though his business records were less than satisfactory. The judge was impressed with the overall evidence showing that the taxpayer was motivated to make money in this venture. Still, it is important to maintain better-than-adequate business records for your activity, and to utilize the records to assess overall performance. The IRS is always impressed if a taxpayer has well laid-out business records.

2.2 Car racing

Drag racing is a very popular sport. These are races in which only two cars participate over a straight, quarter-mile course. There are different categories of drag racing, determined by the rated speed of the car. At the amateur level, the prize money is considerably smaller than in professional races.

It is important to have a plan on how you hope to make a profit in your racing venture. In the case of *Riddle v. Commissioner* (included on the CD), it was not feasible for the taxpayer to make a profit in the local races he entered.

Another drag racing case, also against the taxpayer, further illustrates the importance of operating an activity in a businesslike manner.

Example: *Spear v. Commissioner,* T.C. Memo 1994-354.

Joseph Spear, Las Vegas, Nevada, had a lifelong interest in car racing, particularly drag racing. He decided to convert his hobby into a business. He joined the National Hot Rod Association (NHRA) and entered races sponsored by that organization. He entered anywhere from 14 to 25 races per season and devoted 30 to 40 hours per week to racing and maintenance of his car.

He raced in the highest level of drag racing, known as the "super eliminator" class. He personally mounted and assembled the engine, body, and other accessories on his car.

Mr. Spear upgraded to better cars as time went on. His ambition was to become certified as a "pro stock" racer, although he said in the US Tax Court that his full-time job as a telephone repairman prevented him from putting in enough time to attain this goal. Mr. Spear testified that he figured it would take ten years for him to realize a profit from drag racing, but could not say how that would happen.

He was never able to get a commercial sponsor and in a six-year period he had sizable losses, although he did win or place in several races that yielded modest cash awards.

The court said that his track record in the first six years "certainly did not show or establish that he was moving toward profitability."

The court also said that Mr. Spear did not have a professional racing crew, but relied on friends who occasionally helped him at races. "The absence of a regular, consistent crew indicates that the activity was not conducted on a professional level." The court also noted that Mr. Spear's upgraded cars did not reap larger awards.

The court concluded that Mr. Spear "was dedicated to car racing as a sport, and his love for that activity completely overshadowed the business aspects. The elements of personal pleasure and recreation dominated all semblances of profit."

The court said that Mr. Spear did not engage in the venture in a businesslike manner. His sparse records dealt mainly with racing schedules and the mechanical aspects of his car, rather than the financial aspects of the activity.

The previous example provides the following key points:

1. The taxpayer estimated that it would take ten years for him to finally make a profit, but he failed to provide a budget or other documents to show how that would happen. The court was skeptical because it was not clear whether the taxpayer would attain "pro stock" status, where better prize money was available.

2. The IRS views amateur car racing as a recreational activity, not a business. In order to overcome this, it is crucial that you have a concrete plan for how you will eventually make money at it. It is sometimes necessary to explain to the IRS what the point system means, and how you can eventually earn money from accumulating points.

3. Business records of a racing venture should include items that help analyze the profitability of the activity. There should be a break-even analysis or similar document that you have prepared and a business plan explaining how you intend to make a profit.

4. Employing a professional racing crew rather than relying on friends to help is evidence that you are operating in a businesslike manner.

5. It is important to be able to show that you have enough time to engage in the venture despite a full-time job. Car racing is usually a time-intensive activity, with much time needed for car maintenance and improvement.

It is important to research the feasibility of making money in drag racing before embarking on it. In the case *Emerson v. Commissioner* (included on the CD), the taxpayer was subject to speed restrictions because of a heart condition, which prevented him from making much of a profit in drag racing.

Another kind of racing involves off-road pickup truck racing. The only way to make a profit in this venture is to gain sponsorships because the purses are low. For an example, see *Likes v. Commissioner* on the CD.

3. Racing Sponsorship for Advertising

Until recently, auto racing only presented marketing opportunities to large companies such as McDonald's and Coca-Cola, in which the companies sponsor their own teams and cars. The fact that so many companies are sponsors in motor sports highlights the appeal of the sport as an effective form of advertising. Statistics published by Simmons Market Research Bureau show that racing audiences have the highest level of sponsor recollection of all sports enthusiasts.

In this section you will learn how to successfully take advertising deductions for sponsorship of race car events and learn from business owners who themselves are racing enthusiasts.

Sponsorship can be a way of developing relationships with clients, as you will see in the following case.

Example: *Menard, Inc. v. Commissioner,* T.C. Memo 2004-207.

Menards is a Wisconsin company engaged in retail sales of hardware, building supplies, paint, and garden equipment. John Menard, the principal shareholder, has a passionate interest in car racing. Mr. Menard decided to utilize motor sports to garner publicity for the stores, to attract customers' attention, and to distinguish Menards from its competitors.

He formed an S corporation known as TMI, for the purpose of competing in the Indy 500 races. TMI was used as a separate corporation to shield the Menards Company from liability in the event of racing accidents.

TMI sponsored approximately 100 races in the first two years. Mr. Menard arrived at the races either the day before or the day of the race. He invited vendors, customers, and Menards executives and employees to the events. At the races, he had the opportunity to talk with people about his company's sponsorship, and to develop business relationships with other participants and learn more about their products and services in a personal environment.

The race cars, driver uniforms, and Indy promotional materials exhibited the Menards logo, among the logos of other sponsors.

The expenses of TMI amounted to many millions of dollars, much of which was paid as salaries. Menards did not create or maintain separate accounts in its books and records identifying the TMI expenses as sponsorship fees or advertising expenses. Instead, Menards recorded the TMI expenses in ten different accounts of Menards' corporate division according to expense type, such as "Repairs/Vehicles," and "Gas and Oil." Only costs directly related to advertising, such as logos placed on the cars, were recorded under "Advertising." Menards owned the race cars used by TMI and depreciated them on books, records, and tax returns. TMI's assets consisted only of cash.

When Menards staged grand openings for new stores, TMI participated by sending drivers to sign autographs and providing an Indy car for display. Menards further implemented the racing theme at store openings with a contest in which customers could register to win a mini Indy car.

Mr. Menard enhanced the racing sponsorship by launching an annual "Race to Savings" sale, built around the Indy 500 and Memorial Day weekend. The ads for the sale featured the Menards-sponsored Indy cars. Workers at the stores wore t-shirts depicting these cars.

The US Tax Court held that the sponsorship expenses were ordinary and necessary business expenses of Menards for advertising. The court also said that the amounts in question were reasonable in relation to the company's large gross income. The court said: "The races provided opportunities for Mr. Menard and other Menards' executives to network with vendors and create and maintain goodwill with customers."

The court said that Menards received significant advertising and promotional benefits in return for the sponsorship fees. The court also said: "Indy racing may not be the only form of advertising available to Menards for targeting potential customers, but participation in motor sports is an innovative and exciting method for generating local, national, and international publicity for Menards' business. Menards competitors' decisions to become involved in motor sports also highlights its appeal as a form of effective advertising. Even though Mr. Menard had a personal interest in racing, any personal enjoyment that he gained from Menards' involvement in motor sports was incidental to the benefits Menards' business received through its relationship with TMI."

At the same time, the court criticized the company for poor records in connection with the sponsorship. For instance, there was no written sponsorship agreement. Also, when Menards deducted the TMI expenses on its tax returns, it did not identify the deductions as sponsorship fees or advertising expenses. TMI did not keep books or records of any sponsorship fees received from Menards. Despite these shortcomings, the court upheld the deductions for the most part, with some adjustments made.

The previous example provides the following key points:

1. In order for sponsorship of sporting events to be justified as advertising expenses there must be some fairly clear advertising benefit to your business.

2. As a sponsor of various race cars, Mr. Menard used the opportunity to develop business relationships with other participants in a more personal environment. He also developed good will for his company by inviting employees, customers, and others to the events.

3. The Menards Company won this big case even though company records of the sponsorship were a mess. There was not even a written sponsorship agreement! It was clear auto racing was a personal hobby for Mr. Menard, but the court was convinced, based on all the evidence, that the sponsorship was used as an effective advertising method and that the company made the most of it.

In the following case, a successful businessman failed to convince the US Tax Court that his sponsorship of an auto racing team had an advertising purpose for his business.

Example: *Hopkins v. Commissioner,* T.C. Memo 2005-49.

Michael Hopkins, Dana Point, California, was a successful salesman of plastics products and equipment. He was also a car racing hobbyist. Mr. Hopkins was one of the top performing salesmen at his company and was expected to conduct his own promotional activities. He decided that he would sponsor a racing team as a way of advertising his business.

Under the sponsorship agreement, his business logo was displayed on the race cars driven by the sponsored drivers and on their racing uniforms and helmets. The drivers were required to refer to Mr. Hopkins as their sponsor if and when asked about the sponsors.

Mr. Hopkins deducted the cost of sponsorship fees, race car graphics, signs, clothes, promotional hats, country club dues, and travel costs incurred while he attended various races.

The US Tax Court said that Mr. Hopkins did not prove a "causal nexus" between the sponsorship and the promotion of his business. The court said that Mr. Hopkins' testimony on this point was "general, conclusory, vague, and/or uncorroborated in certain material respects," and that he was not a credible witness.

The court said that Mr. Hopkins simply failed to carry the burden of proof in establishing that there was an advertising benefit for his business as a salesman.

The previous example provides the following key points:

1. According to the court, the taxpayer's testimony was lacking in credibility, and that perhaps made it impossible for him to win the case. Your credibility in any tax matter, whether you are interacting with a revenue agent or giving testimony in the US Tax Court, is of crucial importance. If you come across as vague or contradictory, you will erode your own credibility.

2. The taxpayer also lost because he could not show a reasonable connection between his sponsorship and any advertising benefit for his business. It is important to keep some type of records that show the connection between the sponsorship and business contacts that are generated. If you receive business calls from people as a result of your sponsorship, make a note of this in a memo and file it. Keep copies of emails and correspondence with contacts made as a result of the sponsorship. These records help show a direct connection between the sponsorship and the advertising benefit to your business.

3. Generally, it is a straightforward type of advertising if your business name, logo, and other information are displayed on a team's uniforms, race cars, and banners, and mentioned in announcements. However, in this case the court did not believe the taxpayer's stated purpose. The court seemed to think that the sponsorship was simply a means of paying for his hobby pursuit.

4. Chapter Summary

The IRS tends to view amateur racing ventures with suspicion, because of the small purses and the recreational elements involved. Also, it is often difficult for amateurs to garner much by way of sponsorship fees.

At the professional level, the IRS is much more willing to concede that the activity is a business, not a hobby, because of the high purses available. Professionals are likely to obtain attractive sponsorship deals as well. The IRS will tend to favorably view evidence that you are working with a paid, professional crew.

In order to withstand IRS scrutiny, it's important to prepare a business plan, including profit projections or some type of budget that shows how you hope to make money in racing. Ideally this should be written before you start the venture.

You should maintain a separate checking account for the venture. Sponsorship agreements, as well as partnership, management, and other agreements, should always be in writing. Ongoing business records should include a record of the races entered, the amounts won, and the amount of support provided by sponsors, as well as maintenance records, a time log, and other businesslike records. It is important that you utilize business records to help you evaluate the venture.

You should document what efforts you made to solicit potential sponsors. Hiring a professional agency to solicit sponsors is often a way to get better results. Of course, sponsors are going to pay according to the ability and track record of the race car driver being sponsored.

Ongoing evaluation of your venture should include looking for ways to improve the chances of winning races and garnering sponsorship support. If there is a history of losses, it becomes very important to consider alternatives in your methods of operation.

For instance, you might consider participating in a greater number of races or races with higher potential winnings, even though this may mean traveling further from home.

For information about aircraft- and boat-chartering ventures, please see the CD-ROM included with this book.

PART V
SPORTS AND GAMBLING BUSINESSES

17
SPORTS

This chapter explores situations in which people are engaged in sports activities as trades or businesses. It is usually a part-time endeavor — participating in the particular activity, competing in it for prizes, developing one's abilities, and seeking to ultimately "make it big." It takes time, talent, dedication, and money to fund the activity until profits may be generated.

This chapter focuses on sports that have been given significant treatment in the US Tax Court.

1. Fishing Tournaments

A significant segment of the economy, especially in coastal regions, involves commercial fishing. Of course, fishing is often a very pleasurable hobby, but many individuals seek to turn this hobby into a profitable fishing venture, as discussed in Chapter 16.

Some fishing tournaments offer extremely large cash prizes for the top winners. There are also considerable recreational elements involved, including cocktail parties and dinners held at various marinas around the world. Some individuals,

such as the taxpayers in the following case, might win top prizes, yet still not make a profit because of the high costs of maintaining a yacht.

Example: *Peacock v. Commissioner,* T.C. Memo 2002-122.

James Peacock, Ponce Inlet, Florida, owned several automobile dealerships. For many years he and his wife enjoyed fishing. They decided to participate in the Billfish Series tournaments, which are held at marinas around the world. The tournament awards trophies and cash to those who catch the largest billfish with prizes ranging from $150,000 to $1.2 million.

The Peacocks fished at the tournaments from their luxurious yacht along with their teammates and friends. They had an arrangement among themselves to share any winnings they might achieve.

They won the 1993 Bahamas Billfish Championship and other awards. They earned almost $500,000 in tournament winnings during a four-year period, but had about $1.5 million in costs, or a net loss of $1 million.

The US Tax Court said that Mr. and Mrs. Peacock were undoubtedly experts in fishing, but they never did anything to evaluate or improve the fishing activity's financial performance. There was no budget, balance sheet, income projection, or business plan. "As an individual who had the skills necessary to make his automobile dealerships profitable and successful, we believe that he was, or should have been, sufficiently familiar with business practices to allow him to conduct the fishing activity in a manner evidencing a profit objective had he had one."

The court said that the Peacocks "did not study the fishing activity from the point of view of catching the fish at a cost that would be less than the anticipated revenues which would be connected therewith."

The court said: "The fact that the fishing activity suffered losses year after year and that petitioners took no meaningful action to reverse the tide supports a finding that they were indifferent as to whether the losing trend could be reversed."

The court added that there were cocktail parties and dinners hosted for the contestants. "The tournaments had an atmosphere resembling that of a college spring break and took place in some of the world's most beautiful locations. During the tournaments, the sunny, crystal-clear blue water vacation destinations were the backdrop to sunglassed, beach-attired men and women, five-star restaurants, free-flowing alcoholic beverages, and swarms of revelers consisting mainly of contestants and spectators."

The previous example provides the following key points:

1. Even though the taxpayers won $500,000 in tournaments, it was not possible for them to make a profit because of the high costs of maintaining their yacht. They made no meaningful economic study on the profit potential of tournament fishing.

2. The court believed that the fishing activity was a hobby largely because of the luxurious circumstances and the obvious elements of personal pleasure and recreation.

Some people can make money by organizing fishing tournaments in their region. The principles in the following case apply to any type of venture in which you seek to promote sports tournaments as a business.

Example: *Busbee v. Commissioner,* **T.C. Memo 2000-182.**

Tommy Busbee, Midland, Texas, worked full time as a safety representative and his wife worked as a shipping clerk. Mr. Busbee investigated bass fishing tournaments as a way to make money. He consulted with someone who had organized more than 300 fishing tournaments. He continued consulting with this individual on an ongoing basis.

The Busbees got involved with the Couples Association of Sport Tournaments (CAST) — an established bass fishing tournament. Mr. Busbee became director of the western region of the tournament. This entitled him to use the CAST name to organize local tournaments. Directors can make money by collecting membership fees and hosting regional tournaments, and they are responsible for all expenses they incur. Directors can keep part of the revenue from membership fees.

The Busbees recruited new members to CAST, and printed flyers and business cards to distribute on weekends and evenings during fishing-related events. They rented booths at local boat shows, spoke at fishing clubs, and posted flyers at marinas to recruit new members. CAST helped with advertising in fishing magazines about upcoming tournaments. The Busbees successfully recruited new members and organized six annual tournaments with 30 to 40 couples participating in each one.

They used a separate checking account for the venture and sent out a tournament newsletter to members and sponsors. Mrs. Busbee maintained membership records and detailed records of monthly expenses, including lodging and food.

In time, Mr. Busbee became a supervising director with three regions reporting to him. He also earned some income by organizing a weigh station where people could have their fish weighed and displayed, receive fishing awards, and have their pictures taken.

The Busbees never made a profit in the venture. The US Tax Court said that the Busbees operated in a businesslike manner, particularly evidenced by their promotional and recruiting efforts. The Busbees also devoted substantial time to the venture in spite of their full-time jobs.

The court noted that they reduced expenses by soliciting local sponsors for lodging and meals, and that they had a sponsor who paid for their boat show booth fees.

The court said: "Though there is no question that petitioners derive pleasure from their fishing activity, and petitioners concede that they fish in their own tournaments on occasion, petitioners' passion for fishing does not disqualify them from having a profit objective. The process of organizing and hosting a fishing tournament is physically difficult and requires long hours of work, and, in this case, far outweighs whatever personal pleasure petitioners derive from occasional participation in their own tournaments."

The previous example provides the following key points:

1. Becoming a regional director of an established sports tournament can be a way of making money through membership fees.

2. Promotion of your tournaments and recruitment of new members are crucial elements in making money in sports promotion. It is helpful to send out newsletters and generate word-of-mouth interest.

3. In running tournaments, it is important to maintain records of members and of income and expenses, as well as to have a separate checking account.

4. In this case, the court was impressed by the fact that the taxpayer recruited quite a few new members and sought additional revenue with the weigh station and photo service for tournament participants.

2. Boat Racing

It is hard to convince the IRS that you are using your boat or yacht as a means of making money by winning boat races. There has to be a large enough prize to enable you to make a profit, which is a difficult predicament, as it can be very expensive to maintain a competitive vessel and deploy it around the world in various races.

As you will see in the following case, it is important to investigate the economics of boat racing before investing your time and money into the venture.

Example: *Rexroad v. Commissioner,* **T.C. Memo 1985-189.**

Lyle Rexroad, Norco, California, was a successful partner in a construction company. After attending two boat races as a spectator, he decided that he wanted to enter competitive races and try to make a profit in this sport.

He had no experience with such boat racing, but had previously owned a pleasure boat. He bought a new race boat. He joined two racing organizations that held races. He raced in 15 of the races sponsored by the organization. He had a dismal financial outcome, earning $350 in the course of the 15 races.

He incurred substantial expenses, including depreciation of his race boat. He kept no books and retained only a few receipts that substantiated only part of his claimed expenses.

The US Tax Court found it unbusinesslike for Mr. Rexroad to start a boat-racing venture without having any experience racing boats, and without some kind of preliminary investigation prior to buying the race boat and plunging into the venture. The extent of his experience in boat racing consisted simply of watching two boat races.

The court also faulted Mr. Rexroad for only haphazardly retaining receipts and for not having a business bank account. The court held that there was no profit motive. Thus, the court held that his boat-racing venture was a hobby, not a business.

The previous example provides the following key points:

1. If you are engaging in a boat-racing venture, it is necessary to investigate the economics of the activity before declaring it to be a business. For instance, it is important to figure out what races yield higher-end prizes, to determine if you are eligible to enter those races, and to find out how much it will cost in terms of boat expenses.

2. If you have no prior experience in boat racing, it will be almost impossible to convince the IRS that you are now engaged in boat racing as a business activity.

2.1 Sponsorship of boat racing

Boat racing is a venue that can be utilized as a means of sponsorship that in turn advertises your main business or profession. There are many popular boat-racing events around the world that not only provide significant cash prizes, but also provide opportunities for sponsorship advertising.

Because boating is universally regarded as a pleasurable pastime, the IRS almost always takes the view that you are using boat races simply as a means of pursuing a hobby, not as a way of advertising your main business. It is important, even more so than with auto racing sponsorship, to keep good records showing an advertising linkage between the boat activity sponsorship and advertising benefits for your business.

With boat races, the opportunities for clear visual displays of business names and logos are not as prevalent as in auto racing. For more information about sponsorship advertising see section 5.

In the following case, the taxpayer lost because he failed to adequately get his business name displayed in the boat races he entered.

Example: *Gale, Inc. v. Commissioner,* **T.C. Memo 1960-191 [affd 297 F.2d 270 (6th Cir. 1961)].**

Joseph Schoenith, Detroit, Michigan, owned an electrical contracting company known as "Gale." He purchased a boat and named it GALE I, after his business name, and painted the name in large letters on her hull.

Mr. Schoenith raced his boat several times a year in widely popular powerboat races on the Detroit River. Mr. Schoenith's son, Lee, also participated in the races. Hundreds of thousands of spectators viewed each of the races. There was also significant coverage through radio and television.

He purchased other boats, and printed the name GALE on the hulls, as well as the electrical industry logo. Mr. Schoenith claimed advertising deductions in connection with the boat racing.

These boats won numerous races, including the Gold Cup race in Seattle. However, the boats were not raced for money. Usually the winners received a cup, a tray, or some other similar trophy.

Mr. Schoenith used a picture of a GALE boat on his company's stationery, invoices, and checks. Although his company paid for the boats, they were registered in Mr. Schoenith's name. Mr. Schoenith explained that this was because the American Power Boat Association had a rule that no corporation could own or race a boat.

He made a promotional film of his company's sponsorship of the boats and distributed it as a kind of infomercial to professional and social groups.

Mr. Schoenith garnered considerable publicity in newspapers, magazines, and boat race programs. In the US Tax Court, Mr. Schoenith presented five scrapbooks containing more than 400 pages of clippings concerning his racing activities.

However, the court said that almost none of the articles mentioned his company's sponsorship, and it was hard to see how the sponsorship had any bona fide advertising benefits. Almost all of the clippings were of articles in the social pages, not the sports pages, and the focus was on Mr. Schoenith and his son as sportsmen, although a few described him as a Detroit electrical contractor. The name "Gale, Inc." almost never appeared in the articles in any way that would suggest that the company was owner or sponsor of the race boats.

The court said that while the boats bore the name GALE on their hulls, this insignia could hardly be expected to publicize the company. The connection was simply too subtle.

Mr. Schoenith claimed that his sponsorship was effective because his company's gross sales increased fivefold during the five-year period of his company's sponsorship. The court said that his company's revenue had already been on the upswing prior to the sponsorship and that Mr. Schoenith simply failed to meet the burden of proof in showing that the sponsorship constituted a legitimate advertising expense.

Mr. Schoenith was also unable to convince the court that the races gave him a unique opportunity to solicit new customers for his company. The court said that undoubtedly there were benefits to his business, but that the same would be true of any social relationship.

The previous example provides the following key points:

1. It is important in sponsorships that your company name, logo, or other identifying information be featured at the events in a clear and prominent way. In this case the taxpayer's display of his company's logo was considered "too insubstantial" to provide a legitimate advertising benefit.

2. It is important to keep records showing the connection between your sponsorship and any advertising benefits that resulted. This will help convince the IRS that your sponsorship is a bona fide means of advertising your main business.

3. If your sponsorship generates publicity in the media, that is helpful in amplifying its advertising benefits. However, in interviews with media, be sure to mention that your business is sponsoring the event and keep it at that. Refrain from making statements to the media about how much

fun you are having, because that can give the impression that you are utilizing the sponsorship primarily for recreational purposes.

4. The taxpayer's son also participated in the races. The court did not seem to consider this a problem, but based its ruling on the evidence as a whole.

3. Golf

Attaining professional status as a golfer is a difficult and usually long-term task. If you want to make it into the tournaments provided by the Professional Golfers' Association of America (PGA), you have to be an excellent golfer. You have to go through an apprenticeship at an approved golf course and you have to qualify through tournament points you accrue. You can also qualify as a professional by attending a PGA tour qualifying school.

In the following case the taxpayer became certified as a professional by the PGA, and then set out to make money in tournaments. Although he did not do very well, he nonetheless convinced the US Tax Court that his sports activity was a business, not a hobby.

Example: *Kimbrough v. Commissioner,* T.C. Memo 1988-185.

Donald Kimbrough, Chicago, Illinois, taught golf and other sports at a high school. He had been an avid golfer since his college days. After he completed an apprentice program at a professional golf course, he became a member of the PGA.

He attended a business course for golfers, assisted a professional golfer from whom he took lessons, and devoted a significant amount of time to practicing and improving his golf skills. He practiced golf after school on a daily basis, and in

the summer devoted 12 hours a day to golfing activities.

Mr. Kimbrough decided he could make money competing in golf tournaments. In a five-year period he won only $3,000 in prize money and claimed losses of $18,000. He carefully detailed the expenses he incurred for each tournament and recorded the prize money available at each tournament.

The IRS denied his tax deductions claiming he was engaged in a golf hobby. The US Tax Court sided with Mr. Kimbrough.

The court was impressed by the fact that there were significant cash prizes available at professional tournaments, that Mr. Kimbrough had attained professional status, and that his expenses were fairly modest.

The court said: "Despite the degree of enjoyment petitioner may have experienced, we believe he had an honest and actual objective of realizing a profit from his golfing activity."

The previous example provides the following key points:

1. In professional golf there are opportunities to win significant prize money. Many pros consider their activity to be a business and take appropriate tax deductions for their expenses.

2. The taxpayer took a business course for golfers, which gave him the details of how a pro could make money in golf tournaments, which was very helpful to his case.

3. If you are engaged in golf as a business, you should devote a significant amount of time to improving your golf skills. It is important to attain professional status and to carefully plan which tournaments you intend to enter.

4. Record keeping for a golf activity is somewhat minimal compared to other activities. However, it is necessary to keep records of expenses and revenue, as well as a list of prize money available at tournaments. Ideally, you should have a budget that shows how much you expect to spend and the range of revenue you realistically expect to earn.

The PGA sponsors tournaments for seniors who are amateurs, at which they can win prize money. However, without attaining professional status, it is extremely difficult to withstand IRS scrutiny if you are taking tax deductions in connection with your golf activities — even if you are working towards attaining professional status. For more golf venture examples, see the cases *Heywood v. Commissioner* and *Courville v. Commissioner*, included on the CD.

4. Volleyball

In the following case, the taxpayer devoted herself to developing a career in volleyball and convinced the US Tax Court that her activity was a business.

Example: *Nelson v. Commissioner,* T.C. Memo 2001-117.

Ruth Nelson, who over a period of time resided in several states, had a master's degree in physical education. For many years she worked as a college coach for tennis and volleyball teams. She was regarded as a highly qualified volleyball coach and served as a consultant for various volleyball, sporting, and marketing organizations. She received numerous professional honors and awards. Some of the players she coached were selected to play on US Olympic teams.

She devoted most of her time as coach of the Baton Rouge Volleyball Club. She organized tournaments and obtained sponsorship money from various companies to help pay costs. She produced a training video for which she received royalties. She also designed and marketed her own volleyball shoe that she sold through the club. She conducted summer camps for volleyball training, for which she charged a fee.

Ms. Nelson had to undergo back surgery for an injury, which set back her ability to participate in volleyball activities and forced her to incur costs of hiring additional help. She had to take on other work to generate income, which cut into the amount of time she could devote to the club activities.

Ms. Nelson's back injury worsened and she had to withdraw from working at the summer camp and tournaments. Instead, she did consulting by telephone. She also worked on obtaining corporate sponsors whose logos were placed on the face of prepaid phone cards that she marketed through the club's website. She continued to solicit companies to sponsor club events.

In a 12-year period Ms. Nelson had a net profit of only $2,000 during one year and losses that ranged from $12,000 to $23,000 for the other years.

The US Tax Court was impressed by the businesslike manner in which Ms. Nelson carried on her activities. She had a separate checking account, clear records of receipts and expenditures, and ledgers for the camps and tournaments.

The court said Ms. Nelson had vast experience in volleyball. She also sought the advice of a business consultant, indicating her desire to derive a profit from the venture.

The court noted that in some years, she devoted herself full time to the venture, and in other years she devoted at least 20 to 30 hours a week to the activities. She spent considerable time promoting the camps and other programs, and marketing her volleyball shoe.

The court said that even after her disability and the need to take on phone work, she continued promoting her volleyball programs and tournaments.

The court said that Ms. Nelson, practically a life-long devotee of volleyball, undoubtedly derived great personal pleasure from anything to do with the sport. "Nevertheless, the mere fact that a taxpayer derives a certain amount of personal pleasure from an activity does not, in and of itself, render the activity not engaged in for profit."

The previous example provides the following key points:

1. An individual who acquires significant skill in a given sport, or attains professional status, will stand a good chance of claiming the sport as a business activity.

2. Even if you are an expert in the sport itself, it is important to conduct research or obtain expert advice on how to make money in the particular sport.

3. In this case the court was impressed that the taxpayer diligently applied herself to volleyball in a variety of ways: she ran a summer training camp, organized tournaments, obtained corporate sponsors, and marketed her own volleyball shoe.

5. Sponsorship Advertising for Sports

As mentioned in Chapter 5, a sponsorship enables you to link your business name with an event. The advertising benefit is that your firm shares in the image of the event (in much the same way that a product shares the image of a celebrity endorsing it). This linkage is sometimes referred to as *brandstanding*, and it helps generate public interest and excitement about your product or service. Also, event sponsorship allows you to attend and entertain guests at the events, and to use the events as opportunities to network.

The money you spend on sponsorship fees constitutes advertising, and you are entitled to deduct it as an ordinary and necessary business (i.e., advertising) expense. However, the IRS might take the view that your sponsorship is simply a way of funding your own hobby, rather than a form of advertising for your business or profession.

The IRS might argue that while your sponsorship may have provided social opportunities to meet potential customers or clients, it was not related closely enough to the conduct of your business to have provided you with an advertising benefit. The IRS will say that the expenses were of a social nature and nondeductible.

The following should be observed when taking advertising deductions for sports sponsorships:

- Your business logo or name should appear on uniforms, banners, trailers, signs, rolling billboards — or in other suitable ways — at the sponsored events.

- Public address announcements at the events should make it clear that your business is sponsoring the event. The announcement should also identify your product or service, if possible.

- You should place print ads in the event programs to help draw the public's attention to your sponsorship.

- Keep some sort of record that tracks business contacts you make as a result of your sponsorship. This helps prove that the sponsorship produced actual results in terms of new business. Your record can consist of memos, phone logs, or copies of emails.

- Document any sales or new business that resulted from the sponsorship efforts, again as evidence of the advertising benefits to your business.

- It is best to have a written sponsorship agreement with whomever you are sponsoring. The contract should make clear that your business name or logo will be displayed at the events. The contract should state the amount of sponsorship fees to be paid.

- If you are self-sponsoring your own sporting activity, there should be some written memorandum indicating the purpose of the sponsorship and the ways your business name will be displayed.

- If your business is a corporation or LLC, there should be a Resolution from the Board of Directors authorizing the sponsorship and allocating a budget for that purpose. The Resolution should identify the sponsorship expenses as advertising costs.

- Invite potential or existing customers to the sponsorship events, as well as employees. At the events, make a point of meeting new people who might be potential customers or be helpful to your business.

- If possible, rent a vendor booth inside the sports facility. At the booth you could hand out promotional material about your business. Your ad in the event's program can help drive traffic to the booth.

- If you speak with the media about your sponsorship, be careful not to say anything that could imply that your purpose is to engage in a personal pursuit or that the activity is a hobby. Rather, you should speak about your sponsorship and its connection to your business.

- It is helpful, but not crucial, to have graphics or photos representing your sponsorship on your business stationery, invoices, and checks.

The following case involves sponsorship of the taxpayer's favorite basketball team.

Example: *Bower v. Commissioner,* T.C. Memo 1990-16.

James Bower, West Lafayette, Indiana, was a commodity broker and also owned a rental housing business called "Bower Housing." Mr. Bower had a passion for basketball since he was a child.

Mr. Bower decided that a unique way of making his name known to potential rental and commodity trading clients was to sponsor a basketball team made up of ex-collegiate players.

As part of the promotion, he had the name "BOWER HOUSING" shown in large letters on the back of the team's uniforms. Mr. Bower was also a member of the team, as well as assistant coach. He attended every game played by the team even if he was not participating. The crowds at the games ranged from 200 to 10,000 people.

As the team's sponsor, Mr. Bower paid for the team's travel, lodging, food, promotions, Amateur Athletic Union fees, tournament fees, gym rental, and uniforms. Sometimes pictures of the team would appear in the sports pages of the local paper and the team also received some radio and television coverage.

Sponsorship of the team was Mr. Bower's primary form of advertisement for his brokerage and housing businesses. A majority of his clients were men and were interested in athletic events. Many of his clients would talk to him about his sponsorship of the team. He claimed that his commodity trading client list grew since he started sponsoring the team.

Prior to the games or tournaments, Mr. Bower made a point of meeting with customers who lived in the area and discussing business with them.

The US Tax Court said there was obviously an element of personal pleasure because of Mr. Bower's love of the sport, but that the expenses were reasonably intended to advertise his businesses. The court said that the team's publicity afforded Mr. Bower's businesses with good local and regional advertising to rental and commodity trading customers, and at a relatively low cost.

The previous example provides the following key points:

1. The taxpayer believed that basketball was a particularly popular sport in his region and that basketball audiences would be a good pool of potential customers.

2. The taxpayer made sure that his company's name was printed on the team's uniforms, and at the games he made a point of meeting with local customers and discussing his business with them.

3. While there were clearly elements of personal pleasure and recreation involved, the court was convinced that the sponsorship was a bona fide advertising expense.

For another example of sponsorship advertising in sports, see the case *Ebner v. Commissioner* (included on the CD).

6. Chapter Summary

The IRS regards the playing of sports — except where someone is clearly making money as a pro — as inherently a hobby activity. If you are serious about being an athlete as a trade or business, it is important to operate in a businesslike manner. That means figuring out how you might go about making money in your field before you begin the venture. It also means actively developing and improving your skills, entering tournaments that can help you win prize money, accumulating points that will advance your career, and even trying to get sponsors to help pay for costs. As in other hobby loss areas, it is important to maintain adequate books and records, particularly to help you evaluate the progress you are making from an economic standpoint.

Sponsorship of a sports event gives you an opportunity to meet and/or entertain existing and potential clients, as well as your employees. The IRS often seeks to argue that these costs are not advertising expenses, but a disguised way of paying for your activity. It is important, if you are audited, to emphasize the advertising benefits that your sponsorship provides to your business or profession, and that any personal enjoyment you gain from the activity is incidental to the advertising purpose.

For information about managing a child's sports activities, please see the CD-ROM included with this book.

18
GAMBLING

Gambling winnings are regarded as income and must be reported on your tax returns. However, a special provision of tax law that has existed for many years allows you to deduct gambling losses from your gambling gains. Section 165(d) of the IRS Code says: "Losses from wagering transactions shall be allowed only to the extent of the gains from such transactions."

The deduction may not exceed the amount of your gains. Thus, if you win $1,000 and lose $2,000, you can deduct your loss only up to the $1,000 that you won, and the remainder is simply a loss that you must absorb.

Gambling losses can be deducted against gambling gains whether the particular gambling activity is legal or illegal. Losses from one type of gambling activity are deductible against gains from a different type of gambling transaction. For example, losses suffered at the racetrack can be deducted with respect to gains realized at the casino.

1. Professional Gamblers

While many people who gamble do so with the intent of winning, only a small percentage of people make a profit. Even fewer are professional gamblers. Taxpayers who are amateur gamblers cannot deduct the cost of plane trips, hotel rooms, and meals on trips to Las Vegas or other gambling sites to engage in gambling, even if they have a strong hope or expectation of making a profit.

For professional gamblers, it is another matter. Some people make a living at gambling and declare themselves to be professional gamblers. A professional gambler is someone engaged in gambling as a trade or business. For professional gamblers, gambling is an income-producing activity and they would not engage in it were it not for the fact that income can be produced.

If you are a professional gambler, you can claim ordinary and necessary business expenses in addition to gambling losses, as tax deductions against your gambling winnings. As a professional gambler you have the advantage of deducting transportation, lodging, meals, admission fees, publications, seminars to improve gambling skills, office supplies, bank charges, and other expenses associated with your gambling activity.

In order to qualify as a professional gambler, the IRS will consider whether you pursue the activity on a regular, full-time basis, in good faith, and whether your primary motive is the production of income rather than merely pleasure or amusement. The IRS will usually accept that your occupation is that of a professional gambler if you derive nearly all of your gross income from gambling and if you have no other job.

In the following case, the taxpayer's gambling activity was considered sporadic by the court and, therefore, was considered a hobby and not a business.

Example: *Neymeyer v. Commissioner,* **T.C. Summary Opinion 2002-120.**

Carol Neymeyer enjoyed gambling in Las Vegas. Mrs. Neymeyer decided that she could make a profit at gambling and turned her skills to playing the slot machines. She had some success, but incurred losses. She wanted to deduct travel and meal expenses, in addition to her gambling losses, against her gambling gains.

The US Tax Court said that to be engaged in the trade or business of gambling, one must be involved in the activity with continuity and regularity, and the primary purpose of the gambling must be for income and profit. She played the slot machines only about once a week during the year in question and she did not consult with any professional gamblers or do any research concerning professional gambling. She did not know whether she was supposed to have a professional gambling license. She kept records of her winnings and losses in a notebook, but said she lost it.

The court said that her activity was not continuous or regular enough, and that while she certainly desired to win money, she did not engage in gambling primarily for income and profit. Rather, her activity "more resembles a diversion than a professional engagement. A sporadic activity, hobby, or an amusement diversion does not qualify as a trade or business." Thus, the court only allowed deductions for her losses to the extent of her gains from gambling transactions.

The previous example provides the following key points:

1. If you devote yourself full time to gambling, it is your intended livelihood source, and you have no other job, the activity may be regarded as a trade or business.

2. If your gambling activity is sporadic, or an amusement or diversion, it is a hobby, not a business, and you are not entitled to take deductions for travel, meals, or lodging.

3. If you are a professional gambler, you may be expected to acquire a professional gambling license if one is required in the particular jurisdiction where you gamble.

2. Proving Gambling Losses

Whether you are a professional gambler or a casual gambler, if you do incur gambling losses it is important to maintain records to prove this in order to deduct losses against winnings. You have the burden of proving the existence of losses and the amounts involved. This can be very difficult to establish.

The IRS knows that it is difficult for gamblers to substantiate their losses, so they will often audit individuals who claim to have a "wash" on gambling income. The taxpayer will usually be hard-pressed to substantiate his or her losses, and will end up paying income tax on the money won.

According to the IRS, to prove gambling losses you should maintain a diary with the following information:

- Date and type of specific wager or wagering activity.
- Name of gambling establishment.
- Address or location of gambling establishment.
- Names of other persons, if any, who were with you at the time you gambled.
- Amounts won or lost.

For example, with racetrack wagering you should keep a log identifying each race entered, amounts wagered, amounts collected on winning tickets, and amounts lost on losing tickets. Supplemental records should include unredeemed tickets and payment records from the racetracks.

You might get a pocket gaming diary, often provided by hotels in the vicinity of casinos. The diary must be kept contemporaneously with the winnings and losses in order to be acceptable. Without substantiation of losses, the IRS will tax you on your winnings and disallow any offset for losses.

Larger gambling winnings are usually reflected on Form W-2G (Certain Gambling Winnings) or Form 5754 (Statement by Person Receiving Gambling Winnings) issued by the casino, racetrack, or other gambling venue. This form is issued for winning bets of more than $1,000, and a 20 percent withholding tax is deducted from the amount given to the bettor. In order to avoid this, people will sometimes place numerous small identical bets.

If you keep losing on pari-mutuel tickets, you will still have to explain them if you are audited, since the IRS suspects people pick up losing tickets that others have thrown away to generate false losses. Pari-mutuel tickets are of little evidentiary value unless there is corroboration on top of your own statement that you purchased each and every losing ticket. This can be accomplished by having witnesses present when you place the wagers. However, the best evidence of losses is a contemporaneous diary or similar record of your gambling activities that indicates total winnings and losses for the day, supplemented with whatever receipts and tickets you can save.

Other evidence could be copies of your casino credit records and copies of your casino check cashing records. If slot machines are involved, you can obtain a record of all winnings from the casino by date and time that the machine was played. Often, casinos are very cooperative if you need an official to sign an affidavit verifying that you actually gambled at a particular time and lost a particular amount — assuming they know you and are familiar with your gambling patterns.

If you traveled out of town to gamble, you should keep hotel bills, airline tickets, gasoline receipts, credit card statements, canceled checks, and bank deposits and withdrawals to help corroborate your gambling winnings and losses.

The IRS will not accept as evidence of losses an informal and familiar system of comparing how much money you had in your pocket at the outset of the day, with the sum you had at the close of the day, with the difference representing the gain or loss.

3. High Rollers: Comps

If you are a high roller, casinos will "comp" you by giving you expensive gifts, equal to approximately 50 percent of the casino's anticipated win on your gambling. The value of the comps (e.g., expensive cars, jewelry) can be used to offset your gambling gains.

As you will see in the following case, comps are considered taxable income.

Example: *Libutti v. Commissioner,* T.C. Memo 1996-108.

Robert Libutti, Secaucus, New Jersey, was a high roller at Trump casino in Atlantic City, New Jersey. In 1987, Mr. Libutti gambled on 75 days, playing mainly craps, with an average bet of $15,000 and overall losses that year of more than $4 million. In 1988, Mr. Libutti gambled 179 days and had an overall loss of $3 million. In 1987, Trump gave him $443,000 in cars, jewelry, and vacations, and in 1988, gave him almost $1 million in cars, jewelry, and vacations. The casino was prohibited by law from providing cash comps to patrons, so instead it provided cars (mainly Rolls Royces and Ferraris). Mr. Libutti promptly sold the cars he received and in turn used the funds for more gambling at the casino.

The value of the comps constituted taxable income, just like ordinary gambling winnings. The IRS argued that Mr. Libutti could not deduct his gambling losses against the value of the comps, but only against his straightforward gambling winnings. Mr. Libutti argued in the US Tax Court that the comps were so closely associated with his gambling activity that they should be treated as wagering gains. The court sided with Mr. Libutti and held that such comps constituted taxable income as wagering gains, because they had a strong nexus to the taxpayer's wagering transactions, and therefore could be offset by

his wagering losses. The rationale is that the individual would not receive the comps but for the fact that he gambled extensively at the establishment. He received the comps due to his direct participation in wagering transactions.

The previous example provides the following key point:

1. In this important case, it was held that comps are part of a gambler's winnings. Thus, the value of jewelry, cars, and other property that a casino gives to a high roller customer are deemed wagering gains for tax purposes. That means these gains can be offset, under section 165(d), by wagering losses.

4. Chapter Summary

Very few people are professional gamblers. If you gamble full time and make a career of it, you are probably a professional gambler. As such, you are in the trade or business of gambling and you are entitled to take ordinary and necessary business expenses as tax deductions.

Many people who are casual gamblers try to take tax deductions for their gambling trips, but if they are audited they do not get these deductions.

Of course many people have a serious gambling problem. The tax law allows you to deduct gambling losses only to the extent of gambling gains. The philosophy behind this is that the government does not want to encourage people, with a tax break, to gamble to excess.

PART VI
OTHER BUSINESSES

19
COLLECTIBLES

A collectible is anything that merits being purchased, brought home, displayed, and arranged. Collecting is a great hobby, but it can also be a lucrative business. Many people make their livelihoods collecting and selling things.

Numerous magazines are devoted to collectibles, including *The Curio*, a journal established in 1887. According to the inaugural issue, "in truth, there is nothing that collectors will not collect."

The IRS takes the view that the lives of millions of people revolve around collectibles and that the most prominent purpose of the activity is personal pleasure. The IRS views any collecting activity as a hobby, particularly if the taxpayer fails to make a profit.

Hobbyists and serious collectors have much in common, so it is difficult to differentiate the two because they both —

- collect things that they are interested in,

- organize their collections so they know what they have,

- store their collections carefully to prevent damage,

- let others know that they are collectors, and

- find others who are collecting the same things to compare items and discuss trades.

The main thing that proves you are in the business rather than the hobby of collectibles, is that you make significant efforts to sell the items rather than hold onto them for the pleasure that owning them provides. A serious collector gathers things, but also sells them. A hobbyist will generally shy away from selling anything.

At the same time, some people have a legitimate expectation that, by holding onto certain collectibles, they will eventually be able to sell the items at a significant profit. Long-term gains can be realized by eventually selling assets that are held with the expectation that they will increase in value.

This chapter discusses the two types of activity that can generate tax deductions with collectibles:

1. Engaging in the business of buying and selling collectibles, meaning that you buy items and seek to sell them, either in your home, at trade shows, or in a store.

2. Acquiring and maintaining a collection as an investment for future production of income, much as you would with a stock portfolio.

1. Deductions for Costs Associated with the Management or Conservation of Your Investment Collection

Section 212 of the IRS Code allows you to take ordinary and necessary business deductions for costs of "the management, conservation, or maintenance of property, held for the production of income."

That means that if you hold a collection primarily as an investment — whether art, stamps, coins, or other collectibles — you are entitled to take tax deductions for costs associated with the management, conservation, or maintenance of your collection.

The expenses allowable under section 212 include consultations with investment advisers about your particular investment activity.

Also, you can deduct travel and related costs to attend conventions, seminars, or similar meetings as long as the meetings directly relate to your particular investment activity. Therefore, it would be questionable to deduct costs of attending a seminar on real estate if your particular investment pertains to collecting art. Also, the IRS seeks to ferret out travel expenses that are predominantly for vacations. It is important to show that your trips to conventions, conferences, and seminars have a direct bearing on your particular collection investment.

As for your ability to deduct the costs of travel to auctions to check out objects that you might acquire for your collection, you should always consult a tax professional. In principal they can qualify as deductions. Costs of research about your particular investment are generally allowed as well.

2. Art and Antiques

Walk into anyone's house and right away you'll see art on the walls and artifacts on the tables. Art has been recognized as an investment by leading art connoisseurs. Some of the wealthiest and shrewdest investors in the world buy art with the expectation that it will appreciate in value.

If you collect art as an investment, you are entitled to certain tax deductions. However, while many people collect valuable art, and expect to eventually sell items for a profit, the IRS often takes the view that their primary motivation for the collection is personal pleasure. That is what happened in the following case of a prominent New York couple.

Example: *Wrightsman v. United States,* 428 F.2d 1316 (Ct. Cl. 1970).

Charles and Jayne Wrightsman, New York, New York, were well-known collectors of art. Mr. Wrightsman made his fortune as a lease broker in the oil business and became the largest stockholder, and President, of Standard Oil Company of Kansas.

The couple initially started collecting art as a hobby and eventually had a multimillion-dollar collection. At one point they started treating their collection as an investment that they were holding for the production of income.

They devoted considerable time and effort to their collecting activity. Over the years they became art experts in their own right. A major portion of their typical day was devoted to studying works of art. They engaged in extensive reading in their chosen field of 18th century French art, and engaged in discussions with recognized art experts, museum curators, and others knowledgeable in the art world. They acquired a substantial art library. They traveled extensively to further enhance their knowledge of art and to make their collection known.

The Wrightsmans kept meticulous bookkeeping details of their collection. They maintained records of all acquisitions and detailed records of each work (noting the purchase price, date of purchase, and other details). They cataloged their art in 26 three-ring binder volumes that required a shelf space of about 5 feet. They provided air conditioning and humidity control considered necessary for the preservation of works of art.

The Metropolitan Museum of Art published a five-volume book on the Wrightsman Collection. Many of their works were on loan to museums. Mr. Wrightsman became a member of the Metropolitan Museum's Board of Trustees and served on its Purchasing Committee. Mrs. Wrightsman assisted Mrs. John F. Kennedy in redoing the White House during the term of President Kennedy.

The Wrightsmans claimed deductions in the management, conservation, and maintenance of their collection, claiming that these works were held for the production of income. The costs included insurance, maintenance, subscriptions and services, shipping, hotel, travel, entertainment, and other miscellaneous expenses.

The IRS argued that their art collecting was not an investment, but was primarily for their personal pleasure and enjoyment. The US Tax Court said that their personal lives revolved around their art collection and related activities,

and that the most prominent purpose of their activity was personal pleasure.

The court conceded that Mr. and Mrs. Wrightsman were wary of more risky investments and that they understandably regarded art as an investment. Their collection greatly increased in value and confirmed their financial wisdom. However, the court stated an important principle — that a potential for appreciation is inherent in many, if not most, collecting activities. That means that merely because the Wrightsmans may have expected the value of their collection to increase does not mean they were primarily motivated by an investment purpose rather than the personal satisfaction derived from pursuing a hobby.

The previous example provides the following key points:

1. This case is controversial because the taxpayers had significant evidence of their serious investment purpose behind the collection. They had a meticulous bookkeeping system. Also, they did not want to engage in the stock market, because they considered it too risky. They spent very little time at their New York apartment, where about 80 percent of the art objects were located.

2. The court was influenced by the considerable social aspects that surrounded their art collecting activity. Their social life revolved around it, coupled with extensive art-buying trips to Europe. The court found that their real motivation in collecting was their great love of art and the pleasures it afforded them.

3. The court was probably also influenced by the fact that there was no evidence that the taxpayers ever sold any of their art.

In the following case the taxpayer collected antique glass novelties. The court felt her activity was a hobby mainly because of lack of marketing and sales.

Example: *Stanley v. Commissioner*, **T.C. Memo 1980-217.**

Mary Stanley, Buffalo, New York, was a corporate officer of a steel company that her husband owned. Mrs. Stanley collected antique glass novelties. These included glass toys, figural bottles, and glass novelty dishes. She focused on glass novelties because they were within her price range and she believed the items would increase in value.

After ten years her collection consisted of more than 10,000 items. Of those, she had only several dozen items that were intended for resale. She insured her entire collection.

Mrs. Stanley sent out notices to antique dealers on a mailing list she compiled from trade journals, illustrating items she wanted to acquire and items she was willing to sell or trade. She frequented antique trade shows and shops throughout the United States.

Mrs. Stanley added to her collection by purchase or trade, and sought to increase the variety and quality of items in her collection. She replaced damaged items with ones of the same type in better condition. She tried to acquire rare items that would be more desirable for customers than the more common items.

She wrote a book about her collection, called *A Century of Glass Toys*, which was published. The book contained photographs of 1,250 glass novelties from her collection, accompanied by brief descriptions. The book was sold in various museum shops, but Mrs. Stanley received no royalties from the publisher.

After a dispute with the publisher, she sold the book herself. She advertised the book by direct mail to antique dealers and collectors of glass novelties, and placed advertisements in trade journals. She sold 637 copies as a result.

The book helped to establish Mrs. Stanley as an authority in the field of glass novelties and attracted attention to her collection. She also wrote articles in various trade journals. Various newspapers and magazines published articles of personal interest about Mrs. Stanley and her collection.

She displayed the collection throughout her three-story house. Most of the collection adorned home furnishings, while some parts were in display cases. Her collection was not open to the public during regular hours.

Mrs. Stanley did not have a separate checking account for the activity and she did not list her glass novelties venture in the phone book. However, Mrs. Stanley cataloged and described each item in her collection, and listed the cost of acquisition. She kept detailed records of her book sales. She kept copies of all correspondence concerning the collection.

The US Tax Court said that her records may have had "the trappings of a business," but this was "as consistent with a hobby as it is with a business."

The court noted that very few people actually came to look at her collection. In an average year only a few dealers would view her collection, and only by appointment. Members of clubs and her college alumnae group viewed the collection on private tours she conducted, but nothing was sold to these visitors.

The court noted that her house was zoned for residential use, not commercial activity, and she never applied for a variance permit.

The court said that Mrs. Stanley was sincere in her expectation that the collection would appreciate in value over time. However, the court said that "a potential for appreciation is inherent in many, if not most, of the items which have traditionally been collected as a hobby, e.g., stamps, coins, works of art, for the pleasure afforded by the acquisition and possession of the collection itself. The mere fact that a collector is aware that the value of his collection may increase does not mean that he is primarily motivated by an expectation of profit rather than the personal satisfaction derived from pursuing a hobby."

The court said that Mrs. Stanley's primary purpose was not to hold the collection for the production of income, but for personal satisfaction, and that she could not deduct her expenses connected with the collection.

Moreover, Mrs. Stanley never had the collection appraised. She testified that she reinsured her collection for double their cost, but the court did not believe that the potential for appreciation was enough to support a finding that Mrs. Stanley could ultimately make a profit through sales. Moreover, the court said that Mrs. Stanley had no plans to sell any of her collection.

The court noted that while Mrs. Stanley acquired many rare items that could be easily marketed, "virtually all those engaged in a hobby of collecting similarly seek to acquire rare items, not primarily for potential profit, but for a value placed on the rarity itself."

The previous example provides the following key points:

1. The taxpayer argued that she was engaged in two types of activity: one, that she was buying and selling collectibles as a business; and two, that the collection was held for the production of income as an investment. The court said that the activity had the trappings of a hobby, and that hobbyists often hold onto items with the expectation that they will increase in value.

2. The taxpayer wrote articles about her collection and even got a book published about it. The court said these publications were consistent with a hobby and that nothing in the articles indicated that anything was offered for sale. While it is useful to write articles about your collection in the press, this in itself does not distinguish the activity from a hobby.

3. It is important in a collectibles business to have a separate phone line dedicated to the activity, a listing in the White Pages and Yellow Pages (under the appropriate heading, e.g., "Antique Dealers"), a separate checking account for the venture, and for your location to be zoned for retail sales.

4. If you display your collection in your home, dedicate one room for that purpose rather than scattering the items throughout the house where they are obviously enjoyed as home furnishings.

5. If you are in the trade or business of buying and selling collectibles, there should be efforts to market items through advertising or other means. In this case people were invited to see the collection by invitation only.

6. Make sure you have the collection appraised periodically if you are holding it with the expectation that it will appreciate in value.

In the case *Dailey v. Commissioner* (included on the CD), the taxpayers also claimed that they considered their collection to be an investment, and they sought, unsuccessfully, to deduct the costs of trips to Europe to acquire more for their collection.

2.1 Antique shops

Many people decide to open antique shops in a storefront while others open shops in their homes. Either way, the IRS considers "gift shops" an area of special concern because of the potential for underreporting of income, as well as the hobby loss rule.

Sometimes audits will target retired individuals, as in the following case.

Example: *Barcus v. Commissioner,* **T.C. Memo 1973-138.**

Leonard Barcus, New Rochelle, New York, was manager of an optical plant. He and Mrs. Barcus decided to turn their long-standing antique collecting hobby into a business. They read literature on the antique business and operated their antique venture in their home, under the DBA "Marlen House."

They claimed that 95 percent of their household antique furnishings were for sale. On the third floor of their home they separated antiques that were not for sale. They stored a considerable number of items in the basement.

They had no sign on their house indicating that antiques were for sale and they did not advertise in newspapers, magazines, or any other outlets.

Mr. and Mrs. Barcus deducted maintenance costs of their house, telephone and utility bills, automobile mileage, and the costs of trips to Europe during which they went antique hunting.

Mrs. Barcus gave lectures on antiques and opened her house to charitable organizations, but there were very few actual customers coming to look at the collection.

The US Tax Court said that Mr. and Mrs. Barcus used their antiques as furnishings in their home. They "enjoyed purchasing antiques, enjoyed living with beautiful antiques in their home, and engaged in the purchase and sale of these items more as a way to reduce the cost of living in a home furnished with beautiful antiques than for the purpose of making a profit on the purchase and sale of those antiques."

The court said that they tended to acquire items that they personally liked and wanted to have in their home — rather than items that they could sell for a profit. Over the years, they bought many more items than they sold.

They held items over long periods of time and they refused to sell some items even when offered significant prices. For instance, they held onto a pair of oriental horsemen purchased for $125, even though they had been offered as much as $2,400 for the pair.

They reported a small profit in one year. However, the court said that this was a manipulated profit because the taxpayers simply underreported their true losses.

The previous example provides the following key points:

1. To operate an antiques business in your home, it is important to conduct the activity in a businesslike manner. That means that your residence is zoned for retail sales, your business is listed in the White Pages and the Yellow Pages, you have a sign out front, and you engage in some sort of advertising or promotion.

2. For any hobby loss situation, it is important to not artificially "create" a profit year

by manipulating accounts or by declaring a drastic reduction in costs — unless of course you actually did reduce costs to the extent indicated.

3. In this case, the taxpayers refused to sell some items despite being offered significant prices and this was further evidence of a hobby motive. If you hold onto items despite the fact that you are offered reasonable prices for them, this suggests that the items have sentimental or personal value to you, and that you are not really interested in selling them.

Many people decide to open up an antique shop in town, where there are other shops and some foot traffic. Operating out of a storefront instead of your home does not automatically mean that you are operating a business rather than a hobby.

Example: *Estate of Brockenbrough v. Commissioner,* **T.C. Memo 1998-454.**

Edward Brockenbrough worked as a pilot for Delta Airlines and his wife was a flight attendant. After he retired they bought a farm in Gay, Georgia, town with several antiques stores. They decided to buy a building in town and opened an antique store called "Olde Bank Antiques." Mrs. Brockenbrough ran the store and Mr. Brockenbrough helped out.

While they were away they relied on friends to run the store. They put a few advertisements in the local paper, but had very few sales. After about five years of not making a profit, they decided to gradually sell off their inventory. Two years later, they sold their remaining inventory at an auction and sold the building.

They deducted the antique store expenses against their principal sources of income.

The US Tax Court held that the antique store was not a business, but had more elements of a hobby.

Mr. and Mrs. Brockenbrough had no business plan. They did very little advertising. They had no experience operating a retail store or other business experience, and they did not seek any advice about how to improve their ability to make a profit.

The court noted that they waited two years after they knew the business could not be profitable before they finally liquidated their inventory. During that period they continued to depreciate the building and incur expenses.

The court also said that it was not businesslike for them to rely on unpaid friends to run the store when they were away.

The previous example provides the following key points:

1. Prior to starting an antique shop, it is important to investigate the feasibility of making money at it, and to document your efforts in this regard. If you do not honestly believe you can make a profit in a venture, it is inappropriate to claim it is a business.

2. With an antique or gift shop it is important to advertise or otherwise engage in efforts to attract customers. It is important to hire people who have experience working in a retail store.

3. If you decide to wind down a venture because it is not making the profits you had hoped, it is prudent to proceed diligently to sell off your inventory, so as to help minimize further losses.

4. With an antique shop or gift shop, it is important to know what items you have sold and what is in your inventory.

3. Rocks and Crystals

Millions of people are avid collectors of rocks, crystals, and other minerals. Other types of collectibles fall into this category, such as fossils and meteorites.

Most of these people are hobbyists, but those who sell crystals, rocks, and other mineral items often are engaged in a full-time business. There is a huge market of people interested in buying these beautiful objects. Many vendors do the trade show circuit, selling their collections across the country. Others set up shop at home. Vendors need to keep on top of the market, find good sources of supplies, and use their best efforts at making sales.

In the following case, an individual claimed that his rock collecting activity was a business, but he failed to conduct the activity in any way that resembled a business.

Example: *Griesmer v. Commissioner,* T.C. Memo 1999-147.

Wilbur Griesmer, Cleveland, Ohio, was a factory worker for most of his life. When he retired, he started a collection of rocks and minerals, particularly meteorites, which he believed were quite valuable.

He claimed he was in the business of selling rocks and minerals. He incurred losses over a period of several years. Mr. Griesmer had a modest retirement income, but nonetheless the losses helped reduce his taxable income. He never offered any of his specimens for sale and he kept no records of his activity.

The US Tax Court held that he did not conduct the activity with the requisite profit objective. "The ultimate goal of an activity engaged in for profit must be to realize a net profit from the activity so as to recoup losses sustained in prior years."

The court noted that Mr. Griesmer maintained no books or records, and he did not have any special skill or expertise with regard to meteorites. He did not have a single dollar in gross receipts and he did not offer any part of his collection for sale. Rather, he generated significant tax benefits by offsetting losses from his collection activity against his retirement income and dividends.

The previous example provides the following key points:

1. Most people who are in the trade or business of selling rocks, crystals, or other mineral items devote a significant amount of time in marketing their inventory, in contrast to the situation in this case.

2. Needless to say, if an individual never offers items for sale, and does not even keep books or records, the activity is clearly a hobby, not a business.

4. Stamps and Coins

Many people claim they buy and sell stamps or coins as a business. This breaks into two types of situations:

1. It can be an activity in which you buy and sell stamps or coins for profit.

2. The activity can be an investment, where your principal purpose is to manage and maintain your stamp or coin collection, eventually disposing of it to reap a profit.

Either way, there is a business purpose — the near-term or long-term production of income.

Remember, if you claim that you are holding your collection as an investment for the production of income, your tax deductions are governed by the provisions of section 212 discussed earlier in this chapter (see section 1.). Certain things cannot be taken as write-offs.

For people who are engaged in buying and selling stamps or coins as a business, there is a huge retail market consisting of individual collectors as well as other dealers. Those who are earnest about making money in this area, whether on a large or small scale, will actively seek to sell items, rather than hold onto inventory. Also, those who regard this venture as a business attend stamp expos, take out vendors' tables at meets and trade shows, and otherwise actively buy and sell their inventory.

Both hobbyists and serious dealers usually want to hold onto stamps or coins that could significantly appreciate in value. By holding onto these assets, one can eventually sell them at significantly higher prices than the present market bears.

It is no surprise that many people regard collecting stamps or coins to be an investment. However, a taxpayer's mere statement that the collection is really an investment and is expected to appreciate in value is not enough to claim the collection as an investment. You will have to provide evidence that your predominant motive is to maintain the collection as an investment, rather than for the pleasure the collection affords you.

The following example is the leading case on this point, which ruled in favor of the taxpayer's claim that his stamp collection was an investment.

Example: *Tyler v. Commissioner,* 6 TCM 275.

George Tyler, Newtown, Pennsylvania, was a highly wealthy individual. He started stamp collecting in the 1920s because he was impressed with the investment possibilities in stamps as described to him by friends. He sought the advice of a professional philatelist who published a journal for other stamp collectors. Mr. Tyler spent a fortune on stamp collections as recommended by his adviser (who also functioned as his broker), hoping that the collection would increase in value and that he could eventually sell it for a profit, subject to capital gains tax instead of ordinary income tax.

Mr. Tyler, for his part, was not particularly interested in stamps. He did not attend functions of the American Philatelic Society and did not read philatelic publications. However, he spent countless hours organizing his collection of 500,000 stamps into albums, with the help of his adviser.

His bookkeeper maintained records of his purchases and sales of stamps in exactly the same manner as he maintained records for his other investments. He insured his collection and he opened a separate bank account, that he used for all transactions relating to stamps.

After the stock market crash in 1929 the value of his stamp collection plummeted, and he decided to sell much of his collection because he needed the money for a new house. He sold more stamps at a loss in 1938, after he decided it was only a question of time before there would be another world war. The sales resulted in a net loss of more than $210,000, and he sought to deduct this loss against other income.

The US Tax Court held that Mr. Tyler's testimony was credible, but more importantly, that he sought out expert advice and followed that advice in the purchase and sale of stamps. Also, the court was impressed by the fact that he maintained businesslike records of his activity.

The court noted that Mr. Tyler obviously took great pleasure in his stamp collection, but that his desire to make a profit was the most important motive that led him to acquire his collection, and that his personal pleasure in collecting stamps was secondary. The court concluded that Mr. Tyler's principal motivation was to carry on an enterprise for profit. Thus, the loss sustained was deductible.

The previous example provides the following key points:

1. To collect stamps or coins as an investment you should consult a knowledgeable investment adviser, with the understanding that you wish to realize long-term gains for your collection. If you do not have expertise in a given area, it is important to rely on individuals who can advise you on how to proceed in the venture. Follow the advice obtained unless you have good reason not to.

2. Find a good dealer from whom you can start acquiring your collection. Familiarize yourself, through expert advice and research, with which stamps or coins are likely to be good investment opportunities. Research this as much as you might research a stock you are contemplating buying.

3. If you are already an expert in stamps or coins, you may be qualified to make your own investment decisions, based on your experience and understanding of the market for these items.

4. You should keep abreast of market prices, and if you have opportunities to sell certain items at a profit, you should seriously consider doing so. Again, this is much like dealing with the stock market in terms of decision making. Often it is wise to hold onto valuable property with the expectation that it will further increase in value.

5. Your records should be clear enough to indicate the contents of your inventory, your acquisition costs, and your selling prices. You should also have copies of invoices for each item sold.

6. Your collection should be insured against fire and theft.

7. You should periodically obtain a written appraisal by an experienced philatelist for your stamp collection, or numismatist for your coin or paper money collection.

8. Remember that under section 212 you are only entitled to deduct certain costs associated with the management, conservation, or maintenance of property held for the production of income.

Many people who buy and sell stamps as a business focus their attention on "first day of issue" stamps. The US Postal Service releases new stamps on a specific day at a specific location. Since 1930, a special cancellation bearing the words "FIRST DAY OF ISSUE" along with the date and town of issue, has been applied to stamped items given to the Postal Service on the first day the stamp is issued. This service is provided by the US Postal Service at no charge, other than the cost of the stamps.

A "first day cover" is an envelope that bears a stamp postmarked with a "first day of issue" cancellation. In some instances, the envelope includes a decorative design, usually related to the subject matter of the applied stamp. By the 1940s, hundreds of thousands of first day covers were routinely prepared by collectors for every newly issued stamp and had become an important part of stamp collecting.

Example: *Feistman v. Commissioner,* T.C. Memo 1982-306.

Eugene and Lorraine Feistman, Sepulveda, California, had full-time jobs as a probation officer and a teacher, respectively. They collected stamps and coins for many years as a hobby, and then decided to set up a business called "Feistman Stamps, Coins and Accessories."

They operated at a loss for several years. There were two US Tax Court cases concerning their activities. They lost the first case. In that case the court said that they had poor record keeping, they did not operate the activity out of an office or store, and they carried on the venture much in the same way as when they considered it to be a hobby.

After they lost, they changed methods of operation. They devoted a single room in their house to the activity. They spent considerable time purchasing first day covers. They visited customers, attended trade shows, and set up tables at swap meets where they offered stamps for sale. They also attended auctions to purchase collections of stamps. They kept a log of revenues, inventory purchases, and expenses. They obtained a Business Tax Registration Certificate issued by the city, bearing the classification "Retail Sales." They maintained a separate bank account for the venture.

The second tax case considered these changes, and ruled that the Feistmans' activity was a business, not a hobby.

The court noted that they spent considerable time purchasing first day covers for each new stamp issued and bought large quantities of them — an amount far in excess of the requirements of a hobby. Also, they regularly displayed stamps for sale at shows and swap meets. They had a growing inventory, an increased level of activity, and a fairly steady march towards actually making a profit. The losses were declining and in one year they actually made a modest profit.

The court said that it was quite difficult to identify the precise time at which the venture became sufficiently independent from the initial hobby activity to constitute a business.

The previous example provides the following key points:

1. The taxpayers were seriously intent on buying and selling stamps as a business. They changed methods of operation from how they operated as a hobby, focused on first day covers, and operated in a more businesslike manner. The court felt that the large quantity of first day covers they bought indicated a business, rather than a hobby.

2. The taxpayers actively engaged in marketing their collection by taking out tables at trade shows, swap meets, and other venues.

3. The taxpayers kept good business records, including a log of revenues and expenses, and a complete inventory. They had a separate checking account for the venture and obtained a retail sales license from the city.

5. Model Railroads

A number of people make a living selling new and antique model trains. As with any venture, it is necessary to conduct the activity in a businesslike manner and show some degree of diligence in selling your wares. In the following case, a model train enthusiast failed to convince the US Tax Court that his activity was a business.

Example: *Lencke v. Commissioner,* **T.C. Memo** 1997-284.

James Lencke, Lafayette, Indiana, collected model railroads since childhood and displayed his elaborate collection in the basement of his home. Mr. Lencke was very knowledgeable about model railroads.

After retiring from his job as an insurance agent, he visited model railroad shows and sought advice from various vendors on how to make money with model railroads. He then started a venture called "Red Caboose." He decided to focus on selling model railroad items to wholesalers.

He attended model railroad shows in order to display and sell merchandise, but his main focus was mail-order sales. He used the trade shows as a way of attracting mail-order customers.

He advertised in model railroad and toy magazines, and published a flyer describing his venture and listing his merchandise for sale. Mr. Lencke distributed the flyers at trade shows. He created business cards and obtained a retail merchant certificate. He and his wife carefully selected merchandise for each show and gauged pricing according to prices that were published in model railroad magazines, Sometimes they adjusted their prices downward to meet competition from other vendors. He and his wife kept track of which items sold well and which items needed to be re-ordered. They deducted costs of table rental fees, postage, advertising, utilities, banking fees, and travel expenses.

The venture sustained sizable losses for a number of years, yet Mr. Lencke failed to change methods of operation other than to stay at less expensive hotels while attending trade shows.

Gross receipts were quite small in the first three years then increased to $8,000 and up to $16,000 in subsequent years, but losses regularly exceeded the income from the activity.

Mr. Lencke did not have a business plan and he did not consider how to improve the profitability of his activity. He did not obtain a separate phone line for Red Caboose.

The US Tax Court held that his model railroad activity was a hobby, not a business. The court said that his business records were on the haphazard side. The court said that Mr. Lencke commingled the records of Red Caboose with his personal records and recorded sales in his personal appointment book, and that much of his expenditures involved personal expenses.

The court noted that Mr. Lencke was able to use the losses to offset substantial pension income, and that the venture provided him and his wife with a method for achieving tax savings while enabling them to pursue his lifelong hobby activity.

The previous example provides the following key points:

1. This case could have gone either way. The taxpayer exerted considerable effort to sell model railroads to buyers and garnered significant revenue in some years. The court seemed more influenced by what it characterized as poor records, the lack of a business plan, the lack of a separate phone line, sloppy sales records, and the commingling of funds.

2. The court was also influenced by the taxpayer's lifelong hobby interest in model railroads, and the fact that the significant and ongoing losses enabled him to offset his tax liability from his sizable pension income.

6. Chapter Summary

Collecting is unique for everyone. In the process of collecting, you continue to learn. As you build any collection, you apply skills in identifying, selecting, discriminating, evaluating, classifying, and arranging items.

The main difference between a hobby and a business or investment in this area is the taxpayer's intention to market the items. A hobbyist usually does not want to sell anything in their collection.

If you are collecting for the purpose of selling the items, it is important to actively engage in marketing efforts at trade shows, flea markets, and expos. It is also important to advertise in trade journals and local newspapers, and on the Internet.

If you are collecting as an investment, you are entitled to certain tax deductions for the management of your investment under section 212 of the IRS Code. You should have an investment adviser familiar with the art, antiques, coins, or stamps that you are collecting.

A serious collector will examine the market to determine how supply and demand affect the value of the collectibles. It is important, if you are in the venture as a vendor or as an investor, to obtain expert advice on marketing strategies, trends in your field, as well as what to buy, what to sell, and when to sell.

Whether you are a vendor or an investor, it is important not to inflate tax deductions, or to deduct personal expenses, as this could give the impression that your sole motivation is to reduce your income tax liability. The IRS may scrutinize situations where people have other income that is substantial, maintain a luxurious lifestyle traveling and visiting European auction houses, and do not make money from their collectibles.

Overall, the quality of your business records is very important in this area, perhaps more so than in other hobby activities. It is crucial to maintain a current inventory of your collection, to have a separate checking account and dedicated phone line, to have business cards, and to issue sales invoices for anything you sell.

20
TREASURE HUNTING

Treasure hunting on land and in the water has captured the imagination of the public in recent years. People who are serious about locating shipwrecks or prospecting for gold usually devote more than the equivalent of full-time work to the endeavor. Such ventures require optimism, perception, perseverance, and planning.

The hobby loss rule comes into play with individuals who, on a small scale, get involved in treasure hunting on the cheap. You can buy metal detectors and look up maps of abandoned gold mines to try your hand at treasure hunting. You can have a good deal of fun at this and it does not entail much by way of costs, compared to full-scale shipwreck recoveries. However, if you claim your prospecting or treasure hunting activity is a business rather than a hobby, you will have to convince the IRS.

1. Shipwrecks

Making money hunting for shipwrecks is an expensive endeavor and highly speculative. In order to fund shipwreck-salvaging operations, private investors are needed. Finding backers who are financially able and willing to invest in the undertaking is no easy task because the undertaking is a gamble. If unsuccessful, the investors will lose their money. If the recovery is successful, there is the inescapable push by investors to make a profit by selling recovered artifacts.

There is considerable preliminary research needed to decide which wrecks to recover, and to prepare for the daunting challenge of finding them. You need to collect and assemble all available information that might assist in the actual search for and location of the particular ship.

Archaeologists are usually part of the team, as they know how to care for and preserve the items salvaged. A great deal of machinery and equipment is needed to conduct a salvage operation. For example, you might need equipment that can recover heavy objects (such as an anchor), as well as delicate items (such as gold coins, china, or pottery), without damaging them. Sometimes certain equipment needs to be specially designed, manufactured, and assembled for the project.

Example: *Harrison v. Commissioner,* T.C. Memo 1996-509.

Frederick Harrison, Sr., Marlton, New Jersey owned and operated trucking and solid waste removal businesses. He became interested in underwater treasure salvaging. He investigated several possible opportunities, met with people who had invested in salvage operations, and read books on treasure hunting.

He ended up forming a joint venture with an operation called "International Recoveries." The operation was headed by an individual who was an expert in salvage operations. Mr. Harrison investigated the background of International Recoveries before deciding to participate in this venture, and studied business plans and maps that were shown to him concerning sunken treasure.

He had no budget for participating in the venture, but agreed to provide $50,000 in costs, and managed to negotiate a greater percentage of profits than was originally offered him. Mr. Harrison also paid for metal cages that would be lowered to protect divers from sharks and other underwater dangers.

During a one-year period his total expenses came to $201,000. The venture had three expeditions off the Florida Keys and the Gulf Coast.

Mr. Harrison spent considerable time working with the salvage team. He drove a truck carrying heavy equipment from Arizona to the Texas coast, he spent 35 to 40 days working long hours each night manning pumping equipment operations, and when he was away from the group he kept in touch by calling in for progress reports one to three times a week. He also frequently contacted the captain of the vessel to determine if any progress was being made. The three operations failed to find anything of value.

The US Tax Court held that he was engaged in the venture as a business, not a hobby, and allowed his tax deductions. The court said: "Careful investigation of a potential business to insure the best chance for profitability strongly indicates an objective to engage in the activity for profit. While a formal market study is not required, a basic investigation of the factors that would affect profit generally is."

The court said that while Mr. Harrison was not an expert in treasure hunting, he did align himself with experts and this gave the venture an opportunity to be successful.

The court said that Mr. Harrison's record keeping left something to be desired (he simply kept handwritten notes of the expenditures made), but that this did not negate his profit motive. "Lack of record keeping is not determinative of intent. Treasure hunting is not the type of business where thorough records of gains and losses are necessary to a successful operation."

The court noted that treasure hunting is an activity likely to generate only costs, with no income until a find is made, at which time the income will come in a lump sum.

The court said that Mr. Harrison entered the activity "with the belief that if treasure were found the return would be so great that all of his expenses would be recouped and a substantial profit would be realized."

The court said that Mr. Harrison spent a significant amount of time on the activity, and that the nature of the time spent could hardly be called recreational or pleasurable. "He was not merely an investor who made the occasional inquiry into the operations; petitioner participated in the daily operations ... negotiated contracts, arranged equipment rentals, and transported equipment."

The court also seemed impressed that Mr. Harrison only participated in the venture for one year, after which he abandoned it because he didn't think it could be profitable at that point.

The previous example provides the following key points:

1. In this case, the taxpayer won despite the lack of adequate business records, primarily because he carefully investigated the treasure hunting venture before investing in it, and he spent a considerable amount of time and effort monitoring the project.

2. In this case, the court took a sympathetic approach to the inadequate business records and the lack of a budget. It is important to have evidence of adequate or better-than-adequate business records to rebut the allegation that the venture is merely a hobby.

3. The court noted that treasure hunting can require a period of time during which there are significant costs, and that it is a highly speculative venture, but one that stands a chance of reaping great sums of money if and when one finds something valuable.

4. The taxpayer incurred substantial costs, but bailed out after the venture proved unsuccessful. Abandoning an unprofitable venture is evidence that your primary motive is to engage in an activity for profit.

In the case *Reed v. Commissioner* (included on the CD), the taxpayer researched locations of ancient shipwrecks, bought sophisticated equipment, and became an expert in his own right on treasure hunting. He convinced the US Tax Court that his treasure hunting activity was a business, not a hobby.

2. Gold Prospecting

Gold prospecting is another intriguing area of treasure hunting. You will see in the following case how important it is to research a prospect before you convert your hobby into a business.

Example: *Hezel v. Commissioner,* **T.C. Memo 1985-10.**

William Hezel, St. Louis, Missouri, was an engineer. He became interested in prospecting as a hobby — that is, looking for gold treasures on land sites — and soon decided he could make money at it.

He entered into a written agreement with an individual named Ankarlo, who was familiar with the gold mining regions of Arizona and New Mexico. Under this agreement, Mr. Hezel paid $4,000 for Ankarlo's prospecting services, and the two agreed to pool their efforts to find a certain gold brick treasure that was rumored to be buried in Socano County, New Mexico. They searched several sites and dug up a number of dry holes, but found nothing of value.

Mr. Hezel sought to deduct his modest exploration costs of $4,600, which included the $4,000 fee paid to his prospecting partner.

The US Tax Court denied the deductions, ruling that the treasure hunting activity was a hobby. The court said that there were no business records other than the contract with Ankarlo. Mr. Hezel had no prior experience in treasure hunting other than having read a "gold-hunter's book," and Ankarlo admitted in court that he had never found gold in previous searches. The court also noted that Mr. Hezel spent very little time on the activity — only about a week — and he also apparently enjoyed side trips into the desert areas of Arizona and New Mexico.

The previous example provides the following key points:

1. In order to do prospecting as a business you need to plan a little better than in this example. It is certainly helpful to hire someone who is an experienced prospector, but in this case the taxpayer hired someone who had zero success in prior searches.

2. In this case there were no business records at all, other than the written contract with the prospector. The court felt that while there was a written contract engaging the other party's prospecting services, it was not enough to convert a hobby interest into a business.

3. Business records should include evidence of investigation and research you conducted before embarking on the particular prospecting venture.

3. Chapter Summary

Speculative activities qualify as a business, rather than a hobby, if the individual has an honest intention to be engaged in a business and make a profit. In the area of treasure hunting, people may incur substantial expenses and great risk of danger in hope of a substantial reward. To some extent, treasure hunters are gamblers, but many of them have struck it rich with their finds. The motto, "Nothing ventured, nothing gained," is prevalent in this field.

The IRS tends to view dilettante-type treasure hunting as a hobby. In order to withstand IRS scrutiny and support your claim that the activity is a business, not a hobby, it is important to do a preliminary study. You should research historical records (such as manifests and cargo shipping records) and the site or sites you and your associates wish to explore. Estimate how long you think it might take, what kind of booty you can expect to find, what equipment you will need, what dangers are involved, and any other information relevant to your particular project.

21
VACATION RENTALS AND TRAVEL CONSULTING

Making money by owning your own resort, lodge, or bed-and-breakfast (B&B) can be profitable, but also time-consuming. Some people begin with the idea of a vacation retreat for family and friends, and then decide to develop the place into a resort complex.

Under the hobby loss rule, the IRS is mainly looking to see whether the vacation rental is more than the family's personal retreat. The IRS will look to see what efforts were made to get paying customers. As in other hobby loss situations, it is important to maintain adequate books and records of the venture, as well as to generate business by advertising.

Advertising is important to any vacation rental business. It is helpful to have a website and a brochure with a synopsis of what you offer and pictures of the rooms and amenities. In order to promote your venture, it is important to advertise with travel agents, realtors, and in guidebooks. If you establish good relations with various travel agents, you can become one of their regular referrals. They will expect a commission for these re-

ferrals. If your business is a B&B, there are brokers that can list your inn.

You might also list your services in a number of national travel magazines. You should develop a mailing list of customers and keep in touch with them to help generate word-of-mouth advertising, solicit repeat business, offer special discounts, or announce special events in your community that they may want to attend.

This chapter mainly focuses on operating vacation getaways in a businesslike manner, but there is also a section discussing travel consulting as a business.

1. Bed-and-Breakfasts

The IRS targets people who claim to be operating bed-and-breakfasts, if they have a very low occupancy rate and do little to advertise or promote their business. The IRS believes that the taxpayers are mainly interested in taking significant tax deductions for the costs of maintaining their homes.

As you will see in the following case, it is important to advertise your B&B.

Example: *Hogan v. Commissioner,* **T.C. Summary Opinion 2003-8.**

James Hogan, Killbuck, New York, owned a six-bedroom house and worked full time as an elementary school principal. He decided to convert his house into a B&B venture. He filed a DBA in his county and operated under the name "Camelot Inn." Mr. Hogan had no prior experience operating a B&B, and he did not consult with any experts before starting the venture.

During the four years that were considered, he had losses each year ranging from $26,000 to $55,000. He deducted costs of advertising, car and truck depreciation, insurance, mortgage interest, legal services, office expenses, repairs and maintenance, supplies, taxes and licenses, travel and meals, and utilities.

Camelot Inn was not going to get drive-by business because it was off the beaten track, so Mr. Hogan advertised in local publications and, at times, reduced the price charged for rooms. He maintained simple but adequate books and records of the activity and had a separate bank account for the business.

The US Tax Court said that while the books and records were adequate, Camelot Inn was not operated in a businesslike manner. Mr. Hogan had no experience running such a venture and never investigated how to make money operating a B&B. The court said that, given his full-time employment as a principal, he had very little time to devote to making the venture profitable.

Mr. Hogan argued that he expected the property to appreciate in value and offered a formal appraisal as evidence. However, the court said that the accumulated losses of the venture exceeded the residence's appreciation in value.

The court said that Mr. Hogan was primarily motivated by the ability to use the losses to reduce his gross income, because these reductions led to substantial tax savings for him. The court concluded that he did not operate the activity with an intent to make a profit, and disallowed his deductions.

The previous example provides the following key points:

1. If you have no prior experience operating a B&B, it is important to investigate beforehand how you might make a profit from this activity.

2. In operating a B&B it is usually important to advertise in order to attract customers, especially if the location is off the beaten track.

2. Resorts

The IRS views with suspicion family-run "resorts" where there are few outside guests and little advertising or promotion. If a family-operated resort incurs a history of losses, the IRS will argue that the venture is nothing more than a family vacation retreat and deny the tax deductions. Thus, it is very important when undertaking such a venture to make sure the lessons learned from the following cases are observed.

Example: *Baldwin v. Commissioner,* **T.C. Memo 2002-162.**

This case was previously mentioned in Chapter 19 in connection with tax deductions for the taxpayer's aircraft.

Lucian Baldwin III, a wealthy bond trader in Winnetka, Illinois, found vacation property at Lake Superior. It consisted of 5,000 acres, with a lodge complex and numerous buildings and quarters.

He wanted to develop it as a lodge that could be rented for corporate retreats. He hired a general contractor to restore the lodge and to make major improvements. He had personal living quarters built for his family and he hired a full-time caretaker.

Only invited guests, relatives, and business acquaintances used the lodge. No efforts were ever made to rent rooms to the public. In fact, Mr. Baldwin decided not to operate it as a commercial lodge because he did not want to curtail his family's use of the facility or open it to strangers, yet he claimed the lodge as a business and took substantial deductions against his income as a bond trader.

Mr. Baldwin billed one of his other companies for every night spent at the lodge by his family, friends, and business acquaintances. He said this was evidence that he was conducting a rental business.

Mr. Baldwin insured the lodge as his personal residence and insured all the recreational vehicles at the lodge as his personal property. He never had title to the lodge transferred into the corporate entity that he utilized to operate the lodge.

The US Tax Court said the primary use of the property was as a vacation retreat for the Baldwins. The renovations were designed primarily to enable the Baldwins to use the lodge as their personal residence. The court said that while there were occasional business guests, that in itself did not support a conclusion that the lodge was a business.

The court said that Mr. Baldwin did not engage in any meaningful research regarding the likelihood of operating a lodge for profit. He made no effort to evaluate the operating costs. Neither Mr. Baldwin nor his advisers had any significant experience operating a vacation rental facility.

The court said that Mr. Baldwin failed to obtain licenses or permits to operate a commercial facility under Michigan law, the lodge was not insured for business use, and there were no state liquor tax returns or sales tax payments on gross receipts.

Also, the court noted that the property cost $4.3 million and Mr. Baldwin invested about $2.5 million in improvements, plus millions more in operating costs. At the time of trial the property was appraised at $3.8 million.

The previous example provides the following key points:

1. In this case the evidence was overwhelming that the resort property was for the exclusive use of family, friends, and invited business guests. It was simply a private family retreat.

2. The resort was not operated in a business-like manner. There was no effort made to attract customers and the property was not licensed to be used as a commercial facility. The insurance on the property was not for commercial purposes. The renovation and decoration of the lodge was designed solely with the family's needs in mind.

3. The taxpayer argued that in addition to operating a commercial property, he made improvements with the expectation that he could sell the property for a profit. However, his costs were so high that it was difficult to see how he could make a profit even if he did sell the property at the value he presented.

If you decide to purchase a resort outside of the United States, it is a good idea to research the laws and regulations for running the business in the foreign country. The taxpayer lost because of lack of research, in the case *Monfore v. U.S.* (included on the CD).

A long history of losses could indicate that your venture is not run in a businesslike manner, which is what happened in the following case.

Example: *Morring v. Commissioner,* **T.C. Memo 1995-403.**

Clinton Morring, New Alexandria, Pennsylvania, enjoyed scouting since age eleven. He established a venture called Appalachian Trails, which was located on his property and consisted of an outdoor recreation center with outfitting for backpacking, camping, and similar outdoor activities for scout, church, and family groups.

He built campsites, trails, and parking areas. The property was located near state parks, camping sites, and forests, so it had much to offer people interested in the outdoors.

He maintained informal records of expenses and receipts, and opened a separate bank account for the venture. He kept a logbook of equipment and utility costs. He had no outside advisers, but relied on his own experience in outdoor recreation.

He had one telephone number for himself, but also had it listed as Appalachian Trails. The venture was listed in the Yellow Pages and he put up road signs pointing to the center.

His promotional efforts for Appalachian Trails were sporadic. He distributed pamphlets to local churches, scouting groups, and acquaintances. He sometimes invited people to a slide show regarding Appalachian Trails. He hoped that if the venture became profitable, he would engage in it full time and quit his day job as a factory worker.

Mr. Morring sustained losses during a 20-year period, for which he took tax deductions to offset his main source of income.

The US Tax Court said that despite some businesslike records, there were too many facts

suggesting the activity was not a business. The court said that Mr. Morring's full-time job severely limited the amount of time he could devote to the venture and that his promotional efforts were minimal. The court noted that at times Mr. Morring allowed groups to use the facilities for free or for minimal charges. Also, he never developed a written business plan or sought expert advice regarding running an outdoor recreational center.

The court said that while Mr. Morring was experienced in outdoor recreational activities, he had no experience running a recreational center as a business. The court said that under the current manner of operating the activity, Mr. Morring stood very little chance of ever making a profit.

The court said that Mr. Morring's main motivation was his enjoyment of scouting activities and his desire to promote a sense of community. "The activity is commendable because of the social accomplishment. Petitioner's own testimony is that he derived personal pleasure from the outdoor activity and would have much preferred spending his days in such outdoor activities instead of in the factory work he was required to perform to support his family."

The court said that regardless of the worthiness of Mr. Morring's venture, he did not operate Appalachian Trails with an actual and honest objective of making a profit.

The previous example provides the following key points:

1. The strong element of personal pleasure and recreation, and the taxpayer's love of scouting and outdoor activities, suggested that this venture was a hobby.

2. There was some evidence of a businesslike manner of operating the venture, including a separate checking account, a listing in the Yellow Pages, and adequate records of income and expenses. This was not

enough to overcome evidence of the taxpayer's personal pleasure and recreation in the venture.

3. Giving free access or charging only minimal fees to users of a resort facility is not businesslike. However, at times it is a useful form of promotion to provide complementary accommodations to people who can help promote your venture (such as travel agents, travel writers, or business people who want to plan retreats for their companies).

4. A long history of losses (20 years in this case) is overwhelming evidence that the venture is not conducted in a businesslike manner.

In the case of **Furey v. Commissioner** (included on the CD), the taxpayer claimed he was engaged in a hotel development enterprise. He took substantial travel and entertainment deductions, but never got any project going. The US Tax Court held that his real motive was pleasure and recreation.

The following is a case where the taxpayer was able to prove that certain setbacks in running his resort were due to circumstances beyond his control, and this helped convince the US Tax Court that he was operating a business, not a hobby.

Example: *Akerson v. Commissioner,* T.C. Memo 1998-129.

Steven Akerson, an American taxpayer living in Costa Rica, was a physicist in solar energy. He worked in Costa Rica manufacturing and installing solar powered equipment. In addition, he decided to buy a five-room hotel equipped with a restaurant and pool, and located on a bay.

He purchased ten adjoining acres for the resort. He bought four sailboats to attract guests and he installed a solar powered generator to purify water.

Mr. Akerson kept accurate books and records of the resort's income and expenses. He printed brochures to advertise the resort. He saved on costs by doing all of the repair work himself. He hired an attorney to tend to legal issues, who also helped manage the resort when Mr. Akerson was away.

It was hard for tourists to reach the property because the government had failed to pave surrounding roads. Also, despite promises from the phone company to provide telephone service, there was none. There were also international tensions in the region that adversely affected tourism.

Mr. Akerson made a net profit in two years, but lost money over six years.

The US Tax Court said that Mr. Akerson honestly intended to make a profit in the venture. While the losses may have been greater than desired, it was largely due to the political difficulties in the region and the lack of proper access to the resort.

The court said that Mr. Akerson came across as very believable in his testimony. The court said: "Generally, a taxpayer's unimpeached, competent, and relevant testimony may not be arbitrarily discredited and disregarded by the Court."

The court concluded that he had a profit motive in operating his resort activity.

The previous example provides the following key points:

1. The taxpayer came across as a very credible witness and this helped convince the court that he had an honest intention of operating the resort as a business, not a hobby.

2. If there are financial setbacks beyond your control, or other circumstances (such as the political unrest in this case), it is important to gather and keep information to help prove this. Evidence of setbacks that are beyond your control is important to explain losses.

3. The taxpayer had an overall businesslike manner in operating the resort. He disseminated brochures, did repair work himself (thus saving on costs), and hired an attorney to write up documents as well as to assist in managing the resort. Also, the taxpayer actually did make a profit in two years, and this was helpful to his case.

If there are setbacks due to market conditions that help explain losses, it is important to keep evidence of the circumstances just as the taxpayer did in the case of *Allen v. Commissioner*, included on the CD.

3. Travel Consulting

Many people work as travel agents or travel consultants, whether in a firm or as independent contractors. Travel agents and consultants usually make a small commission on sales they make, but one of the great benefits of this work is the opportunity for free travel.

As a travel agent or consultant you can get "familiarization trips," or FAM trips, which give you an opportunity to become familiar with a travel-related area, a particular tour or cruise, or a specific program. Sometimes FAM trips are sponsored by government agencies or other groups that pay the costs.

Some people who consider themselves travel consultants have very few clients and devote little time or effort to actually advising people about travel or booking tours. The IRS believes that some travel consultants are really hobbyists trying to write off their pleasure trips around the world.

It is important for travel agents and consultants to operate in a businesslike manner. You should have business cards and stationery, a dedicated phone line, a listing in the phone book, and records of each tour or trip you have booked.

If you spend time providing advice — which comprises a great amount of a travel consultant's time — it is a good idea to keep phone logs or memoranda about consultations you have provided. This can be documentary evidence to prove that you are engaged in a business.

If you consider yourself a travel agent or consultant, it is crucial to obtain credentials from a travel training school.

As with any business venture, you must promote it. In the following case the taxpayer had inadequate promotion for her business.

Example: *Kelly v. Commissioner,* T.C. Memo 1997-185.

Kathleen Kelly, Virginia Beach, Virginia, worked full time as a career management specialist. She was very interested in the social and political unrest in Haiti and wanted to do something to help Haitians.

She decided to form a venture called "Too Close To Home." The main purpose was to promote tourism to Haiti. She tried to generate business during her lunch hours and in her spare time, and claimed this was a business activity.

She rented a booth at a festival where she handed out balloons printed with messages about supporting Haiti tourism. She organized an art show to benefit the orphans of Haiti and sent out postcards announcing this event. She organized a Haitian tour for four people and traveled there with the group.

She incurred about $8,000 in losses that she deducted from her taxes. She kept no business records at all. She had a separate bank account for the venture, but did not keep any records detailing the purpose for which funds were expended.

The US Tax Court concluded that Ms. Kelly did not carry on the activity in a businesslike manner. Although she had a separate bank account for the venture, it was not used exclusively for the venture, as she paid personal expenses (such as her insurance premiums) from the account. The court also noted that Ms. Kelly had no expertise in providing tours and no special knowledge of Haiti. Also, she devoted very little time to the activity.

The previous example provides the following key points:

1. The taxpayer did organize a small group of tourists to visit Haiti, but that did not make a profit and she did little by way of seriously promoting her venture. The US Tax Court felt that handing out imprinted balloons at a festival was not enough. Also, the taxpayer had no business records other than canceled checks.

2. The main point of having a separate checking account for a venture is to avoid commingling of personal funds with those used in the venture. In this case, the taxpayer had a separate checking account for the venture, but still commingled funds by writing checks from that account for personal expenses.

4. Chapter Summary

Developing a vacation rental or travel consulting business is no simple matter. Many people do make a profit in these areas. However, some people are motivated primarily by tax deductions for property or travel expenses.

The key is to prove that you are actively promoting your business to get customers. You should also have a separate checking account, accurate books and records, and if you do not have experience in the industry you are pursuing, you should seek advice from others who are familiar with how to make money in your type of venture.

The CD-ROM included with this book contains information on many more types of hobbies that can be turned into businesses, such as treasure hunting, and vacation rentals and travel consulting.